THE PRESE OF CONSUMER THEORY

The Implications
for
Social Welfare Theory

Third Edition

Timothy P. Roth

University Press of America,® Inc.
Lanham • New York • Oxford

Copyright © 1998 by
University Press of America,® Inc.
4720 Boston Way
Lanham, Maryland 20706

12 Hid's Copse Rd.
Cummor Hill, Oxford OX2 9JJ

Library of Congress Cataloging-in-Publication Data

Roth, Timothy P.
The present state of consumer theory : the implications for social
welfare theory / Timothy P. Roth. —3rd ed.
p.   cm.
Includes bibliographical references.
1. Consumption (Economics) I. Title.
HB801.R687   1997   339.4'7'01—DC21   97-40090 CIP

ISBN 0-7618-0944-9 (pbk: alk. ppr.)

Contents

FOREWORD

Proceeding from rather simple beginnings, the study of demand phenomena has developed, over the years, into a major area of economic research. Significantly, it is an area that continues to present serious intellectual challenges to scholars seeking to explain observed consumption behavior. We know, of course, that the predictive power of standard demand models is not as great as we might wish. And, indeed, such success as we have had in estimating demand relations has come about more because of improvements in statistical technique and computational capacity than because of refinements in the conventional theory of demand as such. It is true that, when properly considered, the theory of demand cannot avoid dealing with such elusive notions as value, utility and rationality. This situation surely makes for difficulties. Nevertheless, it is also apparent that while contributions to the postwar demand literature have covered a wide range of topics, the main thrust of these writings has been toward the extension and refinement of the classical theory of demand. Critics of this approach, including Professor Roth, argue with reason that the problem lies here. That is, although traditional demand theory has been able to bring about some advances in knowledge, it presupposes the existence of an idealized, frictionless world and, thus, has corresponding limitations.

From the standpoint of an increasing number of modern scholars, demand theory must be pushed in some fundamentally new directions, The work of behavioral economists has suggested that individuals are only boundedly rational, that decision making is a costly process, and that, in practice, people make choices among alternatives that do not conform to the predictions of orthodox utility analysis. Similarly, exponents of the New Institutional Economics accept the concept of bounded rationality, but go on to emphasize the roles that transaction costs, asymmetrical information and opportunism play in shaping economic behavior - and in determining the very institutional environment in which choice takes place.

The present book has special value precisely because it undertakes systematic investigation of these new areas of discussion. By reviewing the relevant literature, and giving due attention to underlying methodological issues, Roth is able to present a lucid account of the state of contemporary consumer theory and its problems. Further, Roth argues that since an economy characterized by bounded rationality and costly transactions produces outcomes that differ significantly from those implied by the frictionless neoclassical model, the body of welfare economics now widely used to evaluate policy requires reconsideration.

What has to be kept in mind of course is that the new theoretical structure being explored, which seeks to replace mainstream doctrine, is still in the process of formulation, and does not yet possess the logical rigor, elegance and seeming precision of, e.g., orthodox general equilibrium theory. The promise of improvement offered by the new developments is clear, but much work has to be done to consolidate the gains in understanding made so far. Interestingly, at the inaugural conference of the International Society for New Institutional Economics held recently in St. Louis, both Nobel prize winners Ronald Coase and Douglass North warned that a long period of time may have to elapse before a truly satisfactory formulation of the neoinstitutional paradigm is realized. However this may be, we can be grateful that this book will help ease the path to reconstruction.

Eirik G. Furubotn

September 1997
Private Enterprise Research Center
Texas A&M University
and
Center for the Study of the New Institutional Economics
University of the Saarland
Federal Republic of Germany

PREFACE TO THE THIRD EDITION

The preface to the second edition suggested that the methodological issues addressed in the first edition had gone largely unattended in the demand literature. On the other hand, I observed that "While demand theorists have generally not embraced the notion of cognitive limits, the new institutional economists regard economic agents as 'intendedly rational, but only limitedly so.'" Emphasis was placed on the notion that proponents of the new institutional approach sought, by modifying some of its behavioral and other postulates, "to expand the reach of neoclassical theory."

The third edition is motivated by the following considerations: (1) The theoretical and empirical demand literature continues to grow. (2) The emerging literature reflects a more receptive view of the methodological issues addressed in the first two editions. (3) The new institutional economists have become increasingly circumspect about the logical structure of "hybrid models"; of models which retain some of the behavioral and other postulates of the received neoclassical theory, while taking explicit account, inter alia, of bounded rationality and of positive transaction costs. Finally, the earlier editions did not include an explication of the implications of bounded rationality and other features of observable reality for the New Social Welfare Theory; a theory which takes as one of its points of departure the received, ordinal utility theory. Accordingly, the third edition incorporates a new chapter appropriately entitled The Implications for Social Welfare Theory. The discussion suggests that a decision environment characterized by bounded rationality, information asymmetries, opportunism, positive transaction and decision costs and endogenously determined preference and value structures militates against the specification of both the efficiency frontier and the Social Welfare Function.

ACKNOWLEDGMENTS

I wish to thank my Administrative Secretary, Gloria Armistead, for her continuing help and support. Special thanks are also due to Sigrid Westphal without whose "computer virtuosity" this project would not have been completed.

Chapter 1

Some Thoughts on Models and Model Building

Methodological discussion, like calisthenics and spinach, is good for us.....
Paul A. Samuelson

INTRODUCTION

That much has been written about the theories of utility and demand is a brute fact familiar to all economists. What is also clear even--perhaps particularly--to the dispassionate observer is the fairly homogeneous character of much of the work:

> . . . it would seem that any observer must be struck by one central characteristic of the received work on the theory of the consumer - the tendency of so many studies to accept the objectives and basic preconceptions of earlier models without much change . . . the main thrust of post-war writing has been toward the extension and refinement of the classical theory of demand that has come down to us through Marshall, Hicks, et al [Ekelund, Furubotn, Gramm 1972, p. 57].[1]

This is not to say that theoretical and empirical work has been confined solely to stretching the analytical limits of the traditional or ordinal utility analysis. Neither should a suggestion be broached that the received doctrine has been devoid of intellectual or "scientific" achievement. Theoretical lacunae have been at least tentatively filled, and new frontiers have been penetrated via systematic extensions and revisions of the traditional model. I have in mind, for example, the revealed preference approach due to Samuelson (1938); a formulation which, while logically equivalent to the ordinal utility theory [Houthakker 1950], nevertheless sheds light on the logical foundations of demand theory.[2] Other examples abound: The work on the indirect utility function [Hicks 1956, 1958] which has led, inter alia, to important new developments in the theory of index numbers [Theil 1975]; the utility tree formulation and the literature derivative of it [Strotz 1957; Sono 1961; Green 1964; Muth 1966; Furubotn 1967, 1974]; the Lancastrian "New Approach" [Lancaster 1966a], and the work on choice under uncertainty pioneered by von Neumann and Morgenstern (1947), Friedman and Savage (1948) and others. More recently, Stigler and Becker have proffered an intriguing hypothesis relating to the intertemporal stability of preference structures; an hypothesis which, while empirically untestable, has important implications for empirical work [Stigler and Becker 1977].

While the list is by no means exhaustive, it is heuristic. Much interesting and important work has been done. It remains true, however, that

> (an) examination of demand theory indicates, if anything, that great effort remains to be applied in this area which is so fundamental to the entire corpus of economic theory and policy [Ekelund, Furubotn, Gramm 1972, p. 93].[3]

Granting this, my purpose here is to undertake a critical evaluation of the received doctrine and to proffer, based upon this evaluation, a menu for future work.[4]

I shall argue that there is a clear need for a reorientation of effort in this important area; a reorientation that is, moreover, technically feasible.[5]

While the catalysts to this effort have been many, Professor Knight's elegant statement has contributed most to the warp and woof of the final product:

The treatment of demand is the branch of economic theory in which methodological problems are most important and most difficult. This is because it is here that behavior facts are most inseparably bound up with motivation and that objective data call most imperatively for interpretation by subjective facts and meanings [Knight 1944, p. 289].[6]

Having come this far, it is important to indicate the nature of the evaluative criteria to be employed. As a general rule, I shall not be concerned with either the mathematical derivations or the deductive processes inherent in the extant models. The efficacy of this approach follows from the compelling logic of Professor Leontief:

> In the presentation of a new model, attention nowadays is usually centered on a step-by-step derivation of its formal properties. But if the author - or at least the referee who recommended the manuscript for publication - is technically competent, such mathematical manipulations . . . can . . . be accepted as correct [Leontief 1971, p. 2].

Of course, it does not follow that the mathematical structure of the various models will not be of interest. Indeed, as we shall see, an explicit consideration of the mathematical structure of a model can be quite revealing.[7] It can shed light on such substantive questions as these: To what sort of decision environment does the model have basic relevance, and under what circumstances does the predictive power of a model collapse? The point to be emphasized is that:

> . . . reconsideration of the mathematical structure of a model frequently raises questions of the greatest significance for economic interpretation. In effect, we are forced to reexamine our assumptions about the real phenomena under investigation and make sure the economic problem is well posed [Ekelund, Furubotn and Gramm 1972, p. 63].

This last point serves as my point of departure.[8] What is at issue is the efficacy of the assumptions upon which a particular theoretical edifice is built. As we shall see, the efficacy of a particular set of assumptions turns on the answers to the following questions: a) What is(are) the purpose(s) of the model?, and b) What are the conditions requisite to the achievement of the model's objective(s)? Unfortunately, as Professor Leontief points out,

> By the time it comes to interpretation of (the model's) substantive conclusions, the assumptions on which the model has been based are easily

forgotten. But it is precisely the empirical validity of these assumptions on which the usefulness of the entire exercise depends [Leontief 1971, p. 2].

If one adopts the view that a theory should be both explanatory and informative, that it should provide at least a tentative answer to the question "Why?", then rigorous conditions must be met. Included among these is the "empirical validity" of the model's assumptions [Nagel 1963; Melitz 1965; Wong 1973]. On the other hand, if the avowed purpose of a model is simply "prediction", realism of assumptions is not mandatory; it is simply judicious [Melitz 1965; Wong 1973]. It follows that before it can be established that a <u>sine qua non</u> for its usefulness is the empirical validity of its assumptions, a model's purpose must be unambiguously established.[9] Granting this, before an explicit statement of the evaluative criteria to be employed can emerge, we must "plant our methodological feet." We must ask ourselves, "What is it that we want our models of consumer behavior to do?"

THE PURPOSES OF MODELS

The question, "What is it that we want our models of consumer behavior to do?" is answered according as we adopt a particular methodological posture. Because each has gained wide acceptance among economists, our interest centers on the following methodological positions: a) descriptivism, b) instrumentalism, and c) the view that a theory should be both explanatory and informative.[10]

That an understanding of the nature and the implications of the three positions is of interest to a philosopher of science is obvious. That the same understanding is of practical significance to an economist is perhaps less clear. What is fundamentally at issue, however, is the role of the theories which the economist brings to bear in analyzing systematically the complex phenomena which come under his purview. And it is precisely the economist's perception of the role of a theory that must determine the character and content of the assumptions upon which that theory is built. To see this, we must first undertake a systematic review of the alternative methodological positions.

THE DESCRIPTIVIST VIEW

The descriptivist view holds that theories are only descriptive of observable experience; that they can never be explanatory. An influential proponent of this view is Paul Samuelson. On his view, a) a theory is just a description of observable experience; a convenient, mnemonic representation of empirical reality [Samuelson 1963, p. 236; 1956, p. 1171]. It follows that b) "knowledge" consists essentially of observable reports; indeed, all well-known theories in science are expressible in terms of basic statements [Samuelson 1965a, p. 1167]. The latter are understood to have a specific spatio-temporal reference.

Samuelson's rejection of the view that theories are explanatory is itself explicable [Wong 1973, p. 319]: a) He regards explanations as ultimate, and b) It is his view that apriorism must be avoided and that, therefore, theories must be expressed in terms of basic statements.

While it would be redundant simply to reproduce Professor Wong's elegant critique of Samuelson's methodological position, it is essential that the rudiments of the argument be understood. In his view [Wong 1973, p.320]:

> Explanations are not ultimate. We can give explanations of explanations. Samuelson mistakenly identifies the explanatory view with an essentialist view. Essentialism aims at ultimate explanation which is neither capable nor in need of further explanation.[11]

So much for the view that explanations are ultimate. On Samuelson's rejection of apriorism, Wong is equally persuasive [Wong 1973, p. 320]:

> Samuelson has rightfully condemned apriorism, the view that all phenomena can be explained as consequences of self-evident first principles, the truth of which is independent of all possible experience. But the alternative . . . is not to ground theories in observational statements. For such a program is impossible to achieve because of insurmountable difficulties, both logical and epistemological.

The difficulty arises from the logical form of a theory: A theory includes at least one unrestricted universal statement; a statement with no spatio-temporal reference. And, as Wong has emphasized, ". . . an unrestricted universal statement is not equivalent to a finite conjunction of observational statements . . . " [Wong 1973, p. 320].[12]

All of this suggests that the position that well-known theories in science are expressible in terms of basic statements [Samuelson 1965, p. 1167] is, at best, fallacious. Indeed, all the theories cited by Samuelson in support of his position claim to be universal.[13] To put the matter differently, each of the theories cited includes at least one unrestricted universal statement. It is clear that these theories cannot, therefore, be expressible as basic statements.

There are, moreover, epistemological grounds for rejecting the view that theories must be grounded in observational statements: We simply do not have an independent language in which to ground theories. Indeed, "All observational terms are theory laden" [Wong 1973, p. 321]. That is to say, all observational statements and terms implicitly assume theories; constructs which, via their logical structure, go beyond observational statements.[14]

From what has been said, it is clear that the logical foundations of the descriptivist position are, at best, tenuous. Indeed, one could plausibly argue that implementation of descriptivist strictures would consign economists to the role of observers of empirical reality. Consistent employment of basic, to the exclusion of universal statements, would not only impede the development of theories in economics; it would prohibit their emergence. Granting this, the methodological position to be adopted here must be found elsewhere. It must, in fact, be either the instrumentalist view, or the view that a theory must be both explanatory and informative. We turn next to the instrumentalist view.

THE INSTRUMENTALIST VIEW

Stripped to its essentials, the instrumentalist view holds that a theory is an instrument for prediction. On this view, ". . . the only relevant test of the validity of a hypothesis is comparison of its predictions with experience" [Friedman 1953, pp.8-9]. Because the theory constitutes the machinery through which predictions about observable reality are to emerge, the descriptive realism of the theory's assumptions is a moot question. Indeed, the only relevant question is [Friedman 1953, p. 15]:

. . . whether [the assumptions] are sufficiently good approximations for the purpose at hand. And this question can be answered only by seeing whether a theory works, which means whether it yields sufficiently accurate predictions. The two supposedly independent tests [test of the assumptions and test of the theory by a test of its predictions] thus reduce to one test.

While much can be said about this, it is clear that there exist no logical or epistemological arguments with which successfully to challenge this position.[15] As the noted philosopher of science Ernest Nagel puts it [Nagel 1963, p. 218]:

> Is [Friedman] defending the legitimacy of unrealistic assumptions because he thinks theories are at best only useful instruments valuable for predicting observable events but not to be viewed as genuine statements whose truth or falsity may be significantly investigated? But if this is the way he conceives theories (much in his argument suggests that it is), the distinction between realistic and unrealistic theoretical assumptions is at best irrelevant, and no defense of theories lacking in realism is needed.

Explanation vs. Prediction: Some Preliminary Remarks

So long as the only purpose of a theory is prediction, the instrumentalist's position is logically impeccable. This is not to say, however, that the position is without difficulty. At the most rudimentary level, the employment of unrealistic assumptions precludes the possibility of explaining the phenomena that come under the purview of the theory [Wong 1973, p. 317].[16] It follows that one cannot employ unrealistic assumptions and at the same time claim that a theory has both predictive and explanatory power. Yet, as Professor Nagel observes [Nagel 1963, p. 212]:

> ... an economic theory (e.g., the neoclassical theory of consumer choice) is a set of statements, organized in a characteristic way, and designed to serve as partial premises for explaining, as well as predicting an indeterminately large (and usually varied) class of economic phenomena.[17]

Thus, if one sets out, as economists are wont to do, not only to predict but to explain a class (or classes) of empirical phenomena

> ... in terms of the mechanisms involved in their occurrence ... [the theory employed] cannot be viewed as [Friedman] suggests that it can, as a 'simple summary' of some vaguely delimited set of empirical generalizations with distinctly specified ranges of application. [Nagel 1963, p. 218].

The Need for Adequate Empirical Interpretation

To this point I have emphasized that the instrumentalist position cannot be reconciled with the explanation of empirically observed phenomena. In asserting that this is so, I have relied mainly upon the weight of Professor Nagel's authority.[18] While I shall presently have more to say about this, I should like for the moment to focus on another issue raised, almost incidentally, by Professor Nagel. In the passage just cited, Nagel refers to ". . . some vaguely delimited set of empirical generalizations with distinctly specified ranges of application." The issue raised here has to do with whether a theory -- regardless of its avowed purpose -- has been given adequate empirical interpretation.

The relevance of the question of empirical interpretation comes readily into focus when it is understood that the statements belonging to any theory can be divided into three subgroups: 1) the theory's "assumptions" or basic "hypotheses"; 2) the set of statements logically deducible from the assumptions as theorems, and 3) the set of statements that specify correspondence; in particular, the correspondences between (a) the expressions embodied in the theory which designate nothing actually observable and are not definable in terms of expressions that are, and (b) the empirically determinable features of actual processes [Nagel 1963, pp. 212-213]. The point is that many of the statements in the first two subgroups specify nothing actually observable.[19] Yet, as Nagel points out, statements containing such terms ". . . cannot possibly explain or predict the course of actual events, unless a sufficient number of theoretical terms .. . are coordinated with observable traits of things" [Nagel 1963, p. 212]. The third group of statements embodied in a theory is, therefore, the set of interpretive rules; the statements that indicate the correspondences between the theoretical terms embodied in the theory, and the empirically determinable features of actual processes.[20] It is the interpretive rules that determine whether or not a theory possesses adequate empirical interpretation.[21]

To establish the relevance of adequate empirical interpretation to the instrumentalist position, one might proceed along two lines of thought. At a rudimentary level, a sine qua non for the ability to confirm (disconfirm) a theory's predictions is the provision of a set of instructions; a set of interpretive rules telling us how to apply the data of a particular case. An example due to Clarkson will serve to clarify the point at issue [Clarkson 1963, p. 74]:

... earlier we made use of the physical law relating to the free fall of a body near the earth's surface ... This 'ideal' law is supposed to be true only for bodies falling <u>in vacuo</u> when near the earth's surface . . . In this case the interpretive rules consist of a set of instructions that identify the factors to take into consideration, e.g., the density of the media, the shape of the object, etc., as well as the effect on the results.

In other words, if we are to be able to disconfirm a theory by checking the correspondence of its predictions to observable reality, we must know how to interpret the facts of the case. This requires that we know the "parameters of the system." A particularly relevant illustration of the point at issue is the presence in the classical theory of demand -- the theory that has come to us through Marshall, Hicks, <u>et al</u> -- of at least one unidentified exogenous variable; namely, the preference structure of the individual consumer. Yet, unfortunately, unless the preference structure is known <u>a priori</u> [Clarkson 1963, p. 99]:

. . . . the set of events over which the law [of demand] is supposed to hold cannot be completely defined or identified. Accordingly, there is an insufficient number of interpretive rules to allow one to determine whether the behavior of the consumer is consistent with the law or not.

Unless a sufficient number of interpretive rules are provided, we are unable to evaluate observed events relative to the predictions of a model. We do not know whether a disparity as between the two constitutes a disconfirmation of the theory, or whether one of the parameters of the system has changed.[22]

The "As If" Construal

That I should have appealed to the "falling body" example to illustrate the need for interpretive rules is appropriate for another reason. Precisely the same example was employed by Professor Friedman in arguing that the assumptions of a model are properly regarded as "as if" statements [Friedman 1953, pp. 16-17]:

It is an accepted hypothesis that . . . the distance traveled by a falling body in any specified time is given by the formula $s = 1/2gt^2$, where s is the distance traveled in feet and t is time in seconds. The application of this formula to a compact ball dropped from the roof of a building is equivalent to saying that a ball so dropped behaves AS IF it were falling in a vacuum.

The implication is that the law of falling bodies can be restated to read [Nagel 1963, p. 216]:

> Under a wide range of circumstances bodies that fall in the actual atmosphere behave AS IF they were falling in a vacuum.

In point of fact, however, [Nagel 1963, p. 217]:

> . . . the proposed paraphrase mistakenly assumes that Galileo's law can be assigned the functions actually performed by statements of correspondence . . .

The statements of correspondence to which Nagel refers are, of course, the requisite interpretive rules.

Unfortunately, even if interpretive rules were to be provided, the "as if" formulation cannot be reconciled with the avowed instrumentalist objective of prediction:

> . . . consider the assertion that businessmen behave AS IF they were trying to maximize profits, or . . . that under certain conditions businessmen behave AS IF they were attempting to maximize profits. Given the requisite circumstances, if any, what can we predict, or in other words, what observable implications can we derive from this 'as if' statement? Unfortunately, no observable implications seem to follow. If businessmen act only AS IF trying to maximize profits, then evidently they do not exactly try to maximize profits, at least not all the time, and perhaps sometimes they do not even try to maximize profits at all. As a result, no specific conclusions about businessmen's actions, however vague and tentative, can be strictly derived from this statement [Melitz 1965, p. 50].[23]

Designed vs Undesigned Classes of Implications

A sketch of the limitations of the instrumentalist approach would not be complete without reference to the implications to which a set of assumptions give rise. It is particularly appropriate that the issue be broached here because it is inexorably bound up with the question of whether or not a theory has adequate empirical interpretation; that is, whether or not a sufficient number of interpretive rules have been provided.

In effect, the instrumentalist position -- at least as it is espoused by Professor Friedman -- holds that false information contained in assumptions may not concern classes of implications which the theory is "designed to explain" [Melitz 1965, p. 46]. Now it is clear that theories may give rise to "undesigned" classes of implications. The corollary is not, however, that contradictory test evidence can be discarded:

> Before any negative results can be safely dismissed, it is necessary to be able to discern the 'undesigned' classes of implications. Friedman views this ability as present to an important degree in economics. According to him, every hypothesis in economic theory is attended by a set of rules defining the class of phenomena which the hypothesis is supposed to explain. While these rules are inexact, and Friedman deplores the failure to devote greater attention to their elaboration, he believes that 'to a considerable extent the rules can be formulated explicitly' [Melitz 1965, p. 47].

The instrumentalist position presumes, in other words, that so long as the requisite interpretive rules are provided, the descriptive realism of a theory's assumptions is a matter of indifference.[24] Given the appropriate interpretive rules, we should be able to determine <u>a priori</u> the class of phenomena to which a predictive theory has basic relevance.

What, then, are some examples of interpretive rules as they are applied in instrumentalist theories? It is in this spirit that Melitz asks [Melitz 1965, p. 47]:

> What, for instance, is a rule determining any one class of 'undesigned' implications of the postulate of profit maximization? . . . Likewise, what are the rules for finding the 'undesigned' classes of implications of the theorem of negatively sloping demand for non-inferior goods?

Even if one were to assume that the appropriate interpretive rules can always be identified, problems remain: It is difficult to conceive of a set of circumstances under which the "undesigned" class of implications might be eliminated without impairing the explanatory or predictive power of the theory. This follows from the fact that in any theory the interrelationships among the statements and definitions that constitute its logical structure may be extremely complex [Melitz 1965, p. 49]. Thus, even if one were able unambiguously to identify the "undesigned" implications, their elimination will impel a modification of the assumption set. Unfortunately,

> Even if elimination of the part of the theory set or the assumption set corresponding to the invalid part of the consequence set were possible, it may not always be desirable to do so for instrumentalism. The corresponding part of the theory set or the assumption set may be required for the generation of the valid predictions [Wong 1973, p. 316].

Moreover, granting the complexity of a theory's logical structure, it is apparent that [Melitz 1965, p. 49]:

> . . . any particular aspect of a statement which appears negligible in itself may nevertheless play an important part in the theory as a whole. Thus, the falseness of any portion of the theory may be an unsuspected cause of many false predictions.

We conclude then that theories frequently do give rise to "undesigned" classes of implications. However, the presumed ability to specify interpretive rules requisite to their identification does not solve all of the attendant problems. Mutatis mutandis, the elimination of the undesigned classes of implications will frequently impair a theory's residual predictive power; it may result in the inability of the theory to generate any valid predictions.

There is, however, an even more fundamental problem: Insofar as the acceptability of a theory depends upon its ability to predict observable events, ALL of the derived implications of a theory must be defensible [Koopmans 1957, pp. 135-142]. Indeed, unless it can be shown that "undesigned" classes of implications can be deleted without impairing the explanatory and predictive powers of a theory, ". . . there is every reason to think all negative findings must be accepted as disconfirmatory" [Melitz 1965, p. 48].

At issue, then, is not simply the ability of instrumentalists to identify and to eliminate "undesigned" classes of implications. At issue is the proposition that SOME of a theory's derived implications may be false without at the same time being disconfirmatory. Whether false implications relate to "designed" or "undesigned" classes of implications is essentially irrelevant. ANY false prediction must be regarded as disconfirmatory.

Finally, there is this: The adoption of the methodological position that the descriptive realism of assumptions does not matter may have deleterious effects on the evolution of economic science.

Scientific Advance as an Iterative Process

Our point of departure is the instrumentalist view that "undesigned" classes of implications can be exempted from empirical verification. It is this view that caused Professor Koopmans to remark that [Koopmans 1957, pp. 139-140]:

> To state a set of postulates, and then to exempt a subclass of their implications from verification is a curiously roundabout way of specifying the content of a theory that is regarded as open to empirical refutation... Before we can accept the view that obvious discrepancies between behavior postulates and directly observed behavior do not affect the predictive power of specified implications of the postulates, we need to understand the reasons why these discrepancies do not matter. This is all the more important in a field such as economics where, as Friedman also emphasizes, the opportunities for verification of predictions and implications derived from the postulates are scarce and the outcome of the verification often remains somewhat uncertain... If, in comparison with some other sciences, economics is handicapped by severe and possibly unsurmountable obstacles to meaningful experimentation, the opportunities for direct introspection by, and direct observation of, individual decision makers are a much needed source of evidence which in some degree offsets the handicap.[25]

If one grants the notion that empirical verification of predictions in economics is always difficult, frequently impossible and typically ambiguous, Koopmans' line of reasoning is persuasive. What is called for is direct empirical verification of assumptions. We must not lose sight of the fact that the empirical verification of assumptions is eminently pragmatic. The evolution of economics as an empirical science hinges, in part, upon efforts designed to compensate for the difficulties associated with the verification of predictions. Following a somewhat similar line of reasoning, Professor Leontief is led to the following conclusion [Leontief 1971, p. 5]:

> True advance [in economics] can be achieved only through an iterative process in which improved theoretical formulation raises new empirical questions and the answers to these questions, in their turn, lead to new

theoretical insights. The 'givens' of today become the 'unknowns' that will have to be explained tomorrow. This, incidentally, makes untenable the admittedly convenient methodological position according to which a theorist does not need to verify directly the factual assumptions on which he chooses to base his deductive arguments provided his empirical conclusions seem to be correct.[26]

One might grant that a set of descriptively unrealistic assumptions may generate a set of valid predictions relating to "designed" classes of implications. One might, in addition, be sympathetic to the view that any "undesigned" classes of implications can, via the specification of appropriate interpretive rules, be identified. One might, even more heroically, accept the view that "undesigned" classes of implications can be eliminated without impairing the predictive power of the theory. Yet having granted all of this, one might still reject the instrumentalist position. The reason is straightforward: The persistent employment of descriptively unrealistic assumptions may impede the evolution of economic science. This, it seems to me, is too high a price to pay.[27]

Generative vs Auxiliary Assumptions

Before proceeding, it is essential that an earlier, somewhat cryptic statement be qualified. Earlier I indicated that a set of descriptively false assumptions may give rise to a set of valid predictions. While the statement is correct, it raises the question of what conditions must be satisfied if confirmatory evidence is to be secured. To put the matter differently, when is a correspondence between observational statements (or predictions) generated by a theory and observable reality confirmatory?

An answer to this question hinges upon a formal distinction as between "generative" and "auxiliary" assumptions [Melitz 1965, pp. 42-46]. The former constitute statements which serve to derive a hypothesis, while the latter consist in statements used in conjunction with the hypothesis to deduce predictions. An example of an auxiliary assumption, while due to Professor Melitz, would come readily to mind to most economists; namely, the familiar ceteris paribus assumption. An example of a generative assumption would be the presumed freedom of entry and exit of producers in perfectly competitive industries.

On Auxiliary Assumptions

Following Professor Melitz [Melitz 1965, p. 43], let us denote a theory or hypothesis as H. Now H may be understood as saying that if certain conditions, $C_1, C_2, \ldots, C_n$ obtain an event E occurs. The point is that the theory does not yield any predictions alone; what is required, in addition, is a set of auxiliary assumptions, A_x, which affirm that $C_1, C_2, \ldots, C_n$ obtain. Given H and A_x, a statement having specific spacio-temporal content, an observational statement may be derived. We shall call this statement the theory's prediction, O.

The question at issue is this: When does the truth of O impart a degree of confirmation on H and A_x? In Melitz's words [Melitz 1965, p. 43]:

> If O is found to be true, then by inductive logic, both H and A_x acquire a degree of confirmation. That is, the outcome increases the probability that both H and A_x are true. However, it may be shown that any evidence contrary to A_x will also play a role in the interpretation of the test result. Given any deviation between A_x and reality, . . . it is . . . possible that the facts fall outside the boundary conditions for testing H. If this possibility should hold, H would be consistent with false results. Thus, as long as the facts do not correspond fully with A_x, the truth of O is not necessarily favorable to H.

There is a symmetry here. Suppose that O is compared with observable reality and found to be false. In this event, it is true that the test result enhances the probability that H is false. It is also true, however, that [Melitz 1965, p. 43]:

> . . . the more the discrepancy between assumed conditions and reality, the greater the chance that the requisite test conditions are unfulfilled. Consequently, the greater is this discrepancy, the less reason there is to expect H to yield true implications, and the less disconfirmatory is the falsehood of O.[28]

It follows that any evidence contrary to the auxiliary assumptions increases the ambiguity of test results. Regardless of the outcome of the comparison of a theory's prediction(s) with observable reality,

. . . any discrepancy between 'auxiliary' assumptions and reality raises some likelihood that the experiment is invalid . . . The realism of 'auxiliary' assumptions, thus, is plainly relevant [Melitz 1965, p. 44].

It is clear, then, that a theory employing auxiliary assumptions which are known a priori to be false may give rise to valid predictions. Unfortunately, given the nature of the test environment, any favorable test results must be regarded as ambiguous; they cannot, in other words, be regarded as confirmatory of H.[29]   This is a difficulty of which instrumentalists must take account. Contrary to Professor Friedman's position, insofar as he is interested in subjecting predictions of theories to unambiguous empirical test, some of the assumptions employed -- notably, the "auxiliary" assumptions -- must be realistic.[30]

On Generative Assumptions

The question that logically follows is, can the same be said of generative assumptions; that is, does the testability of an instrumentalist model turn, in any sense, on the realism of generative assumptions? Let us, following Melitz, assume that the theory or hypothesis H has been derived via the employment of the set of generative assumptions, A_g. Assume, in addition, the existence of a body of evidence opposed to A_g, at least in the context of H. The question is whether this, by itself, will increase ambiguity, or otherwise interfere with the testing of the theory. The answer is that [Melitz 1965, p. 45]:

> Unlike testimony conflicting with A_x, such evidence would not interfere with the interpretation of outcomes of any tests of H. 'Generative' assumptions are not logically required in deducing observation statements. Consequently, whatever the facts with respect to A_g, the results of checking observation statements derived from H and A_x can be unambiguously interpreted as either for or against H . . . Furthermore, concurrent with a large amount of . . . contradictory evidence [relative to A_g] H may enjoy great predictive success and possess high confirmation.

The employment of unrealistic generative assumptions does not, therefore, impede the emergence of testable predictions. Moreover, a correspondence of these predictions with observable reality may be taken -- given realistic auxiliary assumptions -- to be confirmatory of a theory. It does not follow, however, that unrealistic generative assumptions can be employed with impunity. Despite the benefits that accrue as a result of the employment of such assumptions, these benefits are not enjoyed without potential cost.[31] Notable among the costs is the fact that while the falsity of A_g does not increase the ambiguity of test results, it may, in fact, reduce the probability that the derived hypotheses are true [Melitz 1965, pp. 46 and 52]. This follows from the fact that:

> In case A_g is true, then all of its implications, including H, must be true. However, if A_g is false, then some of its implications must be false, and these implications may affect the substance of H [Melitz 1965, p. 46].[32]

The potential costs are, however, not summarized in the statement that the falsity of A_g may reduce the probability that derived hypotheses are true. As has been emphasized, the employment of unrealistic assumptions has implications for the evolution of economic science. Because their use increases the ambiguity of test results, appeal to unrealistic auxiliary assumptions may impede the development of "economic theory." Moreover:

> . . . with regard to 'generative' assumptions, the more unrealistic these assumptions, the weaker the basis for relying on them in order to develop hypotheses or hunches. Hence, . . . tests of economic assumptions are generally useful in testing and appraising hypotheses, and in indicating possible avenues of improvement in theory and hypotheses [Melitz 1965, p. 52].[33]

Our point of departure was that, so long as theory is viewed as a useful instrument for PREDICTING observable events, the instrumentalist position cannot be refuted.[34] It is clear, however, that the falsity of one class of assumptions will jeopardize the integrity of the testing procedure. The falsity of another class of assumptions will reduce the probability that derived hypotheses are true. Thus, while one might, for pragmatic or other reasons, adopt the view that false assumptions are sufferable, he must recognize that ". . . every inaccuracy in assumptions is disadvantageous" [Melitz 1965, p. 59]. There is no escaping the fact that the instrumentalist methodology is not only congenial to, it is an effective catalyst to the emergence and persistence of theoretical lacunae. As Harry Johnson, no stranger to the instrumentalist position, put it,

The demand for clarification of the mechanism by which results can be
EXPLAINED is contrary to the methodology of positive economics . . .
[Johnson 1971, p. 13]. (emphasis mine)

And here, it seems to me, is the crux of the issue: Adoption of the
instrumentalist methodology precludes the possibility of EXPLAINING
phenomena. Yet it does not take much of a logical leap to recognize that
the frequently explicit and, I think it safe to say, almost always implicit
purpose of economic theories is both to predict and to explain observable
events.[35] Indeed, apropos of the central focus of this book, Professor
Nagel points out that:

> . . . an economic theory (e.g., the neoclassical theory of consumer choice) is
> a set of statements . . . designed to serve as partial premises for explaining,
> as well as predicting . . . [Nagel 1963, p. 212].

In summary, two related propositions lead me to a rejection of
instrumentalist methodology: 1) The fact that the employment of false
assumptions will, in general, impede the evolution of economic science,
and 2) The logical impossibility of reconciling the instrumentalist
position with the explanation of observable events. While the first of
these two propositions should require no further elaboration, the second
clearly does. With this in mind, I turn next to a consideration of the
methodological position that a theory is explanatory and informative;
that it must be able to provide at least a tentative answer to the question,
"Why?"

THE EXPLANATORY VIEW

Granting the logic of what has been said, neither the descriptivist nor
the instrumentalist methodological position will be adopted here. The
adopted position may be characterized as the explanatory view.

The logic behind the adoption of this view has in part to do with the
fact that the descriptivist position is untenable, and in part with the
debilitating influence of the instrumentalist methodology. The position
reduces essentially to this: The difficulties associated with the view that
the assumptions of a theory need not be descriptively realistic can be

overcome. What is required is that the theory's assumptions be descriptively realistic. And this, it should be emphasized, must be true of generative, as well as auxiliary assumptions. What is suggested is that by meeting as closely as possible the conditions requisite to achieving explanatory power, the probability that theoretical lacunae will emerge and persist is reduced, while the probability is enhanced that the iterative process to which Professor Leontief refers will be accelerated.[36]

What, then, are the conditions that must be satisfied if a theory is to be explanatory? While much has been written on the subject,[37] Professor Wong's answer is sufficient for our purposes [Wong 1973, p. 317]:

> For a theory to be explanatory it must satisfy a number of conditions. The set of statements which forms the explanation (called the explanans) must logically entail the set of statements which describe what is to be explained (called the explanandum). The explanans must not be known to be false and be independently testable. To be independently testable the explanans must have testable consequences in addition to the explanandum . . . Moreover, to preclude ad hoc explanations the explanans must also include at least one universal law.[38]

The explanans to which Professor Wong refers are the generative assumptions of a theory.[39] In effect, if a theory is to have explanatory power, the generative assumptions cannot be known to be false a priori. Moreover, the generative assumptions must be subject to independent test; they must, in other words, be "richer in empirical content" than that which is to be explained [Wong 1973, p. 317].

It is precisely the emphasis upon the testability of assumptions that makes the explanatory view of theory more congenial: a) to the closing of theoretical lacunae -- or, if you will, to the opening of the "black boxes" of received economic doctrine, and b) to the taxonomy of "answered" and yet-to-be answered questions and, pari passu, to the emergence of improved theoretical formulations.

What, then, is the methodological perspective to be employed in the balance of this book? The following passage captures its essence:

> [the choice] surely is not instrumentalism or descriptivism. Instrumentalism in its single-minded pursuit of predictions goes 'beyond the facts' by considering the truth or falsity of statements to be irrelevant; descriptivism in its pursuit of pure descriptions designs a theory not to go beyond the facts and ends up with a theory being just a restatement of the 'facts' . . .

The choice, then, is not between instrumentalism and descriptivism, but between them both and the view that a theory is explanatory and informative, one which provides an answer, albeit a tentative one, to the question 'Why?' [Wong 1973, p. 324].

I shall adopt the view that a theory in economics should be explanatory.[40] It follows that a critical evaluation of the received models of consumer behavior will turn, in part, on the empirical content of the generative assumptions employed.[41] This is done with a view to determining to what extent a model possesses the potential for explanatory power. This is not to say that explanatory power is the only desideratum. Indeed, in those instances where the model in question clearly possesses neither the realized nor the potential ability to explain consumer behavior, I shall employ other evaluative criteria. Whether the explicit or implicit objective of a model is explanation or prediction, interest centers on whether the model has adequate empirical interpretation; whether, in other words, the requisite interpretive rules have been specified. A related issue is whether the auxiliary assumptions have empirical content. And, finally, I shall have occasion closely to examine the mathematical structure of the various models.[42]

PLAN OF THE BOOK

In Chapter II, I undertake critically to evaluate the traditional model of consumer behavior; the model that has come to us through the works of Marshall, Hicks and others. While much has been written -- and likely will be written -- about this conception of the consumer's decision environment, to ignore this cornerstone of the received doctrine would be to deny us a point of departure or frame of reference with which to compare newer formulations. Emphasis is placed upon the fact that the basic postulates upon which the traditional model is built are not testable. Moreover, it is shown that the model embodies a somewhat truncated view of what might heuristically be called the consumer's "decision process".

The subject matter of Chapter III is the so-called Lancastrian or "New Approach" to consumer theory. The "New Approach" retains a certain symmetry with the traditional model in that it conceives of the consumer's objective function as a single equation construct. The key difference between the two formulations is that the arguments in the Lancastrian utility function are not consumption rates of goods and services. Rather, the objects of choice are understood to be the characteristics of goods and services. This conception of the utility function is somewhat more congenial to the representation of a decision environment involving product differentiation. In effect, product differentiates -- varying forms of particular product types -- are viewed as embodying the same (or similar) characteristics vectors. Given this understanding, the various product differentiates are then distinguished by the characteristics release rates specified by the "consumption technology". This, can -- indeed, has -- led to some important theoretical insights. Nevertheless, substantive problems remain; some of which have been recognized in the literature, and some of which have not. Chapter III is given over to a codification of some of these, essentially methodological, difficulties.

In Chapter IV I examine a model of consumer behavior whose conceptual underpinnings may be found in Professor Strotz's utility tree. Insofar as it conceives of the consumer's objective function as a multi-equation construct, it represents a somewhat more radical departure from the Marshall-Hicks formulation. While there are difficulties, the multi-equation utility function is more amenable to an explicit characterization of the consumer's "decision process" than is either the traditional or the Lancastrian approach. Indeed, the utility tree formulation has found new life as a catalyst to new thinking about the construction of monetary aggregates and, *pari passu*, about the demand for money. For its part, the multi-equation utility function has been invoked, *inter alia*, as a means of representing utility domains defined on such disparate desiderata as goods and services, self-reference and interpersonal relationships. This, in turn, facilitates the formal modeling of such phenomena as internal conflict and "moral tastes" or ethical norms.

Whereas the multi-equation utility function approach places emphasis upon the consumer's decision process and allows for the possibility of changing tastes, the household production function approach presumes that individual consumers' preference structures are stable over time. Both approaches seek, via quite different conceptions of the consumer's decision environment, to come to grips with a long-standing problem in the theory of consumer behavior; namely, the lack of adequate empirical interpretation. Chapter V is given over to an evaluation of the household production function approach; an approach that has begun to receive broader attention in the literature.

In Chapter VI attention centers on the methodological difficulties associated with the received models of consumer behavior; in particular, with the lack of adequate empirical interpretation that attends strict adherence to the classical rationality postulate. It is suggested that the empirical verifiability of consumer theory hinges upon a more explicit characterization of the consumer's decision process in general, and upon his bounded rationality in particular.

Chapter VII takes as its point of departure the notion that "bounded rationality" implies neither nonrationality nor irrationality. Indeed, proponents of the New Institutional Economics argue that adoption of the view that decision makers are "intendedly rational, but only limitedly so" both deepens our understanding of the processes of production and exchange and broadens the reach of economic theory. In short, while Chapter VI focuses on the role of bounded rationality in enhancing the empirical verifiability of consumer theory, the new institutionalists emphasize a broader role; namely, the generation of testable hypotheses which fall under the more general rubric of microeconomics. It follows, pari passu, that the new institutionalist literature is both congenial to and corroborative of the recurring theme developed below: An explicit accounting of limited cognitive abilities is a sine qua non for the evolution of economics as an empirical science.

Chapter VIII, new to the third edition, is predicated on the notion that endogenously determined preference and value structures, bounded rationality and positive transaction costs are fundamental features of observable reality. In effect, agents' decision environments are characterized by path-dependencies, cognitive limitations, information asymmetries, opportunism and, pari passu, positive decision-method, data, selection and transaction costs. At issue are the implications of this understanding of the decision environment for the New Social Welfare Theory; a body of theory based, inter alia, on the received, ordinal utility theory. The logic of the argument suggests that an explicit accounting of these phenomena militates against the specification of both the efficiency frontier and the Social Welfare Function. This, in turn has implications for the conduct of public policy.

In Chapter IX, a Postscript on Empirical Demand Estimation, I explore some additional implications of my analysis. With the continuing disarray in the money demand literature as my point of departure, I argue that no amount of technical virtuosity can salvage econometric models whose genesis is an orthodox conception of the consumer's decision environment. Recent efforts to solve the "missing money" problem are heuristic. The new literature invokes a variant of the utility tree formulation, with consumer goods, leisure and the services of monetary assets as arguments of the branch utility functions. The approach clearly provides a convenient, mnemonic method of rationalizing decisions ex post. Yet the presence of an unidentified exogenous variable -- the decision-maker's preference structure -- militates against empirical confirmation (disconfirmation) of the model. Equally important, the inability to specify adequate interpretive rules means that model specification is heavily influenced by prior beliefs and by "theory" which happens at a cross section of time to be prevalent. It follows that "specification searches" -- whether by Extreme Bounds Analysis or any other essentially taxonomic process -- cannot plausibly be regarded as exercises in "positive economics." A corollary of this is significant potential for mischief. On the one hand, the lack of adequate empirical interpretation ensures that a model can be neither confirmed nor disconfirmed. If "bad" models can never be shown unambiguously to be "bad," neither can we know why some models appear in some sense to "work." On the other hand, specification searches predicated on the model builder's (user's) prior beliefs virtually ensure that, eventually, the "right" results will emerge. The lack of adequate empirical interpretation means, in short, that it is possible in virtually all cases to "give the boss what he wants to hear."

Finally, because the lack of adequate empirical interpretation ensures a role for prior beliefs both in model specification and in the interpretation of results, it follows that public policy recommendations and decisions based on these models must have normative content. Technical virtuosity does not, after all, free the model builder from the influence of his prior beliefs. For the model builder to suggest otherwise is to mislead both himself and his model's users.

NOTES

[1]Indeed, Professor Demestz maintains that "The strong export surplus economics maintains in its trade in ideas and methods with the social sciences...." is (correctly attributed by Gary Becker to) [Demestz 1997, p. 1]:

> ... our relentless and unflinching application of 'The combined assumptions of maximizing behavior, market equilibrium, and stable preferences...

The "Anomalies" section of the <u>Journal of Economic Perspectives</u> has for years begun with the following, introductory sentence:

> Economics can be distinguished from other social sciences by the belief that most (all?) behavior can be explained by assuming that rational agents with stable, well-defined preferences interact in markets that (eventually) clear.

See, for example, [Siegel and Thaler 1997, p. 191].

[2]See also [Clarkson 1963; Richter 1966; Uzawa 1960].

[3]Amartya Sen has summarized the situation in this way [Klamer 1989, p. 147]:

> It is assumed that there is no deep problem with the basic story. The extensions and revisions may, thus, look like consolidating battles, the main war having been won, and the high ground already secured. But the high ground is not secure at all. The most basic element of such modeling, namely the motivation of human beings, is not well addressed.

[4]This, broadly speaking, was G.P.E. Clarkson's intention in his <u>The Theory of Consumer Demand: A Critical Appraisal</u> (1963). However, while I am sympathetic to the general theme pursued by Clarkson, I have reservations about the logical structure of his argument and, in particular, about his proposed program of reform for demand theory. For a critical view of Clarkson see, for example, [Melitz 1965, fn. 22, pp. 44-45]. I shall have more to say about this below.

[5]A recurring theme of this book is the need to develop empirically testable theories of consumer behavior. This will require that more interest and effort center on the consumer's decision process; on the process by which the consumer decides what bundle of comestibles is the one to choose. See, especially, Chapter IV.

[6]See footnote 3, above.

[7]This point will be emphasized, in particular, in Chapter III.

[8]An issue clearly related to a model's mathematical structure is the correspondence of symbolism to reality. We shall therefore keep in mind Professor Georgescu-Roegen's admonition that [Georgescu-Roegen 1970, p. 1]

... in our haste to mathematize economics we have often been carried away by mathematical formalism to the point of disregarding a basic requirement of science; namely, to have as clear an idea as possible about what corresponds in actuality to every piece of our symbolism.

[9]Implicit in Professor Leontief's argument is the notion that models in economics should be explanatory. The following passage serves, I believe, to corroborate my interpretation [Leontief 1971, p. 4].

To penetrate below the skin-thin surface of conventional consumption functions, it will be necessary to develop a systematic study of the structural characteristics and of the functioning of households, an area in which description and analysis of social, anthropological and demographic factors must obviously occupy the center of the stage.

[10]While one might quarrel with the notion that these methodological positions constitute an "exhaustive listing" of the available alternatives, it is equally clear that they have, at least in economics, effectively swept the field. To put the matter differently, while mysticism, sensationalism, essentialism, and so on constitute methodological positions, neither I nor anyone else would argue that they should be adopted in economics. See, for example, [Wong 1973].

[11]For a more detailed discussion of essentialism, see [Popper 1969].

[12]See also [Keita 1992, pp. 74-75].

[13]These include Galileo's theory of falling bodies, the Newtonian theory of gravitation as applied to the n-body problem, and Einstein's special theory of relativity [Wong 1973, p. 320].

[14]The observational term "glass" is, in fact, theory laden. It presumes lawlike behavior. It follows that "We can challenge whether a container is glass by testing the container for properties of a glass" [Wong 1973, p. 321].

[15]See, for example [Wong 1973, p. 323]. While it is true that the internal consistency of the instrumentalist position is not at issue, philosophers are increasingly troubled by the hostility to "'metaphysics' that [the instrumentalist] sees everywhere" [McCloskey 1983, p. 486]. On this view, metaphysics -- in the sense of value judgments, prior beliefs and subjective knowledge -- permeates economics and the other sciences. See, for example [McCloskey 1983, esp. pp. 486-493]. See also Chapter 9, pp. 175-177.

[16]This admittedly cryptic statement will be given more substance below. For the moment, I ask the reader's indulgence in simply taking the statement at face value.

[17]Actually, some economists are persuaded that the scope of the phenomena which can be explained using the "economics tool kit" is so broad that it "suggests the possibility of unifying [all of] the social sciences in an economics-led hegemony" [Demesetz 1997, p. 1].

[18]My invocation of authority may reflect what Professor McCloskey has called the "rhetoric of economics." See, for example [McCloskey 1983], [Mäki 1995] and [McCloskey 1995].

[19]Examples proffered by Nagel include the expressions "vacuum", "gene" and notably, "elasticity of demand at a point." These are examples of what he characterizes as "theoretical terms." [Nagel 1963, p. 212].

[20]The phrase "theoretical terms" is Nagel's characterization. Expressions designating nothing actually observable are referred to elsewhere as "theoretical concepts." See, for example [Clarkson 1963, p. 52].

[21]It is interesting to note that it was the presumed lack of a sufficient number of interpretive rules that led G.P.E. Clarkson to argue that the explanations of economic events proffered by the theories of demand and utility cannot be classified as "scientific explanations." On his view, these "explanations are, in fact, ex post rationalizations [Clarkson 1963, p. 85]. We shall have more to say about this below. See, especially, Chapter II.

[22]This point has not been lost on others. Indeed, in noting that violations of the axioms of revealed preference can be ascribed to changes in taste, Professor Furubotn argues that [Ekelund, Furubotn and Gramm 1972, p. 73]:

> Before observed consumer choices can be interpreted confidently it would seem essential to learn more about individual decision-making behavior under the conditions actually operative in the real world.

Professor Caldwell notes that the same problem attaches to empirical tests of the neoclassical maximization hypothesis. See, for example, [Caldwell 1983, p. 824]. For an alternative view, see [Boland 1981] and [Boland 1979].

[23]As it happens, "as if" statements can serve neither to predict nor to explain. See [Melitz 1965, p. 50]. For a discussion of "break downs" of the "as if" principle, see [DePalma et al 1994, pp. 433-434]. For more on the "as if" construal, see [Russell and Thaler 1985, pp. 1080-1081] and [Mayer 1993, pp. 51-52]. We shall have more to say about this below.

[24]Actually, Professor Friedman's position is stronger than this. On his view, "To be important ... a hypothesis must be descriptively false in its assumptions" [Friedman 1953, pp. 14-15]. The reason for this ostensibly paradoxical claim is that [Friedman 1953, pp. 14-15]:

> A hypothesis is important if it 'explains' much by little, that is, if it abstracts the common and crucial elements from the mass of complex and detailed circumstances surrounding the phenomena to be explained and permits valid predictions on the basis of them alone.

Unfortunately, as Professor Nagel points out, an assumption may be unrealistic in at least three senses, and Professor Friedman is not clear as to the sense in which he uses the word "unrealistic" [Nagel 1963, pp. 214-216]. The result is that one cannot "get his teeth" into the issue at hand. This much can, however, be said: Friedman is correct in asserting that abstraction is a sine qua non for the provision of hypotheses with wide application. It does not follow, however, that abstraction necessarily involves the employment of false assumptions [Melitz 1965, p. 40]. On the contrary,

> ... [while] abstraction facilitates the attainment of truth, [it] does not necessitate the acceptance of false assumptions, or immersion in 'unrealism' of any sort [Melitz 1965, p. 41].

[25]The literature on token economies and experimental economics generally focuses, inter alia, on the problem of postulate verification. See, for example, Chapter 2, pp. 34-37.

[26]Professor Melitz seems generally to agree with the proposition that scientific advance in economics is predicated upon systematic, empirical verification of assumptions. On his view, "... any errors uncovered in assumptions may also be considered as clues regarding the possible improvement of the theory" [Melitz 1965, p. 49]. See, also [Melitz 1965, p. 52].

[27]This is not say that unrealistic assumptions should never by employed. Indeed, following Professor Koopmans, economic theory consists in a sequence of models that seek to represent different aspects of an evermore complicated reality. On this view,

> The study of ... simpler models is protected from the reproach of unreality by the consideration that these models may be prototypes of more realistic, but also more complicated, subsequent models [Koopmans 1957, pp. 142-143].

The presumption is, in other words, that the evolution of economic science involves the construction of progressively "more complicated models"; that is, the employment of "more realistic" assumptions. For more on the "progressive dialogue" between theory development and empirical results see [Smith 1989, p. 168].

[28]An illustration of the point at issue has already been provided. We have seen that violation of the axioms of revealed preference can be ascribed to changes in taste; to a violation, if you will of the ceteris paribus auxiliary assumption. See my discussion on page 9 above. See also [Ekelund, Furubotn and Gramm 1972, p. 73, esp. fn.3].

[29]Some would argue, in fact, that the employment of auxiliary assumptions insulates the hypothesis in question from empirical test. Professor McCloskey invokes the argument of the physicist-philosopher Pierre Duhem [McCloskey 1983, p. 487]: Suppose that the hypothesis H implies a testing observation O; "it implies it, that is, not by itself, but only with the addition of ancillary hypotheses H_1, H_2, and so forth that make the measurement possible .... Then of course not-O

implies not-H -- or not-H₁ or not-H̲ or any number of failures of premises irrelevant to the main hypothesis in question." In McCloskey's view, the hypothesis in question "is insulated from crucial test by the ancillary hypotheses necessary to bring it to a test" [McCloskey 1983, p. 487]. See also [Mayer 1993, p. 90].

[30]See also [Smith 1994, p. 127].

[31]As for the benefits, it is clear that appeal to unrealistic generative assumptions "simplifies the analysis."

[32]See also [Nagel 1963, pp. 214-215].

[33]See also [Leontief 1971, p. 5] and pp. 13-14 above.

[34]See, for example, p. 7 above.

[35]A careful reading of Professor Friedman's "Methodology of Positive Economics" reveals a marked propensity to use the word "explain." Indeed, he uses the word in what is clearly one of the more important passages in the essay:

... in general, the more significant the theory, the more unrealistic the assumptions.... A hypothesis is important if it 'EXPLAINS' much by little... [Friedman 1953, pp. 14-15]. (emphasis mine)

[36]See [Leontief 1971, esp. p. 5]. See also the discussion on pp. 13-14 above.

[37]See, for example [Karl Popper 1957, 1968, 1969].

[38]A universal law is a statement with no spatio-temporal reference. See, for example [Wong 1973, p. 320].

[39]At the risk of some redundancy, there is no question as to whether a theory's auxiliary assumptions must be realistic. Regardless of the methodological position adopted, if the ambiguity of test results is to be reduced, auxiliary assumptions must accord as closely as possible with reality. See the discussion on pp. 15-16 above.

[40]See also [Keita 1992, p. 68] and [Caldwell 1991, esp. p.29]. In effect, I share Professor Mayer's view that "... a thoroughgoing instrumentalism is undesirable because we want to explain as well as predict...." [Mayer 1993, p. 92].

[41]In what follows, I use the terms "theory" and "model" interchangeably. This is not to say that it is not possible to argue that the former might be distinguished from the latter. Professor Papandreou has, for example, adopted the convention that whereas a "model" consists of a set of irrefutable statements, a "theory" consists of refutable statements [Papandreou 1963]. This convention is not adopted here. In effect, I share Professor Melitz's view that [Melitz 1965, fn. 22, pp. 44-45]:

... although general scientific statements may be capable of refutation in principle, as a rule scientific hypotheses are rejected because of disconfirmation, or in other words, on grounds of high probability of error.... Consequently, as long as statements can be disconfirmed, which is true of those in Papandreou's 'models', I do not see why the issue of refutability as such, should be of particular concern.

[42]What is of interest here is not simply the correspondence of symbolism to reality. What is of particular concern is whether the mathematical structure of a model is congenial to its stated purpose(s). As we shall see, this is often not the case. Indeed, under certain circumstances, the mathematics employed may result in the inability of a model to yield predictions relative to phenomena that, presumably, come under its purview. See, for example, Chapter III below.

Chapter 2

Ordinal Utility Theory

We can observe the reaction of an individual to two different sets of prices only at two different times. How can we tell what part of the difference in his purchases is due to the difference in prices and what part to the change in his preferences that has taken place meanwhile?

Joan Robinson

INTRODUCTION

The traditional, static theory of demand is based on the presumption that the individual consumer seeks to maximize utility at a moment in time, subject to an income constraint. In the decision environment contemplated, the consumer's tastes and preferences are taken to be summarized in the single-equation utility function

$$U = f(x_1, x_2, \ldots, x_n). \qquad (2-1)$$

Here, the objects of choice, the x_i, $I = 1, 2, \ldots n$, are interpretable as the consumption rates of the n goods and services. Typically, the number of goods and services appearing as arguments of the utility function is unspecified.[1]

The variables over which the consumer exercises discretion, the x_i, are thought of as yielding utility or satisfaction per unit time. U, then, is understood to represent the flow of satisfaction that occurs, with certainty, as a result of the substitution of the imperfectly substitutable objects of choice, the x_i.[2] Finally, because it is taken to be immeasurable, the metric in which utility is expressed is a subjectively determined ordinal index.[3]

The income constraint follows straightforwardly. Given the consumer's nominal income, y^o, and given the set of prevailing commodity prices, p_i^o, $i = 1, 2, \ldots n$, we have

$$y^o - \sum_{i=1}^{n} p_i^o \cdot x_i = 0 \qquad (2\text{-}2)$$

as the relevant constraint. The simple expedient of maximizing (2-1) subject to (2-2) yields the vector of utility maximizing quantities demanded of each commodity; a procedure that determines one point on each of the demand curves for each of the n goods.[4]

THE POSTULATES

The presumption that a consumer possesses a utility function of the form given by (2-1) is predicated on the assumption that the consumer is rational; that the consumer's behavior is consistent with the following statements: (1) for all possible pairs of consumption bundles A and B, the consumer knows whether he prefers A to B or B to A, or whether he is indifferent among them; (2) only one of the three possibilities is true for any pair of consumption bundles, and (3) if the consumer prefers A to B and B to C, he will prefer A to C.[5]

This set of postulates constitutes the key set of assumptions or axioms upon which ordinal utility theory and, therefore, the Hicksian variant of the theory of demand, is built. What is contemplated is a "scale of preferences" [Hicks 1939, p. 18]; a rank ordering that does not assume the measurability of utility. One of Professor Hicks' singular achievements was the demonstration that ". . . a full theory of consumer's demand at least as thorough-going as Marshall's . . ." [Hicks 1939, p. 18] could be built upon a scale preference; that the quantitative or cardinal concept of utility is not necessary to, in his words, "explain market phenomena."

Significantly, Professor Hicks sought to eliminate references to the cardinality of utility, not only because they are ". . . irrelevant to the problem in hand, and their presence is likely to obscure the vision," but because [Hicks 1939, p. 18]:

> If one is a utilitarian in philosophy, one has a perfect right to be a utilitarian in one's economics. But if one is not (and few people are utilitarians nowadays), one also has the right to an economics free of utilitarian assumptions.

While Professor Hicks did succeed in purging many of the elements of utilitarian philosophy from the classical theory of demand, vestiges of the empirically untestable philosophy remain: "Utility," whether cardinal or ordinal, is not subject to direct observation or measurement.[6]

Presumably with the empirical testability of theories in mind, Professor Samuelson set out to "purge demand theory of vestigial traces of the utility concept" [Samuelson 1938]. His objective was, simply stated, to develop a theory of consumer behavior which avoided direct reliance on the utility concept. Samuelson proposed instead to consider only those conditions that can be expressed in terms of observable price-quantity relations [Houthakker 1961, pp. 706-710; Ekelund, Furubotn and Gramm 1972, pp. 68-73]. The product of his efforts [Samuelson 1938, 1947] has come to be called the Theory of Revealed Preference; a theory whose key generative assumptions are summarized in terms of the so-called weak and strong axioms of revealed preference. The weak axiom requires that if consumption bundle A is revealed to be preferred to consumption bundle B, that B must never be revealed to be preferred to A. The strong axiom -- the axiom that assures the transitivity of revealed preferences -- requires that if A is preferred to B, which is revealed to be preferred to C, . . ., which is revealed to be preferred to Z, Z must never be revealed to be preferred to A.[7]

It has been shown that the set of axioms upon which the ordinal utility analysis is built are logically equivalent to the weak and strong axioms of revealed preference theory [Houthakker 1950, Uzawa 1960]. It follows that a test of the empirical content of either set of axioms is a test of the empirical content of the other.[8]

TESTS OF THE POSTULATES

Many of the recent attempts to confirm the postulates of ordinal utility theory have likely been precipitated by attacks on their factual content.[9] It is not clear, however, whether the catalyst to these apologia has been a desire to establish the explanatory power of the theory, or whether it is felt that more is ultimately at issue.[10] Whatever the precise catalyst to the various tests of the postulates of ordinal utility theory (and, therefore, of the revealed preference theory), this much can be said: Within the context of ordinal utility theory, empirical confirmation of the rationality postulate is a sine qua non for explanatory power. It is for this reason that our interest centers on the test efforts.

While it is possible to conclude that, "In general [experimental results] support the qualitative predictions of neoclassical economic theory" [Tarr 1976, p. 1136], the most appropriate characterization is that the test results are ambiguous.[11] This should come as no surprise. It is, after all, a brute fact that empirical testing of the ordinal utility and revealed preference axioms is not a straightforward matter. The reason difficulties emerge is that the interpretation of test results is ambiguous. Indeed, while the axiomatic or revealed preference approach constitutes a major intellectual achievement,[12] it has not resulted in any significant improvement in empirical research on consumer behavior. Professor Furubotn provides us with this assessment [Ekelund, Furubotn and Gramm 1972, p. 73]:

> Longstanding problems concerning aggregation and interaction have been mentioned as obstacles to applied work . . . but perhaps a more basic source of difficulty lies in the assumption of strict consumer rationality. Both utility theory and revealed-preference theory require that the consumer show highly consistent choice behavior . . . . This rather rigid position . . . is ill adapted to the needs of an empirical science. Before observed consumer choices can be interpreted confidently it would seem essential to learn more about individual decision-making behavior under the conditions actually operative in the real world. This means, inter alia, that the process of human decision-making itself and such factors as uncertainty, the cost of search, the social setting of the choice, etc. must be taken into account by the demand model.[13]

THE SOURCE OF DIFFICULTY IN SECURING EMPIRICAL VERIFICATION OF THE POSTULATES

While the intent of the revealed preference formulation was to rid the theory of demand of "the last vestiges" of empirically untestable utilitarian philosophy, we have seen that: a) the axioms of ordinal utility theory and of revealed preference theory are logically equivalent, and b) that the empirical verifiability of the rationality postulate has not been enhanced by appeal to observable price-quantity relations. Those tests of the rationality postulate that have been conducted have, in all cases, resulted in the emergence of ambiguous test results.

The ambiguity of test results should not come as a surprise. Neither ordinal utility nor revealed preference theory provides us with interpretive rules. This follows from the fact that the interpretation of test results requires: a) an independent means of determining a consumer's preferences, and b) an "adequate" understanding of the way in which preferences change over time (if, indeed, they do change over time).[14] Yet this requires that the researcher have some means of determining whether the consumer's preferences remained the same throughout the series of trials. Unfortunately, neither ordinal utility theory nor revealed preference theory provides the researcher with a means of determining the consumer's preference structure before the experiments begin. It follows that neither of the conditions requisite to the explicit formulation of interpretive rules is satisfied.[15]

If the consumer's preference structure were known to be constant, the researcher could use the data from various trials to test the rationality postulate.[16] But the data from one set of trials cannot, in any event, be used to confirm the truth value of both the constancy of tastes and the rationality postulate.[17] We cannot, in other words [Clarkson 1963, p. 77]:

> . . . use the same collection of data to declare that the preference scale is consistent, that all alternatives were rank ordered prior to the selection taking place, and that the (consumer) chose that set of comestibles that yielded (him) the highest utility.[18]

Because of the presence in both ordinal utility theory and the theory of revealed preference of an unidentified exogenous variable -- notably the consumer's preference structure -- it is not possible to formulate the interpretive rules requisite to the confirmation of the rationality postulate.

Because of the unidentified nature of the consumer's preference structure, the set of events over which utility (and therefore demand) theory is supposed to hold cannot be completely defined or identified. In Clarkson's words [Clarkson 1963, p. 99]:

> . . . there is an insufficient number of interpretive rules to allow one to determine whether the behavior of the consumer is consistent with the law (of demand) or not.[19]

What has been said so far reduces to this: The axioms of ordinal utility theory and of revealed preference theory reduce to the presumption that the consumer is "rational" (and, moreover, that his desideratum is the maximization of utility). The rationality postulate, therefore, constitutes one of the generative assumptions of the two logically equivalent theories. Insofar as the postulate is not independently testable, it cannot be regarded as "realistic." It follows that the two theories cannot be used to explain consumer behavior. On the other hand, the fact that the rationality postulate cannot be confirmed does not, by itself, imply that the two theories cannot be used to predict consumer behavior.

Unfortunately, the predictive powers of the two theories are themselves severely encumbered. This follows from the fact that: a) the falsity of the rationality postulate enhances the probability that the two theories may generate false predictions; b) tests of the theories' predictions must, inevitably, yield ambiguous results. A crucial auxiliary assumption -- an assumption employed in both theories -- cannot be independently confirmed: It is not possible, in other words, to use one series of trials to confirm both that a consumer is rational (a generative assumption) and that his preference structure is constant (an auxiliary assumption). Moreover, because of the inability to specify the requisite interpretive rules, it is not possible unambiguously to determine the two theories' "designed" classes of implications. We do not know, in effect, for which classes of real world phenomena the theories' predictions are supposed to have basic relevance. At most, we are able to say that the intent of the ordinal utility theory must evidently be to make predictions relative to: a) the commodity composition of the consumer's optimal consumption bundle (given his tastes and preferences, a specified level of real income, and the prevailing commodity price vector), and b) changes in the optimal consumption bundle precipitated either by compensated or uncompensated changes in the price vector or in real income (again, given tastes and preferences).

With this in mind, I turn next to a consideration of some recent technical extensions of ordinal utility analysis; extensions intended to sharpen the qualitative predictions of the theory.

TECHNICAL EXTENSIONS OF THE ORDINAL UTILITY THEORY

The mathematical structure of the consumer's constrained optimization problem is summarized, in the traditional model, by equations (2-1) and (2-2). On the assumption that utility function (2-1) is quasi-concave [Wold and Jureen 1953, pp. 81-87; Graaff 1967, pp. 42-43; Gorman 1957, pp. 40-50] and that the arguments of the function are perfectly divisible, a static utility maximizing solution must emerge. The problem, as it is summarized in system (2-1) and (2-2), is cast in the familiar mold of the classical calculus.

While the specific mathematical form imparted to the maximand [equation (2-1)] and to the feasible set [defined by (2-2)] is of significance from a number of points of view, much attention has centered on the possibility that the optimal solution may involve negative consumption rates of one or more of the commodities. That this possibility cannot be reconciled with a static decision environment is obvious. Moreover, casual observation suggests that the number of commodities confronting the consumer is enormous. Hence, a model predicting positive consumption rates of all goods would be at variance with reality. In a word, the presumed static decision environment cannot be reconciled with negative consumption rates of one or more goods. On the other hand, the finite nature of the consumer's budget, the enormity of the array of available goods, and the notion that the consumer will typically choose among variants of the product types confronting him, impel us to recognize that the optimal bundle will involve zero consumption rates of some goods.

These considerations led to a reformulation of the ordinal utility model along Kuhn-Tucker lines; a formulation involving the non-negativity restraints

$$x_i \geq 0, i = 1, 2, \ldots, n. \qquad (2\text{-}3)$$

In effect, the consumer is thought of as being confronted with the constrained maximization problem summarized by equations (2-1) and (2-

2) and the inequality constraints (2-3) [Lancaster 1968, Ch. 5; Wu and Pontney 1967, Ch. 8; Houthakker 1961].

It may at first appear that recasting the consumer's optimization problem along nonlinear programming lines effectively solves the problem outlined above. The difficulty is that the "solution" leads to the emergence of another problem. While there is general agreement as to the quasi-concavity and nonadditivity of (2-1) [Gorman 1957; Green 1964, Chs. 2, 3, 4], there remains a question as to whether satiety phenomena might be introduced into the model.[20] In the Kuhn-Tucker formulation satiety is typically ruled out, and the f_i are assumed positive for all positive consumption rates of the x_i. The predictions that emerge from a model of this sort have been summarized as follows [Furubotn 1974, p. 292]:

(i) The consumer may specialize deliberately in the consumption of a single good and the good chosen may be any one of the n goods available in the system.

(ii) The consumer's decision to specialize in the good does not necessarily come about because his income is low; corner solutions can appear at any level of real income.

(iii) The individual may choose to consume simultaneously each type of consumer good produced in the system.

(iv) The consumer will show an infinite demand for any good that carries a zero price.[21]

The point is that the predicted consumption patterns, optimal commodity bundles involving as few as one or as many as n distinct types of goods, are most implausible. Yet, as Furubotn has emphasized,". . . all that is required to generate these odd behavioral patterns is the 'right' structure of relative prices" [Furubotn 1974, p. 292]. There is, moreover, the additional problem that with n extremely large, as it is in advanced economic systems, the sum of all unit prices will exceed the consumer's finite income. It follows that if the optimal bundle does involve all n goods, the consumer must purchase less than one unit of each or, at minimum, less than one unit of most of the n goods. The interpretation must therefore be that [Furubotn 1974, p. 293]:

... the consumer prefers minute quantities of a great many different goods
to larger (integral) quantities of fewer goods . . . [Yet we know that] While
certain goods are divisible and may be purchased fractionally, the consumer
clearly does not buy all or most commodities in infinitesimal amounts.

Both intuition and casual empiricism suggest the implausibility of this
prediction. Yet any attempt to modify the structure of the ordinal utility
theory to accommodate this objection leads to other difficulties.

If, for example, utility function (2-1) is assumed to be consistent with
Debreu's axiom of insatiability [Debreu 1959, p. 55], the possibility
emerges that the consumer may become satiated with respect to the
consumption of any one commodity, or with the consumption of any
proper subset of the n commodities.[22] Given this interpretation of his
preference structure, the consumer's optimal commodity bundle may then
involve any number of goods from one through n, the number of goods
in the system.

While the explicit introduction of satiety assumptions enhances the
flexibility of the ordinal utility analysis, a balanced assessment of the
modified Kuhn-Tucker formulation must be that [Furubotn 1974, p. 294]:

... regardless of what is done along these lines, the core problem concerning
the equilibrium number of goods remains.

If the utility function is defined so that n distinct ridge lines exist in the
commodity space, extreme solutions of the type N = n cannot be avoided.
That is, at some income levels, . . . the consumer must purchase positive
amounts of all the goods in the system. On the other hand, a failure to
incorporate n ridge lines into the indifference map implies that . . . the
consumer can, presumably, achieve unlimited satisfaction by pushing the
consumption of a free good.[23]

The Number of Goods Chosen at Equilibrium

The question of the number of goods chosen at equilibrium raises
important issues, both at the conceptual and the applied level. From a
methodological point of view, one might plausibly ask precisely what
generative assumptions should be employed. Ruling out satiety
phenomena leads to one set of problems. On the other hand, the explicit
introduction of satiety -- in the form of Debreu's axiom of insatiability --

leads to still other problems. And the problems, in turn, have ultimately to do with the emergence of predictions that cannot be reconciled with the empirical record. Yet we know, based upon our discussion in Chapter I, that if a predictive model is to be accepted, all of its derived implications must be defensible.[24]

Even if one were willing to brush aside the methodological questions, there remains the question of the suitability for empirical work of the Kuhn-Tucker variant of the ordinal utility theory. Professor Furubotn's assessment is, once again, apropos [Furubotn 1974, pp. 294-295]:

> None of the proposed hypotheses concerning the shape of individual preferences is truly satisfactory for applied work because none is able to do any more than rule out unrealistic 'low end' solutions ($N = 1, N = 2, N = 3$, ..., $N - L$). .... High end solutions are inherent in the orthodox Kuhn-Tucker model and can never be ruled out unless the form of the utility function ... is changed drastically.[25]

Having come this far, one might plausibly ask why a question so important as this have not received wider attention. The fact that it has not is perhaps explained by a tendency to rationalize the $N = n$ case; the case in which the number of commodities in the optimal bundle equals the number of goods in the system. One approach frequently employed is to treat a proper subset of the commodities as a composite good [Hicks 1939; Samuelson 1947, pp. 141-146]. That his approach is patently unsatisfactory is, however, obvious. To see this, consider the ordinal utility function

$$U = f(X, Y), \qquad (2\text{-}4)$$

where utility enjoyed per unit time, U, is a function of the consumption rates of commodity X and the composite commodity, Y.[26]

Now, given the composite good interpretation of Y, the statement that he has a utility function like (2-4) asserts that, as a matter of empirical fact, the consumer has a utility function if and only if he buys a quantity of X and Y, given their prevailing prices, such that $y = P_x X + p_y Y$. Here, as before, y is understood to be the consumer's nominal or money income this period, and p_x and p_y are, respectively, the prices of commodities X and Y.

The difficulty is that, because Y represents all the commodities available to the consumer other than X, the sum $p_x X + p_y Y$ must always represent the consumer's purchases. This is so at any cross-section of time, no matter what the commodity composition of the consumer's optimal bundle [Clarkson 1963, p. 54]. It follows that once the composite good is introduced, the concept of a utility function is independent of the truth value of its component parts; it takes on the character of a tautology [Clarkson 1963, p. 18]. Once this is recognized, it becomes a practical impossibility to disconfirm the predictions of the model.

A potentially more satisfactory approach to handling the problem is to view the n goods in (2-1) not as the universal set of all consumer goods in the economy, but rather as a proper subset of the universal set. On this interpretation, the $N = n$ solution appears to be more plausible. Yet even this approach is not without difficulty. The effect of an a priori delimitation of the consumer's choice space is the set of implications: 1) That the commodity composition of the consumer's optimal consumption bundle is invariant with respect to changes in real income, and 2) That the model builder can predesignate the arguments of the individual consumer's utility function. Neither of these implications is, of course, defensible. As Professor Duesenberry has pointed out [Duesenberry 1952, p. 22]

> . . . it seems clear that psychologically an improvement of the living standard consists in satisfying one's needs in a better way. This may sometimes involve consuming something different.

Clearly, the implication that changes in real income cannot be catalysts to changes in the commodity composition of the optimal bundle is at variance with observable reality [Furubotn 1974, p. 298].[27] The notion that the model builder can specify a priori the arguments of the consumer's maximand is not only methodologically unacceptable, it is manifestly absurd.

In sum, a satisfactory solution to the problem of the number of goods chosen at equilibrium has not yet been found. More properly, it has not been found in the context of the orthodox, single-equation utility function.[28]

The Indirect Utility Function

A survey of the extensions of the ordinal utility analysis would not be complete without mention of the indirect utility function. It is conventional to write the utility function in the form given by (2-1). That is, the arguments of the individual consumer's utility function are normally taken to be the consumption rates of various commodities.[29] However, insofar as the demand for each commodity is a function of prices and income, the latter variables can appear as arguments of the utility function. We may conceive of utility as an indirect function of prices and income [Hotelling 1932; Hicks 1958]. On this interpretation, the "indirect" utility function may be written

$$U = Y(w_1, w_2, \ldots w_n), \qquad (2\text{-}5)$$

where the w_i represent price-income ratios:

$$w_1 = \frac{pi}{y}, i = 1, 2, \ldots n.$$

As Professor Hicks has shown [Hicks 1958], (2-5) can be manipulated to yield indifference surfaces and that, moreover, all of the standard propositions of the orthodox ordinal utility analysis and of the traditional theory of demand obtain [Roy 1947].

The relationship of the indirect utility function (2-5) to the orthodox utility function (2-1) is established via the concept of duality [Houthakker 1952]. Thus, if (2-5) is minimized subject to budget constraint (2-2), the result that emerges is formally equivalent to maximizing (2-1) subject to (2-2).

An objective assessment of the indirect utility function formulation might reasonably proceed along these lines: While the indirect utility function is analytically convenient, especially in the construction of cost-of-living indices [Theil 1975, p. 134], it has not significantly altered the orthodox conception of the consumer's decision environment. The perception of the consumer's desideratum, income contraint and choice process remain unchanged. To paraphrase Professor Samuelson [Samuelson 1965b], because the optimization problems involving utility functions (2-1) and (2-5) employ parallel technical procedures, no fundamentally different conclusions about consumer demand can be anticipated. It follows that the methodological and other difficulties associated with (2-1) apply with equal gravity to (2-5). Accordingly, I shall have no more to say about the indirect utility function.

Commodity Indivisibility

Frequently, a meaningful economic interpretation cannot be made of solutions to problems involving continuous functions. While this problem would be especially relevant in the case of stock-flow demand models [Bushaw and Clower 1957, Ch. 5; Hadar 1965], such models are intrinsically dynamic and, as a result, are not considered here.[30] Yet, as we have seen, the problem of rationalizing optimal consumption bundles involving fractional amounts of one or more goods arises in the context of the orthodox flow-flow utility model; in models in which the consumer's preference structure is summarized by a utility function of the form given by (2-1).

Suppose now that at least some commodities confronting the consumer are indivisible. In this event, the standard methods of the calculus no longer retain basic relevance. In effect, formulations of the consumer's optimization problem involving twice differentiable functions must be abandoned. With this in mind, some authors have suggested that the revealed preference approach be adapted to the explicit handling of indivisible commodities [Wagner 1956]. However, both because little progress along these lines has been made, and because the revealed preference approach has already been discussed, my interest centers on another suggestion; namely, that the consumer's decision environment be summarized in terms of an integer programming problem.

Unfortunately, while an integer programming formulation seems an eminently plausible solution to the problem of commodity indivisibility, it may not be a "solution" at all:

The formal apparatus used to analyze consumer behavior has to meet some rather exacting standards . . . .

If it is believed that infinitesimal purchases are impossible, representation of consumer preferences should . . . never lead to a solution calling for any optimum quantity to be non-integral . . . . [Moreover] Since it is difficult to conceive of an individual spending his entire income on a single commodity . . . the shapes of the indifference manifolds should be inconsistent with a maximizing solution of this type. Similarly, the utility function should not permit a solution where all n commodities (i.e., all goods in the system) are to be consumed simultaneously. Quadratic and other standard programming forms do not take account of these requirements. There is, therefore, reason to be skeptical about the worth of extending such methods to integer programming applications in the theory of demand [Ekelund, Furubotn and Gramm 1972, p. 67].

It would appear, then, that computational difficulties aside [Roberts and Schulze 1973, pp. 431-433; Naylor and Vernon 1969, pp. 269-278], it is not surprising that "A comprehensive theory incorporating such changes has not yet been developed. . . ." [Ekelund, Furubotn and Gramm 1972, p. 67].

IN SUMMARY . . .

The extensions and revisions of the ordinal utility analysis that have been undertaken have much in common. They have, by and large, been concerned with the mathematical structure of the traditional model. Indeed, it can be argued that those revisions that have been proffered did not take as their point of departure questions about the traditional conception of the consumer's decision problem in general, or of his presumed desideratum in particular. Rather, the view seems to be that more general and rigorous statements of the rudimentary demand theorems can be achieved via appeal to observed price-quantity relations, as in the case of revealed preference theory, and the explicit introduction, in the case of ordinal utility analysis, of non-negativity and other conditions.

An objective assessment of the post-war demand theory literature must, therefore, conclude that no one of the technical extensions or revisions of the traditional analysis has resolved the fundamental methodological problems. The basic purpose of the traditional ordinal utility analysis re-emerges in each of the model variants discussed; each seeks to make predictions relative to observed consumer behavior. Yet the revealed preference approach is logically equivalent to ordinal utility theory, and each of the technical extensions retains the ordinal utility function as the consumer's maximand. It follows that the problem of the presence of an unidentified exogenous variable -- the consumer's preference structure -- has not been resolved. Because model builders cannot specify a priori what the consumer's preference structure is, they are unable unambiguously to test their models' predictions. The various models' predictions cannot be disconfirmed precisely because a key auxiliary assumption -- that tastes and preferences have remained fixed during the test period -- cannot be independently confirmed.[31] Moreover, without independent knowledge of the consumer's preference structure, interpretive rules cannot be specified; rules that constitute a <u>sine qua non</u> for the identification of a model's designed classes of implications.[32]

What is at issue, then, is the predictive power of the ordinal utility model -- whether in the form proffered by Professor Hicks, or whether in the technically refined form of recent years. The conclusion must, it would seem, be that

> . . . there is reason to believe that disproportionate attention has been given to the elementary model based on indifference curves. The conventional analysis has won the day too completely and, until quite recently, alternative approaches have been generally neglected by the profession. This bias . . . seems especially important, moreover, because of the lack of convincing evidence to show that the predictive powers of conventional demand theory have been improving over time . . . the operational significance of traditional demand analysis is still quite modest . . . . [Ekelund, Furubotn and Gramm 1972, p. 57].

NOTES

[1]An exception is, of course, the pedagogically convenient case in which n is taken to be equal to two; the situation characterized in the usual textbook exposition.

[2]The presumption is that the indifference hyperplanes to which (2-1) gives rise are convex; they are consistent with what has come to be called the principle of diminishing marginal rate of substitution [Hicks 1939, Ch. I; Hicks and Allen 1934]. For a critical view of this rationalization of convexity, see [Knight 1944]. For a more recent, thorough-going discussion of convexity, see [Riley 1977].

[3]An exception is the von Neumann-Morgenstern utility index; an index that is cardinal in the restricted sense that the utility numbers employed provide an interval scale so that, pari passu, differences between them are meaningful. See, for example, [von Neumann and Morgenstern 1947, Ch. I; Henderson and Quandt 1971, Ch. II, esp. p. 47].

[4]Other points on each of the n demand curves can, in principle, be generated. Precisely how this is done depends upon the nature of the demand curves to be derived. At issue is whether real or nominal income is regarded as a parameter of the demand function and, hence, of the demand curve. While the taxonomy of independent variables and parameters is a complex question in empirical work, the demand curve of the Marshall-Hicks tradition is, in fact, a "compensated" or real income constant demand curve. See, for example [Friedman 1949].

[5]The phrase "consumption bundle" may be interpreted in the context of utility function (2-1). A particular consumption bundle, A, contemplates the specification of a unique consumption rate of all (or some) of the x_i commodities appearing in the consumer's utility function. As well shall see, whether or not a particular optimal (or utility maximizing) consumption bundle involves positive amounts of all of the x_i depends on the mathematical structure of the model. This issue is momentarily deferred. For a statement of the sufficient conditions for the existence of a utility function of the form given by (2-1), see [Henderson and Quandt 1971, p. 13]. For a comparison of the epistemological status of the rationality postulate in the Austrian and "Chicago" schools see [Paque 1985].

[6]For a discussion of the implications, inter alia, for social welfare theory, see Chapter VIII, below.

[7]See, for example [Henderson and Quandt 1971, p. 40]. See also [Little 1949; Samuelson 1948; Houthakker 1950; Mishan 1961; Bandyopadhyay 1988].

[8]While its chief purpose is to avoid direct reliance on the utility concept, a number of authors have used the revealed preference apparatus to draw inferences about the properties of the underlying utility function. Professor Fuchs-Seliger uses the theory to argue, for example, that certain properties of income-consumption curves imply continuity of the utility function [Fuchs-Seliger 1980]. In his paper "Fuzzy Revealed Preference Theory," Professor Basu argues that appeal to fuzzy set theory enables the researcher to distinguish what he

characterizes as "degrees of rationality" [Basu 1984]. For more on the equivalence of axiom systems see [Kim and Richter 1986].

[9]For representative critiques of the classical rationality postulate and/or the maximization hypothesis, see [Sen 1995, esp. p. 15]; [North 1994, p. 362]; [Nelson 1995, esp. p. 70]; [Furubotn and Richter 1994]; [Nozick 1994, esp. p. 317]; [Keita 1992, esp. pp. 33, 74-75, 83, 96 and 144]; [Caldwell 1991, esp. pp. 18-19], and [Cosmides and Tooby 1994].

[10]One cannot help but feel that it is the latter that accounts for much of the effort at "shoring up" the rationality postulate. While homo economicus is taken by economists as, in some sense, representative of reality, the concept has not been taken at face value by others [Shubik 1970, pp. 410-411]. See also Chapter VIII, below. The result has been frequent challenges of the rationality postulate and of the presumed desideratum of traditional economic theory; in particular, of the assumption that individual consumers seek to maximize utility. See, for example [Heiner 1983, esp. p. 562; Wilde, LeBaron and Israelsen 1985; Heiner 1985a, esp. p. 260; Heiner 1985b; Slovic and Lichtenstein 1983; Akerloff and Yellen 1985]. See Chapter I and footnote 9, above. For a defense of the maximization postulate see [Bös 1986], [Bös 1987] and [Boland 1981].

[11] Professor Vernon Smith, one of the chief proponents of experimental economics is himself somewhat skeptical about the approach. See, for example [Smith 1985, p. 265 and Smith 1982, pp. 931 and 952]. In particular, he emphasizes that [Smith 1985, p. 266]:

Even if preference theory accounts for many agents' stationary state choices in certain experimental situations, it tells us nothing about the PROCESSES that yield these 'good' 'predictions or why some agents' behavior is not consistent with the theory (emphasis in original).

See also [Heiner 1985a and Friedman 1985].

Finally, the phenomenon of "preference reversal" has been a source of much controversy in the experimental literature. See, for example [Tversky and Thaler 1990], [Slovic and Lichtenstein 1983 and Smith 1985, p. 268]. For more on the preference reversal phenomenon see footnote 14, Chapter 6.

[12]In Professor Houthakker's words, "If we regard [the revealed preference approach] as an attempt at theoretical clarification, it has certainly been successful . . . As far as the foundations of the static theory of choice for a single consumer are concerned, we now know where we stand" [Houthakker 1961, p. 713].

[13]For more on experimental and other tests of the rationality postulate, the maximization hypothesis and expected utility theory see [Knez, Smith and Williams 1985], [Machina 1989], [Russell and Thaler 1985, esp. pp. 1080-1081], [Mayer 1993, esp. pp. 152-153], and [Tversky and Thaler 1990].

[14]The proviso is attached to condition b) to take account of the Stigler-Becker hypothesis referred to above. See p. 21, above. Of course, the possibility that tastes do change over time as a result, inter alia, of advertising activities has not

been ignored. See, for example [Basmann 1956] and [Pessemier 1978]. There is, in fact, a body of evidence [and opinion] which suggests that preferences and values [in the sense of moral tastes] are endogenously determined. See, for example [Buchanan 1994b, p. 76], [Williamson 1993, p. 104], [Stiglitz 1993, pp. 111-112], [Karni and Schmeidler 1990], [Elster 1989], [Bowles and Gintis 1993, esp. pp. 99-100], [Cohen and Axelrod 1984], [Persky 1995], [Throsby 1994, esp. p. 3], [Buchanan 1994a, p. 125], [Baron and Hannan 1994], [Frank 1992, esp. p. 166], [North 1994], [Buchanan 1991, esp. pp. 185-186]. Also see Chapter VIII, below.

[15]In effect, the theory is insulated from empirical disconfirmation. See, for example, [Keita 1992, pp. 96-97]. For more on the ceteris paribus assumption and the ambiguity of test results, see [Persky 1990, esp. pp. 188 and 192-193] and [Aaron 1994, esp. pp. 4-8]. See also footnotes 13 and 14, above.

[16]Professors Stigler and Becker advance the hypothesis that ". . . one may usefully treat tastes as stable over time and similar among people . . . ." [Stigler and Becker 1977, p. 76]. Unfortunately, the predictive and explanatory "success" of their formulation depends critically upon the researcher's knowledge, inter alia, of the shadow price vector confronting the consumer; a fact that complicates the establishment of the relevant interpretive rules. I shall have more to say about the Stigler-Becker thesis in Chapter V.

[17]For more on this point, see [Clarkson 1963, Ch. II, esp. pp. 18 and 75].

[18]Writing at almost the same time, Professor Robinson had this to say [Robinson 1962, pp. 49-50]:

. . . we must sadly observe that all the modern refinements of [the utility] concept have not freed it from metaphysics. We are told nowadays that since utility cannot be measured it is not an operational concept and that 'revealed preference'should be put in its place . . .

[But] it is just not true that market behavior can reveal preferences. It is not only that the experiment of offering an individual alternative bundles of goods, or changing his income just to see what he will buy, could never be carried out in practice. The objection is logical, not only practical . . .

We can observe the reaction of an individual to two different sets of prices only at two different times. How can we tell what part of the difference in his purchases is due to the difference in prices and what part to the change in his preferences that has taken place meanwhile? . . .

We have got one equation for two unknowns. Unless we can get some independent evidence about preferences the experiment is no good. But it was the experiment that we were supposed to rely on to observe the preferences.

See also [Chalfant and Alston 1988].

[19]See also [Melitz 1965, pp. 44 and 47; Ekelund, Furubotn and Gramm 1972, p. 73]. For an illustration of the problems to which the unidentified exogenous variable gives rise see [Bartik 1987].

[20]"Satiety" implies that for one or more of the f_i, $f_i = 0$; that is, the marginal utility of one or more of the goods may be zero.

[21]The phrase "in the system" refers, in Professor Furubotn's analysis, to an advanced economic system in which "...the number of distinct comodities is very large" [Furubotn 1974, p. 289].

[22]The only possibility explicitly ruled out is that the consumer may be satiated with respect to all n commodities so that an increase in the consumption of any one good would not result in an increase in utility.

[23]"N" in Professor Furubotn's notation denotes the number of goods chosen at equilibrium. The "ridge lines" to which he refers are the n loci along which, respectively, the marginal utilities of each of the n goods are equal to zero.

[24]See Chapter 1, p. 12, above. See also [Koopmans 1957, pp. 135-142].

[25]I shall have more to say about the last, rather cryptic portion of the statement in Chapter IV.

[26]The composite good, Y, is sometimes referred to as "Hicks-Marshall" money; the amount spent on all other goods taken together, or the value sum of other expenditures. See, for example [Ferguson 1972, esp. p. 74], and [Hicks 1939, esp. Chs. I, II and III].

[27]Quite apart from the obviously sound empirical proposition that changes in real income can be the catalyst to shifts among product types, it is also clear that quality variations among differentiated forms of particular product types can be of basic relevance. That is, changes in real income can cause shifts among product differentiates; a shift among different forms of particular product types. See, for example [Houthakker 1952, pp. 155-156; Duesenberry 1952, p. 22].

The question of systematic quality variation among goods is not without interest. Indeed, Professor Lancaster has laid great emphasis upon the proposition that it is the qualitative properties of goods that constitute the individual consumer's desiderata; not the goods themselves. See, for example [Lancaster 1966a]. For a critical view of Professor Lancaster's formulation of the consumer's "consumption technology," see Chapter III, below and [Roth 1979]. For a discussion of some of the implications of quality variation among units of the same products, see [Furubotn 1969]. For a model which attacks the same problems as those addressed by Furubotn, while at the same time employing the Lancastrian approach, see [Leland 1977].

[28]I shall have more to say about the "number of goods" problem in Chapters IV and V below.

[29]An exception, already noted in fn. 27, above, is the Lancastrian approach; an approach that treats the objects of choice not as goods and services, but as the characteristics of the goods and services. I shall have more to say about this in

Chapter III.

[30]In the case of a stock-flow utility function, the objects of choice are not limited to flow variables; to the purchase of non-durables per unit time, or to the rental of durable goods' services. In the stock-flow decision environment, the consumer is confronted with an intrinsically dynamic problem; whether to purchase or rent a consumer durable.

[31]As Professor Pollak has suggested, "it is not clear what set of observations would cause economists to abandon the neoclassical theory of consumer behavior . . ." [Pollak 1985, fn. 8, pp. 584-585].

[32]The need to study the process of taste formation and of taste change has been underscored by Pollak. In his words [Pollak 1978, p. 374]:

. . . it is time to reconsider the conventional wisdom that tastes are none of [economists'] business.

Chapter 3

The "New Approach"

The theory of consumer behavior in deterministic situations . . . stands as an example of how to extract the minimum of results from the minimum of assumptions.

Kelvin Lancaster

THE LANCASTRIAN VIEW OF THE TRADITIONAL MODEL

The predictive powers of the ordinal utility analysis are effectively circumscribed by the presence of an unidentified exogenous variable, the consumer's preference structure. It is not surprising, therefore, that the traditional model has come, in recent years, under increasingly robust attack.[1]

What is significant, however, is that with the exception of writers like Professor Furubotn, economists qua economists[2] have taken the traditional conception of the utility function as given, and concentrated on pushing the analytical frontiers of the orthodox formulation [see Chapter II].

It is possible, however, to accept the basic structure of the consumer's constrained optimization problem -- to accept the view that a) utility measured in ordinal terms is the consumer's desideratum, and b) that consumers seek to maximize utility subject to an income constraint -- while, at the same time, to argue that the orthodox statement of the problem is ill-conceived. This is the basic criticism embodied in the Lancastrian "New Approach" to consumer theory; an approach that is increasingly well-received.[3]

Partly because it has gained such wide acceptance, and partly because of its emphasis upon the need for improved predictive power, Chapter III is given over to an explicit consideration of Professor Lancaster's "New Approach". Stripped to its essentials, Lancaster's critique is embodied in the following passage [Lancaster 1966a, p. 132]:

> The theory of consumer behavior in deterministic situations . . . has been shorn of all irrelevant postulates so that it now stands as an example of how to extract the minimum of results from the minimum of assumptions.

Standing alone, the statement is, at best, heuristic; at worst, cryptic. Professor Lancaster is, however, quite explicit about the weaknesses he has in mind:

1. A denial by the model of the relevance of the intrinsic properties of a good [Lancaster 1966a, p. 132]:

    All intrinsic properties . . . have been omitted from the theory, so that a consumer who consumes diamonds alone is as rational as a consumer who consumes bread alone, but one who sometimes consumes bread, sometimes diamonds . . . is irrational.

2. The implication that each good has one, and only one, characteristic; that there is only a one-to-one relationship (in both directions) between goods and characteristics. In a word, the only characteristic of an apple would be "appleness", and the only source of "appleness" would be an apple [Lancaster 1966b, p. 15].

3. The presumption that goods consumed separately have the same type and degree of characteristics as goods consumed jointly. On Lancaster's view, a meal -- treated in the traditional model as a single good -- possesses nutritional and aesthetic characteristics. Moreover, a dinner party, a combination of goods, a meal and a social gathering, may possess nutritional, aesthetic, and intellectual characteristics different from the combination of the same characteristics obtainable from a meal and a social gathering consumed independently [Lancaster 1966a, p. 133].

4. The implicit assumption that consumers are well informed about the goods they purchase; that consumer choices are "efficient" in the sense that for a given dollar outlay consumers secure their desired characteristics bundle [Lancaster 1966a, p. 143].

5. The inability of the traditional model to predict the consequences of the introduction of a new commodity or product differentiation for the commodity composition of the optimal consumption bundle Lancaster 1966a, p. 133; Lancaster 1966b, p. 20].

THE CONSUMPTION TECHNOLOGY

The New Approach views consumption as an activity [Lancaster 1966a, p. 133]:

. . . in which goods, singly or in combination, are inputs and in which the output is a collection of characteristics. Utility or preference orderings are assumed to rank collections of goods indirectly through the characteristics they possess.[4]

The presumption is, therefore, that the consumer's utility function may be defined in characteristics space; specifically, that

$$U = U(z) \qquad (3\text{-}1)$$

where the vector z, the various goods' characteristics, constitute the direct ingredients of the consumer's preferences. The problem is that the consumer cannot purchase "characteristics." Rather, he is confronted with an array of purchasable economic goods; commodities that embody these characteristics in various combinations and amounts. Thus, granting that (3-1) can be maximized subject to one or more constraints, the optimal characteristics vector, z^*, must, somehow, be transformed into a consumption bundle involving purchasable economic goods.

The means by which this transformation is effected is the "consumption technology." The structure of the model is such that (3-1) is thought of as being maximized subject to the constraints imposed by the consumption technology, the nominal income of the consumer, the vector of goods' (or activities') prices, and a set of non-negativity conditions imposed on the goods, activities and characteristics.

Case 1: No 1:1 Correspondence Between Goods and Activities

For the case in which there is no one-to-one correspondence between goods and activities, the consumption technology is representable by the families of equations:

$$z = By \qquad (3\text{-}2)$$

and

$$x = Ay \qquad (3\text{-}3)$$

As (3-2) is written, the presumption is that each consumption activity, y_k, produces a fixed vector of characteristics, z_i, and that the relationship is both linear and objective.[5] (3-3), then, contemplates a situation in which the relationship between the level of activity k, y_k, and the goods consumed in the activity is linear and objective.[6]

Granting this, the logic of equation systems (3-2) and (3-3) is straightforward: Given that there is no one-to-one correspondence between goods and activities, equation system (3-2) is insufficient to the consumer's purposes. The maximand, utility function (3-1), is defined in characteristics or z space. But, insofar as the characteristics are secured via the consumption of activities, the initial problem confronting the consumer is to uncover, subject to the constraints summarized above, the optimal activity vector, y*; a vector defined in characteristics space. Hence, it must be possible, given the relevant constraints, to solve the system

$$y = B^{-1}z \qquad (3\text{-}4)$$

for the optimal activity vector. The solution presumes that the consumer's budget constraint can be transformed into characteristics space. For the case in which there is a one-to-one correspondence between goods and activities (a case discussed below), there is no transformation problem; the prices of the activities are given by the goods prices, p_i. If there is no one-to-one correspondence between goods and activities, a transformation of goods prices into activities prices must be effected. In any case, a transformation is possible [Lancaster 1966a, pp. 140-144].

Granting the solution to the initial or stage one optimization problem, the consumer is confronted with another problem: For the case in which there is no one-to-one correspondence between activities and goods, the optimal activities vector, y*, must be transformed into an optimal goods vector, x*. This is the role of equation system (3-3).

Some Thoughts on Case 1

So far as it goes, all of the above proceeds quite plausibly. The difficulty is that the solution involving system (3-4) presumes that the inverse of B, B⁻¹, exists. Yet B⁻¹ will exist if and only if B is both square and non-singular. The problem of singularity is handled quite straightforwardly: Professor Lancaster brings to bear the key auxiliary assumption embedded in the model; namely, the assumption that B contains no linear dependence [Lancaster 1966a, p. 138].

Despite plausible reasons to suppose that B will not always be non-singular, let us assume, for the moment, that it is.[7] In this event, we are still confronted with the requirement that B be square. We have the requirement that the number of characteristics equal the number of activities.[8] Now there is no reason to suppose that this requirement will be satisfied. Yet, if it is not satisfied, B⁻¹ does not exist, and the optimal activity vector, y*, cannot be secured. Put another way, equation system (3-3) cannot be employed: Without an optimal activity vector to inject into (3-3) the consumer is unable to solve the stage II problem; namely, the transformation of the optimal activity vector, y*, into the optimal consumption bundle -- the vector x* defined in terms of purchasable economic goods. The consumer is confronted, in short, with "goods indeterminacy."

This has important methodological implications: In a decision environment in which the number of activities does not equal the number of characteristics -- a plausible state of affairs -- the model is incapable of predicting which goods vector will be chosen at equilibrium. For a model whose genesis included the perception that the traditional model is incapable of making predictions about important classes of phenomena,[9] this is a serious problem.

Case 2: A 1:1 Correspondence Between Goods and Activities

Assume now a one-to-one correspondence between goods and activities.[10] In this event, the consumption technology reduces to

$$z = Bx, \qquad (3\text{-}5)$$

and the optimal goods vector may be secured, provided that we may write

$$x = B^{-1}z. \qquad (3\text{-}6)$$

This is a point to which I shall return below. The decision environment is such that the prices of the activities are given by the goods prices, p_i. There is, therefore, no need to transform the budget constraint into characteristics space [Lancaster 1966a, pp. 140-141]. The difficulty here, as before, is that the solution of the now single-staged optimization problem requires that B^{-1} exist. As before, this requires that B be both square and non-singular.

As we shall see, the requirement that B be square results, under rather plausible conditions, either in an a priori delimitation of the consumer's choice space, or in goods indeterminacy. For the moment, however, our interest centers on the requirement that B be non-singular.

Some Thoughts on Case 2

To facilitate the exposition, I have to this point ignored the implications of one of Lancaster's key "auxiliary" assumptions; namely, that the consumption technology is non-singular. In the decision environment in which there is no one-to-one correspondence between goods and activities, this means that both the B and A matrices are non-singular. In the decision environment in which there is a one-to-one correspondence between goods and activities the assumption reduces to the presumed non-singularity of B [see equation system (3-5)].

Granting for the moment that B is square, what does it mean to assume that B is non-singular? To focus the discussion, suppose that the consumer is confronted with a two characteristics- two goods (=activities) world. System (3-5) could then be written

$$z_1 = b_{11}x_1 + b_{12}x_2$$
$$z_2 = b_{21}x_1 + b_{22}x_2$$
(3-7)

where, by assumption,

$$B = \begin{bmatrix} 2 & 4 \\ 4 & 8 \end{bmatrix}$$

Under the circumstances envisioned, $|B| = 16 - 16 = 0$, so that B is singular. In this event, the consumption technology violates the auxiliary assumption, and B^{-1} cannot be secured. To put the matter differently, equation system (3-7) involves two characteristics but, effectively, only one good (=activity). It follows that system (3-7) cannot be solved for the optimal goods vector -- irrespective of the properties of the consumer's utility function, the prevailing goods (=activities) prices, and the consumer's income.

The central issue -- apart from whether or not the number of characteristics equals the number of goods (=activities) -- is this: Are there circumstances under which B may be singular? The answer, on purely a priori grounds, must be yes.

To see this, consider the following simplified example; an example employing the consumption technology envisioned by equation system (3-7): Think of z_1 as "fever reduction," and z_2 as "reduction of muscular aches and pains." In the present context, the goods (=activities) x_1 and x_2 may be thought of as differentiates of the product type "cold relief medicine."

Given this somewhat rarefied decision environment, is singularity in the consumption technology linking the two characteristics to the two cold relief medicines possible? Is it possible, for example, that at any consumption rate, x_2 will release twice as much z_1 and z_2 as does x_1? Alternatively, is it possible that a specified amount of z_1 and z_2 can be secured with one-half as much x_2 as x_1?[11]

Casual empiricism suggests that the answer to each of these questions must be yes. There is ample evidence to suggest, for example, that for some consumers, the same level of generalized cold relief -- involving, in other words, a specified vector $[z_1^0, z_2^0]$ -- can be achieved using less of one aspirin brand than another. Insofar as this is so, a consumption technology of the sort envisioned by equation system (3-7) cannot be precluded -- at least on a priori grounds. Yet, if such a consumption technology does obtain, a solution to the consumer's decision problem cannot be secured.

The presumption must be that if such a state of affairs can plausibly be envisioned for a two characteristics - two goods (=activities) world, the probability is greatly enhanced that singularity will obtain in a "more realistic" decision environment; one in which the number of characteristics and goods (=activities) is large.

Granting all of this, one might reasonably question whether Professor Lancaster's non-singular consumption technology has an empirical counterpart. There is, in short, reason to suppose that one of the model's auxiliary assumptions is false.

We know from the discussion in Chapter I that the falsity of an auxiliary assumption increases the ambiguity of test results. This, of course, is an undesirable state-of-affairs. Yet the difficulty here is even more rudimentary: The point is not that the singularity of the consumption technology may increase the ambiguity of test results. It is that singularity of the consumption technology prohibits the emergence of predictions relative to the consumer's optimal consumption bundle. Yet without predictions with which to compare observed consumption patterns, there can be no test of the model's predictive power. While this statement is elementary, it is by no means innocuous: For a model whose avowed purpose is prediction, the inability to generate predictions is the worst of all possible debilities.[12]

ON THE AMBIGUITY OF TEST RESULTS

Even if we were to accept that B is non-singular, we are still left with the requirement that the number of goods equal the number of characteristics. Yet, as Professor Lancaster notes [Lancaster 1966a, p. 133]:

> In general - and the richness of the approach springs more from this than from anything else - even a single good will possess more than one characteristic.

Indeed, emphasis is laid upon the fact that in "simple societies" the number of characteristics exceeds the number of goods. On the other hand, it is claimed, quite plausibly, that in "complex societies," the number of characteristics is less than the number of goods [Lancaster 1966a, p. 138].

It follows that in the case either of a "simple" or a "complex" society -- indeed, in all cases of practical importance -- the number of characteristics (r) will not equal the number of goods (n). In this event, either some a priori delimitation of the decision environment must be effected (the case of r>n), or the model may yield a non-unique solution (the case of r<n). Thus, in the case of a simple society, Lancaster tells us ". . . we concern ourselves only with the particular n-dimensional slice of the r-dimensional utility function implied by that technology . . ." [Lancaster 1966a, p. 138].

The passage just quoted implies an a priori delimitation of what might heuristically be called the consumer's choice space. What is contemplated is the explicit use of a patently unrealistic auxiliary assumption; namely, that the number of characteristics is equal to the number of goods. It is known that in the decision environment envisioned, the number of characteristics exceeds the number of goods! While it is clear that its mathematical structure impels the model's user to employ the assumption, the methodological implications are equally unambiguous: The employment of unrealistic auxiliary assumptions increases the ambiguity of test results.[13] In effect, the greater the discrepancy between assumed conditions and reality, that is, the actual decision environment, the greater the probability that the requisite test conditions are not fulfilled. It follows that evidence favorable to the model's predictions is not necessarily confirmatory. On the other hand, neither can evidence unfavorable to the model's predictions be regarded as disconfirmatory. Whether one contemplates a decision environment of the "simple" or the "complex" society type, tests of predictions yielded by the New Approach are necessarily ambiguous.

To see that this must be so not only for the case of the "simple" society just considered, suppose now that the number of characteristics is less than the number of goods; assume, in other words, the case of the "complex" society. Whereas in the "simple" society the New Approach is impelled to an a priori delimitation of the consumer's choice space, here we have the troublesome state of affairs that ". . . for every point in characteristics space the consumer has choice between different goods vectors" [Lancaster 1966a, p. 139]. Thus, given a specified level of nominal income and the family of goods prices,[14] p_i, the consumer may be indifferent among a number of alternative goods vectors. In other words, under the circumstances envisioned -- the case of a "complex" society -- the New Approach leads once again to "goods indeterminacy."

Precisely because the equilibrium is not unique, the model is incapable of predicting which goods vector will be selected at equilibrium.[15]

In the "complex" society decision environment, more than one goods vector may emerge as an admissible solution to the consumer's constrained maximization problem. Clearly, then, choice among these competing goods vectors cannot be taken as confirmatory or disconfirmatory of the model's predictions precisely because the model cannot yield a unique optimal solution.

As has been emphasized, one of the catalysts to the New Approach is the traditional model's inability always to make predictions about the commodity composition of the optimal consumption bundle. Unfortunately, whatever else is said about it, the New Approach suffers from the same debility.

ON THE DESIGNED IMPLICATIONS OF THE NEW APPROACH

Among the weaknesses of the traditional model explicitly mentioned by Lancaster is its inability to predict the consequences of the introduction of a new commodity [Lancaster 1966a, p. 133; Lancaster 1966b, p. 20]. Presumably, then, included among the designed classes of implications of the New Approach are phenomena broadly related to the emergence of new commodities. Unfortunately, while it is a relatively straightforward matter to include new commodities in the consumption technology, methodological difficulties once again emerge. Ultimately, these difficulties center, at least in the case of a "simple" society, on the specification of the consumer's maximand.

To see this, consider once again the case of a "simple" society; a society in which the number of characteristics (r) exceeds the number of goods (n). In these circumstances, as we have seen, the emergence of an optimal solution to the consumer's constrained optimization problem is predicated on an a priori delimitation of his choice space [Lancaster 1966a, p. 138; see also p. 59, above].

The difficulty, in the present context, is that to deliberately exclude characteristics for which no goods counterpart(s) can be found is to impede the emergence of one of the model's designed classes of implications: The delimitation of the r-dimensional utility function to n dimensions denies the possibility of the emergence of effective demand for goods which do not now exist (in the sense that no good can be found that embodies a desired combination of characteristics). In effect, the model is incapable of predicting the emergence of a "better mouse trap." Yet, it is generally assumed that the perception on the part of producers of effective demand for a good embodying a somehow differentiated characteristics vector will, ceteris paribus, result in the development, production and sale of that good. Granting this, if certain characteristics are excluded from the consumer's preference function, how are we to predict -- or even to rationalize ex post -- the emergence of a new good? If the characteristics embodied in the new good do not appear as arguments of the maximand, how are they to evidence themselves in the market?[16]

It is not clear, then, that the New Approach is capable of closing one of the theoretical lacunae admittedly present in the traditional model. Given its mathematical structure, the New Approach is simply not capable of generating predictions of basic relevance to one of its designed classes of implications.[17]

THE PSEUDOINVERSE AND THE PROBLEM
OF GOODS INDETERMINACY

While the potential singularity of the consumption technology and, or, asymmetry of numbers of goods and characteristics do present technical difficulties, these problems are not insurmountable. The analytical integrity of the New Approach can be preserved without requiring -- to borrow a phrase of Solow's -- a willing suspension of disbelief. If, on the other hand, a willing suspension of disbelief is not required, a willingness to accept an approximate solution to the consumer's problem is mandatory. It is possible, in other words, to secure an approximate solution to the consumer's choice problem; to solve for an approximation of the optimal goods vector, regardless of the properties of the consumption technology. What is required is appeal to what has been variously characterized as the general reciprocal, the generalized inverse, and the pseudoinverse.

It is now recognized that the notion of the generalized inverse was developed by E.H. Moore in Part I of his "General Analysis"; a work published in 1935 as Volume I of the Memoirs of the American Philosophical Society [Greville 1959, p. 38]. While Moore referred to the construct as the "general reciprocal," and others have referred to it as the generalized inverse, "pseudoinverse", a characterization due to Max Woodbury, is perhaps most appropriate.

However it is characterized, the essence of the pseudoinverse is that it constitutes the generalization of the inverse of a matrix to include all matrices, rectangular as well as square. The basic relevance of the pseudoinverse to what has been said is immediately clear: In those circumstances in which the consumption technology is not amenable to inversion, employment of the pseudoinverse will yield an approximate solution to the consumer's choice problem.[18]

The definition of the relevant pseudoinverse varies according as the consumption technology -- matrix B -- is of maximal rank, or is of rank less that its smaller dimension. I shall, for present purposes, concentrate on the case of an rxn matrix B of rank equal to the smaller dimension.[19]

As we know, Lancaster contemplates two distinct decision environments: 1) The case of a "simple society" in which the number of characteristics (r) exceeds the number of goods (n), and 2) The case of a "complex society" in which the number of characteristics is less than the number of available goods.

The Simple Society

In the situation envisioned, the consumption technology is given by the rxn rectangular matrix B. Here we have that the number of characteristics (r) is greater than the number of goods (n), and that the matrix B is of rank n; that is, B is of maximal rank.

We now define the pseudoinverse of B as

$$B^\tau = (B^T B)^{-1} B^T \qquad (3\text{-}8)$$

where B^T denotes the transpose of B [Greville 1959, p. 38].[20]   It is significant that appeal to B^τ will yield a nxl solution vector x. That is, the solution will involve the "approximately optimal" consumption rates of the n goods -- despite the fact that there are r>n characteristics; that there are, in other words, "redundant" characteristics.

In effect, appeal to the pseudoinverse gets us "off the hook." When the consumption technology is of maximal rank we need not do as Professor Lancaster suggests. We need not ". . . concern ourselves only with the n-dimensional slice of the r-dimensional utility function implied by that technology . . ." [Lancaster 1966a, p. 138].   Employment of the pseudoinverse does, in these circumstances, allow us to avoid some of the logical conundra attendant to an a priori delimitation of the consumer's choice space. On the other hand, two observations are in order: 1) Appeal to the pseudoinverse does not yield the optimal solution; it yields an approximate solution the interpretation of which will be made clear below. 2) In the likely event that the consumption technology, B, is not of maximal rank, we are again confronted with the problem of effecting an arbitrary choice among columns and rows of B in securing its pseudoinverse. This, of course, is equivalent to an a priori delimitation of the relevant choice space.[21]

The Complex Society

Here, the consumption technology is given by the rxn rectangular matrix B. In this instance, however, the number of characteristics (r) is less than the number of goods (n), and the matrix B is of rank r.

The pseudoinverse of B is now given by

$$B^{\tau} = B^{T}(BB^{T})^{-1} \qquad (3-9)$$

Appeal to (3-9) will yield a nxl solution vector x. It follows that the solution will yield the "approximately optimal" consumption rates of the n goods -- despite the fact that there are n>r goods; that there are, in effect, "redundant" goods.

Some Additional Remarks

While these results are of interest, it is clear that there is no reason to suppose that a rectangular consumption technology will be of maximal rank. Indeed, I suspect that this would be a special case. We must, in any case, admit of the possibility that the consumption technology may be summarized in terms of a nonzero matrix B whose rank may be less than its smaller dimension.

It is not my intention here to deal with this case in any systematic way. I have a rather more modest objective in mind; namely, to use this case to make clear the nature of the "approximate solution" referred to above. For the nonzero consumption technology B whose rank is less than the number of characteristics (or goods, whichever is the smaller dimension), the solution of the system $z = Bx$ is given by

$$x = B^{\tau}z + u \qquad\qquad (3\text{-}10)$$

where B^{τ} is the pseudoinverse of B, and u is any vector orthogonal to the column-space of B^{T} [Greville 1959, pp. 41-42]. The practical significance of this is that when the system $z = Bx$ does not admit of an exact solution, (3-10) yields a "best" solution in the sense of least squares. In effect, Bx is as close to z as it can be made, in that the sum of the squared residuals is minimized [Greville 1959, p. 42; Lancaster 1969, p. 305]. It is in this sense that the generalized or pseudoinverse yields an "approximate" or "best" solution.

In a sense, then, we have come full circle. Our point of departure has been that under rather plausible conditions the consumption technology of the "New Approach" results in goods indeterminacy. The claim has been, in other words, that in those circumstances in which the consumption technology is singular and/or the number of goods does not equal the number of characteristics, the commodity composition of the optimal consumption bundle is indeterminate.

What this discussion has shown is that, at best, the pseudoinverse yields an approximately optimal solution. The key idea emerges unscathed; namely, that under conditions that are likely to obtain, the "New Approach" does not yield the optimal consumption vector -- irrespective of the properties of the consumer's utility function, his income, and the prevailing goods prices.

IN SUMMARY . . .

It is the mathematical structure of the New Approach that impels the use of auxiliary assumptions that either may be false, or that are known to be false a priori.

Consider first the presumed non-singularity of the consumption technology. While linear dependence will not necessarily obtain, there is reason to believe that, in any decision environment of practical importance, the technology will be singular.[22]   To argue that non-singularity must be assumed if the commodity composition of the optimal consumption bundle is to be determinate does not alter the fact that the ambiguity of test results is greatly enhanced. If the technology is singular, the requisite test conditions will simply not be met. Hence, whatever test results emerge, they cannot be taken as unambiguously confirmatory or disconfirmatory of the theory.

Even if it were known that the consumption technology is, as a matter of empirical fact, non-singular, methodological difficulties remain: Unless certain rather restrictive conditions are met, the New Approach is incapable of predicting the commodity composition of the optimal consumption bundle. Indeed, for the case in which there is no one-to-one correspondence between goods and activities, unless the number of characteristics equals the number of activities, a transformation from activities to the optimal goods vector cannot be effected.

Unfortunately, the predictive power of the New Approach is not enhanced by the assumption of a different decision environment; one which, upon first inspection, would appear to be more congenial to it. Even if one were to assume a one-to-one correspondence between goods and activities -- an analytically convenient, but terribly rarefied state-of-affairs -- the model retains a potential for collapse.

Beyond this, there is the possibility that the number of characteristics (r) may exceed the number of goods(n); a situation from which the only avenue of escape is an a priori delimitation of r-n characteristics. On the other hand, the number of characteristics (r) may be less than the number of goods (n).[23] Clearly, operational counterparts for this situation abound. Yet, in this situation, for every point in characteristics space, the consumer has choice among different goods vectors. Hence, for a given level of nominal income, and a family of goods prices, the consumer may be indifferent among an array of alternative goods vectors. The model would, in this event, be incapable of predicting which goods would be selected at equilibrium.

Whether, in other words, $r \gtrless n$, the mathematical structure of the model requires the employment of a crucial auxiliary assumption; namely, that $r = n$.[24] In those circumstances where the assumption is known to be false, there is no escaping the fact that the ambiguity of test results must be greatly enhanced.

Finally, for the case in which $r>n$, the elimination of r-n characteristics results in the inability of the New Approach to predict the emergence of new goods. While this may be acceptable for some models of consumer behavior, it constitutes a theoretical lacuna in the context of the New

Approach; an approach which is proffered as an analytically superior alternative to the traditional model; a model which, on Lancaster's view, "has nothing to say" about consumer reactions to new commodities.

The following assessment of the New Approach would therefore seem appropriate: While explicit attention to goods characteristics suggests a number of promising avenues of research,[25] the New Approach is severely encumbered by the mathematical requirements of the consumption technology.

NOTES

[1]See Chapters VII and VIII, below.

[2]I make a distinction here as between those individuals who regard themselves as "economists" (the economists qua economists) and the somewhat more eclectic, essentially interdisciplinary researchers sometimes referred to as "behavioral scientists." Herbert Simon and his followers are typically included among the latter group.

[3]A search of the literature reveals few articles whose point of departure is the limitations of Professor Lancaster's New Approach. One such article, due to Hendler, concludes that the "... efficiency frontier is objective only under certain restrictive assumptions" and, therefore, that "the 'new approach' ... becomes an interesting and important special case of consumer choice rather than a general model of consumer demand" [Hendler 1975, p. 199].

While I find no reason to quarrel with Hendler's basic conclusion, the New Approach can be shown to suffer from an even more serious debility. In considering explicity only the situation most congenial to Lancaster's formulation -- the case of a 1:1 correspondence between goods and activities -- Hendler notes several implicit assumptions embedded in the "New Approach"; notably, that the analysis requires either the utility independence of characteristics per "consumption unit" (UIC) or the "mixability" of goods per "consumption unit" [Hendler 1975, p. 197]. It is this, he claims, that delimits the range of applicability of the model [see also Ladd and Zober 1977, esp. p. 90 and pp. 92-93]. The argument developed below establishes, however, that even if one were to grant UIC, or the "mixability" of goods per "consumption unit", or both, the model is still subject to collapse. If the consumption technology is singular -- a situation for which operational counterparts abound -- the model is incapable of predicting which goods will be chosen at equilibrium; it is subject to what I characterize as "goods indeterminancy". This is not a point at issue in Hendler's analysis: The consumption technology embedded in his equations (2) and (3) is non-singular. Yet while it is non-singular, the consumption technology characterized by Hendler's equations (8) and (9) may give rise to "goods indeterminancy". Insofar as the number of goods (=3) exceeds the number of characteristics (=2), the situation is formally equivalent to Lancaster's "complex" society; a situation in which the utility maximizing goods vector may not be unique. For examples of applications of the New Approach, see footnote 25, below.

[4]A meal, on Lancaster's view, is not a good; it is a combination of goods. It is, in short, an example of a consumption activity.

[5]"Objective" meaning, presumably, that the relationship between each consumption activity and the vector of characteristics it produces is a technological phenomenon; it is, in other words, independent of the consumer's tastes and preferences.

[6]In what follows, I shall not discuss the implications of, and the problems associated with, the presumed linearity of the consumption technology. Suffice it to say that it is a restrictive assumption; one which may serve to limit the classes of phenomena to which the New Approach might fruitfully be applied. See, for example [Ladd and Zober 1977, p. 93; Lucas 1975, pp. 167-168; Sargan 1972].

[7]An illustration of a possible source of linear dependence is provided below. Discussion of the singularity of B is momentarily deferred.

[8]Lancaster himself indicates that "The leading structural property of the consumption technology is the relationship between the number of characteristics (r) and the number of activities (n), ..." [Lancaster 1966a, pp. 137-138].

[9]See Item #5, page 53, above.

[10]The case assumed by Lancaster "unless otherwise stated" [Lancaster 1966a, p. 138].

[11]These are precisely the circumstances characterized by the consumption technology embedded in equation system (3-7).

[12]Actually, the model may yield an approximation to the optimal consumption bundle, no matter what the characteristics of the consumption technology. There does exist a generalized or pseudoinverse for any matrix, whether rectangular or singular (see pp. 61-64, above). Appeal to the pseudoinverse will not, however, yield the uniquely optimal consumption vector.

[13]See, for example, Chapter I, pp. 15-16, above. One could, I suppose, claim that the assumption that the number of characteristics equals the number of goods has the character of a generative rather than an auxiliary assumption. Yet if one accepts this view, all that is achieved is that one set of conundra is substituted for another: If the assumption is treated as generative, and it is known a priori to be false, then some of the model's implications must be false [see p. 17, above]. Yet, insofar as the acceptability of a theory depends upon its ability to predict observable events, all of its derived implications must be defensible [Koopmans 1957, pp. 135-142; see also p. 12, above].

[14]Again, given a one-to-one correspondence between goods and activities, the goods prices are the activities prices.

[15]There is a conceptual difference as between the goods indeterminacy contemplated here, and that to which I referred above. In the present case, the "consumption technology" is incapable of predicting which of an array of alternative goods vectors will be chosen at equilibrium. In the earlier case -- the situation in which a one-to-one correspondence between goods and activities does not obtain -- unless the number of activities equals the number of characteristics (and the B matrix is non-singular), an optimal solution to the two stage optimization problem cannot be secured. See p. 55, above. In either case, the optimal goods vector is indeterminate.

[16]At another level, by concentrating on the n-dimensional slice of the r-dimensional utility function, we preclude the possibility of systematic search for goods that do possess the characteristics for which no market analogue can readily be found.

[17]At best, the New Approach may be used to rationalize choice of a new commodity ex post; that is, after its emergence. It may be argued, of course, that Professor Lancaster never intended that the model be capable of predicting the emergence of new commodities. Yet, while this interpretation of Lancaster's intentions is admissible, his intentions are, in fact, ambiguous. What is lacking, in the final analysis, is the set of interpretive rules requisite to establishing what are the "designed" classes of implications [see pp. 10-13, above].

[18]To facilitate the exposition attention will center on the case of a one-to-one correspondence between goods and activities; on a decision environment in which the consumption technology reduces to the B matrix [equation (3-5)]. The nature of the "approximate solution" to which I have referred will be made clear below.

[19]The general case of a nonzero consumption technology B whose rank may be less than its smaller dimension requires somewhat more expansive treatment [see, for example, Penrose 1955, Greville 1959, and Peter Lancaster 1969]. In any event, the discussion of the maximal rank case is heuristic.

[20]Note that (3-8) reduces to the ordinary inverse when $r = n$.

[21]The case of a nonzero matrix (here, consumption technology) of rank less than its smaller dimension is briefly discussed below. The reader interested in a rigorous treatment of this case is referred to [Lancaster 1969, pp. 303-307].

[22]As has been emphasized, the potential for singularity of the B matrix is great. All that is required, broadly speaking, is that there exist an array of differentiates of a particular product type, each embodying the same characteristics vector, but with differing characteristics release rates. If, for just one product type, any two differentiates have characteristics release rates such that one is a linear transformation of the other, the consumption technology is singular. Yet, if one is to accept the "twice as effective as. . ." rhetoric of the ad-men, this phenomenon abounds in the product markets. Whether it does or not is, however, a moot question. If such a linear transformation is possible for just two goods out of the tremendously large array of available goods, a transformation from the optimal characteristics vector to the optimal goods vector is impossible.

[23]It should be noted that, just as in the $r>n$ case, if the consumption technology is not of maximal rank, securing its pseudoinverse would require an arbitrary choice among rows and columns of B. This would mean that some of the available characteristics and goods would be eliminated from the relevant choice space.

[24]See fn. 13, above, for a different interpretation of the nature of this assumption.

[25]Not the least of which appear to be the construction of hedonic price functions [Anderson 1985; Edmonds 1985; Whalley 1985; Shonkwiler and Reynolds 1986; Unnevehr 1986; Veeman 1987; Ohta 1987; Thompson 1987; Howell and Peristiani 1987; Murdoch and Thayer 1988; Jones 1988; Stanley and Tschirhart 1991; Asher 1992; Lenz, Mittelhammer and Shi 1994; Nerlove 1995; Feenstra 1995], and a characterization of the decision process involved in occupational choice -- a suggestion due to Professor Lancaster himself [Lancaster

70   *The Present State of Consumer Theory*

1966a, pp. 145-148]. Employing a model which distinguishes between product characteristics (in the Lancastrian sense) and consumption services obtained from products, Ladd and Zober explore some additional applications of the "New Approach" [Ladd and Zober 1977]. It is significant that the Ladd and Zober variant does not employ some of the Lancastrian model's most frequently criticized assumptions; namely, the assumptions of nonnegative marginal utility, linearity of the consumption technology, and the presumption that utility is independent of the distribution of characteristics among products. Their model does not, however, come to grips with the issues raised here. For a critical analysis of the hedonic cost approach as applied to water delivery see [McQuire and Ohsfeldt 1986].

The "New Approach" has, in any case, been widely employed. Researchers have set out, inter alia, to estimate the demand for automobile characteristics [Atkinson and Halvorsen 1984; Agarwal and Ratchford 1980; Goodman 1983]; for physician services [Custer 1986]; for housing [King 1976; Palmquist 1984; Bajic 1984; Fallis and Smith 1985; Fleming and Nellis 1985; Barnett 1985; DeBoer 1985; Follain and Jimenez 1985; Ozanne and Malpezzi 1985; Scotchmer 1985; DeBorger 1986; Parsons 1986; Phipps 1987; Atkinson and Crocker 1987; Gabriel 1987]; for fertilizer [Shaw 1982]; for "quiet" [McMillan, Reid and Gillen 1980]; for "amenities" [Graves and Knapp 1985; Bartik 1988]; for hospitalization costs [Chernichovsky and Zmora 1986] and for nutrients [Eastwood, Brooker and Terry 1986]. In addition, the analysis has been extended to dynamic decision environments [Abelson and Markandya 1985] and to decision environments involving risk [Brumat and Tomasini 1979]. The implications of the approach for industrial organization [Caves and Williamson 1985] and for applied welfare economics have been explored [Stahl 1984], and an attempt has been made to "expand the attribute space" so as to permit of the analysis of a "large class of consumer situations which cannot be handled" by the Lancastrian model [Barmish 1984]. For other applications see [Grunert 1989; Giannias 1990; Encarnacion 1990; Brucks and Schurr 1990; Bitros and Panas 1990; Mullen and Wohlgenant 1991; Grunewald, Faulds and McNulty 1993; Cropper 1993; Burton 1994; Ramezani 1995; Chern, Lochman and Yen 1995: Hui, McLean-Meyinsse and Jones 1995]. Finally, for a heuristic discussion of hedonic methods see [Triplett 1986].

Chapter 4

The Multi-Equation Utility Function

With extreme diffidence, I suggest another utility representation in which each person consists of more than one, possibly many, utility functions.

Henry Aaron

THE GENESIS OF THE MODEL

In the discussion of the technical extensions of the ordinal utility model (Chapter II), much of our interest centered on the character of the equilibrium. Of particular interest is the fact that, unless appropriate inequality constraints are introduced, the traditional model may yield an optimal consumption bundle involving negative consumption rates of one or more goods. This is a logical conundrum to be avoided -- at least in the context of a static model of utility maximization. It was recognition of this possibility, and of the attendant methodological difficulties, that led to a recasting of the traditional model along Kuhn- Tucker lines. The simple expedient of constraining the model to solutions involving non-negative consumption rates had two effects: 1) It meant that the methods of the classical calculus no longer had basic relevance. The consumer's constrained utility maximization problem was now a problem in nonlinear programming. 2) More significantly, the introduction of inequality constraints raised the question of whether satiety phenomena might optimally be introduced into the model.

As has been emphasized, satiety is typically ruled out in the Kuhn-Tucker formulation, so that the f_i, the marginal utilities, are assumed positive for all positive consumption rates of the x_i, $i = 1, 2, \ldots$, n. Unfortunately, this variant of the traditional model results in the emergence of implausible predictions as to the character and content of the optimal consumption bundle [Chapter 2, pp. 37-39]. Without the explicit introduction of satiety conditions, the predicted consumption patterns may involve as few as one or as many as n distinct types of goods. The first possibility has no empirical counterpart, while the second is simply not reconcilable with the finite nature of the consumer's income. The problem, however, is that any attempt to modify the structure of the Kuhn-Tucker variant so as to eliminate these implausible predictions leads to still other difficulties.

Utility function (2-1) may, for example, be assumed to be consistent with Debreu's axiom of insatiability. Given this interpretation of the consumer's preference structure, the optimal consumption bundle may then involve any number of goods from one through n, the number of goods appearing in the consumer's maximand. It follows that while the flexibility of the Kuhn- Tucker model is somewhat enhanced -- at least insofar as the admissibility of solutions ranging from one through n is concerned -- the central problem remains. The introduction into the commodity space of n distinct ridge lines enhances the possibility of "high end" solutions; of solutions involving all n goods.

While other "solutions" have been proffered, they too have been shown to be unequal to the task of resolving the problem of the number of goods chosen at equilibrium. We have seen, for example, that treatment of a proper subset of the goods confronting the consumer as a composite good is patently unsatisfactory. The construct $U = f(X,Y)$ is not a utility function at all; it is a tautology. Precisely because Y is taken to represent all the commodities available to the consumer other than X, the sum $p_X X + p_Y Y$ must always represent the consumer's purchases.[1] Once the composite good convention is introduced, the concept of the utility function is independent of the truth value of its component parts. Tests of predictions that emerge from it can therefore be neither confirmatory nor disconfirmatory.

One last avenue of escape has been attempted. It has been suggested that we view the n goods in (2-1) as a proper subset of the universal set of goods confronting the consumer. Presumably, an optimal solution involving all n goods would, on this interpretation, be somewhat more palatable. Unfortunately, the effect of such an a priori delimitation of the consumer's choice space is methodologically disastrous. For this approach to be acceptable, we should have to be reconciled to the notions: 1) That the commodity composition of the consumer's optimal consumption bundle is invariant with respect to changes in real income, and 2) That it is possible to predesignate the arguments of the individual consumer's maximand. Whatever else one says about it, it is clear that [Furubotn 1967, p. 44]:

> . . . an individual . . . will shift from one subset of goods to another as changes in income and prices take place. Normally, substitutes abound; and particular physical or social needs can be satisfied by any of a large number of similar commodities. These alternative commodities may be in the same class or, as Professor Duesenberry has stressed, in different classes. But whatever the absolute qualities of the goods involved, . . . the consumer . . . will tend to select only one or a few variants from among the alternative commodities which can be used for a specific consumption purpose. Further, the commodity composition of the equilibrium mix will tend to vary systematically with changes in the economic conditions reflected in the constraint.

The problem of the number of goods chosen at equilibrium is inexorably bound up with the question of how consumer theory might adequately deal with variation in the commodity composition of the optimal consumption bundle; with variations precipitated by changes in the consumer's decision environment.

The Utility Tree

One of the earliest attempts to handle the problems just outlined took the form of the so-called utility tree. While Professor Strotz was the first to explore the empirical implications of the utility tree [Strotz 1957], its intellectual underpinnings go as far back as Irving Fisher's 1927 article [Fisher 1927; see also Leontief 1947]. The essential idea embodied in the new formulation was that the utility function can be conceived of as a tree; a tree whose branches correspond to budget categories such as food, transportation, and clothing [Strotz 1957, p. 271].

The presumption is that the consumer's decision process may be characterized as involving two stages. At stage one a decision is made as to how income should be allocated among branches, given all prices. Then, at stage two, the various budget allotments are allocated across the commodities in the respective branches -- with no further reference to purchases in other branches. For the moment our interest centers on an explicit characterization of the utility tree:

$$U = U[V^A(x_{a1}, x_{a2},...,x_{aa}), V^B(x_{b1}, x_{b2},...,x_{b\beta}), ..., V^m(x_{m1}, x_{m2}, ..., x_{m\mu})].$$

$$(a + \beta + ... + \mu = n) \tag{4-1}$$

Here, the commodities in each of the M branches correspond to specific budget categories. In this conceptual scheme, utility is related, in an immediate sense, to a set of intermediate variables $(S_1, S_2,...S_M)$ but each of these, in turn, depends on certain of the n primary commodities in the manner specified by the relevant branch utility function. Utility, U, is assumed to depend non- additively upon the branch utility functions. This, in turn, means that (4-1) is weakly separable. Broadly speaking, this means that there is room for complex association among the intermediate variables $(S_1, S_2,...S_M)$ in the generation of utility. In effect, some or all of the M intermediate variables may be interdependent in the sense that:

$$\frac{\partial \left[\frac{\partial U/\partial S_i}{\partial U/\partial S_j} \right]}{\partial S_h} \gtrless 0 \tag{4-2}$$

Were (4-1) to be subject to the strong condition of separability, the requirement would be that (4-2) vanish. This, in turn, would imply that utility must depend additively on the intermediate variables [see, for example, Ekelund, Furubotn and Gramm 1972, pp. 77-78]. Granting all of this, (4-1) is thought of as being maximized subject to the budget constraint:

$$\sum_{i=1}^{n} p_i \cdot x_i = y \tag{4-3}$$

where, as before, the p_i denote the prevailing goods prices, and y is nominal income.

The point to be emphasized is that the structure of the model is such that it can accommodate changes in the budget allocation across branches. In Professor Strotz's words [Strotz 1957, pp. 272-273]:

> If the prices of the [goods] remain fixed the only thing that can alter the [consumption rates of the goods] is a change in the amount of income allocated to [the various branches]. The allocation to [any branch] may alter either (a) because y changes or (b) because a change in one or more prices in branch I causes a change in V^1 for a given expenditure on the commodities in branch I.[2]

The difficulty with what may appear to be a step in the right direction is that the model does not solve the problem of choice among goods within each branch. There is nothing in the model to preclude the possibility that the consumer will be predicted to consume positive amounts of each -- or simply most -- of the commodities appearing within a given commodity branch. While I shall have more to say about this momentarily, a number of additional observations are in order.

First, it is clear that the matter of goods classification is an empirical question. More precisely, the question of which commodities should be included in a given branch utility function cannot be settled on a priori grounds [Kraft and Kraft 1975, p. 258]. While the question might be settled in a trivial sense by following the admonition that "Commodity subsets are formed on the basis that similar commodities should be grouped together" [Kraft and Kraft 1975, p. 258], it is manifestly clear that the enormous array of available goods limits the taxonomic process to a rather high degree of aggregation. The results of some rather heroic data manipulation by Kraft and Kraft, for example, led to the conclusion that their "case I" represents the "best possible grouping for this body of data" [Kraft and Kraft 1975, p. 260]. Yet "case I" contemplates a "branch I" involving "Food and beverages," and a "branch II" involving "Clothing and shoes; shoe cleaning and repair; Cleaning, dyeing and pressing."

An objective assessment of the utility tree approach must conclude that, given the enormous number of product types, and given the number of available differentiates of each product type, the state of the art is such that the result of any handleable taxonomy is the emergence of an array of goods whose nature is faintly reminiscent of the composite good to which we referred in Chapter II. Insofar as this is so the suitability of the utility tree approach for theoretical work is jeopardized. Ceteris paribus, the higher the degree of aggregation, the more tautological the character of (4-1). The model may, therefore, not be so accommodative of empirical application as might originally have been supposed.

Finally, as has been suggested, there is nothing in the model to preclude the emergence of an optimal consumption bundle involving each -- or simply most -- of the commodities in a given branch function. On the presumption that some degree of disaggregation had been achieved in assigning the arguments of the various branch functions, it is conceivable that the maximization procedure may yield an optimal bundle involving each of the arguments in the "food" branch function. The same may be true of the clothing, transportation and other branch functions. The difficulty here is straightforward: Both a priori logic and casual empiricism suggest the implausibility of such a prediction. We know that particular physical or social needs can be satisfied by any of a large number of similar commodities. Moreover, product types are typically available in numerous differentiated forms. Add to this the fact of quality differences and it is manifestly clear that the process of consumer choice has a mutually exclusive character. Consumers do not buy clothing of all extant quality levels, or furniture of all possible designs [Furubotn 1967, p. 48]. It is this logic that led to the emergence of a new conception of the consumer's maximand; a construct that follows the organizational pattern of the utility tree, but whose implications more closely accord with observable experience [Furubotn 1967].

THE MULTI-EQUATION UTILITY FUNCTION

To facilitate the exposition, consider a decision environment involving only four distinct commodities: $x_1, \ldots, x_4$. Assume, however, that the first two goods (x_1 and x_2) have generally comparable properties, and that it is possible to use either one to meet a particular class of physical and, or, social need. Following the convention adopted earlier, we denote the particular satisfaction arising from this sort of consumption by the variable S_1. S_1, therefore, represents a particular branch of the utility tree but, in this instance, the branch has two forms. We have, then, the alternate branch utility functions for the first area of consumption

$$S_{1j} = {}_jf(x_j), j = 1, 2 \qquad (4\text{-}4)$$

Analogously, commodities x_3 and x_4 can be used to satisfy a second type of consumption need. The branch utility functions for this area are, therefore

$$S_{2k} = {}_kf(x_k), \quad k = 1, 2 \qquad (4\text{-}5)$$

Given (4-4) and (4-5) we may write the consumer's utility function as

$$U_i = {}_if(S_{1j}, S_{2k}), \quad i = 1, \ldots, 4 \qquad (4\text{-}6)$$
$$j = 1, 2$$
$$k = 1, 2$$

As (4-6) is written, there are four definable branch or utility subfunctions. This follows from the fact that S_1 can be secured in one of two ways, and can combine with an S_2 produced via the consumption of either x_3 or x_4. On the assumption that branch one, S_{1j}, pertains to food and S_{2k} to clothing, the consumer is presumed to decide what his indifference system is with respect to any pair of commodities representing food and clothing. In effect, a separate indifference map is associated with each subfunction of (4-6). Apart from the requirement that items of both food and clothing be taken, the indifference curves for any given subfunction have properties similar to those of the traditional ordinal utility function [equation (2-1)].

Each of the utility subfunctions in system (4-6) is thought of as being maximized subject to an appropriate budget constraint:

$$y_0 - p_1x_1 - p_3x_3 = 0$$
$$y_0 - p_1x_1 - p_4x_4 = 0 \qquad (4\text{-}7)$$
$$y_0 - p_2x_2 - p_3x_3 = 0$$
$$y_0 - p_2x_2 - p_4x_4 = 0$$

The maximization process results in the emergence, at stage one, of a set of competing suboptima. As the system is conceived, the stage one solution involves four competing commodity bundles. The optimum optimorum is secured at stage two via the simple expedient of comparing the utility levels obtainable from the four alternatives. Thus, given the consumer's preference structure and income level, and given the prevailing goods price vector, the commodity bundle $[x_1{}^0, x_3{}^2]$ may emerge as the most satisfying; as the "best of the best".

The significance of this result is that it can be reconciled with the facts. Consumers do choose among differentiates of given product types, and the solution vector $[x_1^0, x_2^3]$ means that the consumer has, at this cross-section of time, rejected product differentiates x_2 and x_4. Moreover, the model can accommodate still another observable phenomenon; namely, changes in the commodity composition of the optimal consumption bundle as the level of real income changes. All that is required is that one or more of the parameters of system (4-7) be changed; that, for example, the price of x_3 be increased. In this event, it is likely -- though not necessary -- that the price change will result in the emergence of an optimal commodity bundle involving different goods. It is not implausible to assume, for example, that the increase in the relative price of x_3 may result in the consumer's opting for the other differentiate; namely, x_4. Once again, this result is not necessary; it is simply possible. It is this possibility that makes the model congenial to observable reality: The commodity composition of the optimal consumption bundle is not invariant with respect to the level of real income. Indeed, relatively small changes in the parameters of the constraint system can result in shifts in the commodity composition of the optimal consumption vector.

It is in this sense that the multi-equation formulation is superior to the single equation utility tree. The latter lacks the flexibility inherent in the multi-equation approach. As has been emphasized, one of the difficulties associated with the utility tree is that the model may yield an optimal consumption bundle involving all of the goods appearing in a given branch function. In this not-unlikely event, the model would yield the implausible prediction that at a cross-section of time the consumer chooses each of the available differentiates satisfying a particular physical and, or, social need.

While the multi-equation approach is relatively more accommodative of real world phenomena than is its intellectual precursor, problems remain. Of particular concern are the problems that inhere in the classification of goods. Just as in the utility tree approach, if an operational counterpart for the model is to exist, goods must be classified according as they satisfy specific physical and, or, social needs. As has been emphasized, this taxonomic process is by no means trivial. As generalization of the system proceeds -- that is, as (4-6) and (4-7) are modified to accommodate n goods[3] -- the number of branch or utility subfunctions grows. Yet a prerequisite for the specification of the arguments of the various subfunctions is some perception of the "facts." There is simply no escape: Goods taxonomy is an enormously complicated empirical problem. This is true at any cross-section of time, and it is certainly true in an intertemporal decision environment in which new goods appear and preference structures may change. While difficult, the problem is not intractable. To see this, we turn next to a variant of the multi-equation model.

A Variation on a Theme

The multi-equation utility function is designed to provide a rationale for the process of consumer choice among differentiated forms of various product types. However, as we have seen, the earliest variant of the multi-equation approach shares a problem in common with the utility tree approach. Simply stated, the problem is one of goods taxonomy. The problem can, however, be circumvented. What is required is the adoption of a simple convention.

We begin by assuming upper and lower limits to the number of different commodities the consumer will, at any cross-section of time, consume [Furubotn 1974]. The limiting values, H and L, can be thought of as structural parameters of the multi-equation system; parameters that will likely vary from one consumer to another. For a decision environment involving n goods, we should expect $H<n$ and $L>1$, so that the consumer chooses among proper subsets of the n available goods.

With this convention adopted, the various commodity combinations are determinate. We know that the number of distinct subsets (S_r) of size r that can be chosen from among n commodities is

$$S_r = \begin{bmatrix} n \\ r \end{bmatrix} = \frac{n!}{r!\,(n-r)!} \qquad (4\text{-}8)$$

Then, on the assumption that commodity subsets can range in size from L to H, the total number of definable subsets (E) is

$$E = \sum_{r=L}^{H} S_r. \qquad (4\text{-}9)$$

Now it is from this array that the consumer will choose one commodity subset; the optimum optimorum referred to above. In Professor Furobotn's words [Furubotn 1974, p. 299]:

. . . depending on what choice is made the qualitative character of his consumption will be one sort or another. Any commodity in the universal set (1, 2, ..., n) can be represented in the consumer's final selection, but the total number of distinct goods in any solution is never less than L nor greater than H.

The singular advantage of the approach is that, while the consumer is thought of as choosing among subsets of the n available goods, rationalization of the choice process is not predicated upon a priori goods classification. In effect, one empirical problem is substituted for another; for the problem of goods classification we substitute the problem of estimating the structural parameters L and H. The latter problem is manifestly more tractable than is the former. In the case of L, we know that a consumer in a modern economy combines a relatively large number of goods in satisfying physical and social needs. Moreover, we should expect relatively more diversification in consumption patterns the greater the wealth position of the consumer. It seems clear, in other words, that "Complex and continuing needs . . . insure that the consumer will normally operate with a rather large L parameter" [Furubotn 1974, p. 300]. On the other hand, H will in all cases of practical importance be less than n. This follows from the fact that virtually all goods are subject to significant quality variation. This suggests that the consumer will never demand all or even most of the variant items available [Furubotn 1974, p. 300].

Granting all of this and using (4-8) and (4-9) the consumer's maximand is representable as

$$
\begin{aligned}
U_1 &= {}_1F(x_1, x_2, ..., x_L; \alpha_1) \\
&\quad \vdots \\
U_a &= {}_aF(x_1, x_2, ..., x_{L+1}; \alpha_a) \\
&\quad \vdots \\
U_v &= {}_vF(x_1, x_2, ..., x_{H-1}; \alpha_v) \\
&\quad \vdots \\
U_E &= {}_EF(x_1, x_2, ..., x_H; \alpha_E)
\end{aligned} \tag{4-10}
$$

Each of the utility subfunctions in (4-10) has as its arguments a particular subset of the n available consumer goods. The notation does not suggest, however, that any two subfunctions involving the same number of goods embody as arguments the same goods vector. The subscripts denote nothing more or less than the number of goods appearing in a particular subfunction.

The family of scale factors, α_i allows for the fact that some of the commodity subsets in (4-10) are not likely to be very appealing, given their commodity composition [Furubotn 1974, p. 302]:

Since a utility subfunction $_iF$ concerned with, e.g., L goods can embrace any L items whatsoever, it follows that the commodity composition of the subfunction can be quite specialized. If the L goods in question should all happen to be variant forms of clothing ..., the level of satisfaction (U_i) yielded by any combination of these L goods must be relatively low . . . [this] can be suggested in formal terms by the magnitude of the scale factor [α_i].

As in (4-6), each of the utility subfunctions in (4-10) is assumed to possess mathematical properties analogous to those of the traditional ordinal utility function [equation (2-1)]. There is, however, this difference: While the individual indifference hypersurfaces are convex, satiety conditions are assumed. Each subfunction is taken to have interior ridge lines beyond some level of real income. This eliminates the possibility of predicting infinite product demand. On the other hand, the imposition of satiety conditions does not here carry with it the implications deducible from (2-1). The assumption of interior ridge lines for all goods does not, in other words, imply that above an income threshold, the individual must necessarily consume n (or even H) goods per time period. Rather [Furubotn 1974, p. 302]:

. . . the consumer can be conceived as moving from one utility subfunction to another in response to data change and, thus, of consuming any number of goods from L to H.

As before, the choice process is presumed to proceed in two stages. At the first stage, the individual utility indexes in (4-10) are considered in a series of distinct optimization problems. Thus, for each subfunction in (4-10) such as

$$U_1 = {}_1F(x_1, x_2, ..., x_L; \alpha_1) \qquad (4-11)$$

there must exist appropriate budget and nonnegativity conditions:

$$y - \sum_{i=1}^{L} p_i x_i = 0 \qquad (4\text{-}12)$$

$$x_i \geq 0, \quad i = 1, 2, ..., L. \qquad (4\text{-}13)$$

The maximization of (4-11) subject to (4-12) and (4-13) yields the optimal consumption bundle for this particular subset of goods 1, 2, . . ., L.[4]

Following an analogous procedure for each of the E-1 other utility subfunctions yields an array, E, of competing suboptima. It is from this array that, at stage two, the consumer selects "the unique commodity bundle that will provide the greatest possible utility and constitutes his ultimate equilibrium choice" [Furubotn 1974, p. 303].

THE IMPLICATIONS FOR CONSUMER BEHAVIOR

The point of departure of this chapter was the notion that the orthodox ordinal utility model does not adequately handle the problem of the number of goods chosen at equilibrium. Moreover, the problems that inhere in the orthodox formulation have also to do with the qualitative character of the optimal consumption bundle. In particular, no matter what satiety conditions are imposed, the model is simply not accommodative of two observable phenomena; namely, choice among differentiated forms of various product types, and systematic variation as real income changes, in the type and form of goods consumed.

These considerations were the catalyst to a series of new conceptions of the consumer's maximand. The utility tree formulation is congenial to the formal consideration of consumption categories; of the notion that subsets of the available goods are uniquely adapted to the satisfaction of certain classes of physical and, or, social needs.[5]   This result is not secured without cost, however. At the heart of the empirical application of this simple idea is a taxonomic process; a process by which, in principle, each of the n available goods is assigned to a consumption area or "branch." At one extreme, the level of aggregation within consumption branches is so heroic as to be vacuous. In the limit, such goods as "food," "transportation," "clothing," and "furniture" become somewhat akin to the Hicks-Marshall composite good, a rarefied conception that imparts a tautological character to the utility function [see Chapter 2, pp. 40-41]. Predictions yielded by such a model are nontestable because they cannot be disconfirmed. An individual consumer will always consume positive amounts of "food," "transportation," "clothing," and "furniture." At the other extreme, the systematic specification of the commodity composition of each branch proceeds at some risk. The risk is that the utility tree formulation cannot preclude the emergence of predictions that are known a priori to be false. Of particular concern is the prediction that the consumer will take positive amounts of each -- or simply most -- of the goods appearing in a given branch.

In contrast, because specialization or, at minimum, limited diversification within branches is an empirical reality, the multi-equation formulation has much to commend it. In its earlier guise [Furubotn 1967], the model came to grips with the reality of limited diversification; with the fact that at any cross-section of time, consumers do not consume all of the goods differentiates adapted to the satisfaction of a particular need. Moreover, the model is capable of rationalizing changes in the commodity composition of the optimal consumption bundle as the level of real income changes. What the model failed to do was to resolve the problem of goods taxonomy; a problem whose solution emerged in a variant of the multi-equation model.

The problem of goods classification was circumvented by the simple expedient of recognizing that observable consumption patterns involve a minimum and a maximum degree of diversification. Appropriate modification of the system permits determination of the number of definable subsets without requiring prior specification of the commodity composition of each. Moreover, the model's predictions accord with observable experience: The consumer's equilibrium position is seen to involve selection among product variants, and the commodity composition of the optimal consumption bundle is in part dependent upon the level of real income.

ON THE AMBIGUITY OF TEST RESULTS

While the qualitative predictions of the multi-equation utility function accord with experience, methodological difficulties remain. At the most rudimentary level, the various models lack interpretive rules. At one extreme, we have the utility tree formulation. While it is a single equation construct, it is the analytical antecedent of the multi-equation formulation.

As we have seen, taxonomic problems result in a level of commodity aggregation that renders the model's predictions vacuous. At the other extreme, the multi-equation construct admits of so exhaustive an a priori listing of alternative commodity subsets that virtually any observed consumption pattern can be rationalized. The implication is clear: The lack of adequate empirical interpretation increases the ambiguity of test results. A comparison of observed consumption patterns with the various model's predictions can never be disconfirmatory. Given the generality of the models' predictions, virtually any observed consumption behavior can be claimed to fall within the models' designed classes of implications. Alternatively, given the presence of an undefined exogenous variable -- the consumer's preference structure -- test results that appear to be irreconcilable with the models' predictions can always be ascribed to "changes in taste."[6]

THE THEORY AS EX POST RATIONALIZATION

The predictive powers of the multi-equation formulation are quite limited. Yet there is a sense in which emphasis upon predictive power misses the point. It seems clear that the purpose of these models is not so much to generate testable predictions as it is to provide a convenient and heuristic ex post rationalization of observed consumption behavior. As Professor Furubotn has suggested [Furubotn 1974, p. 304]:

> The new utility formulation is conceived in abstract terms and merely represents a convenient way of rationalizing the choice problem.

While the avowed purpose of ex post rationalization does not have the inherent intellectual appeal of prediction or explanation, this relatively more modest undertaking has much to commend it.[7]

As we know, a sine qua non for explanatory power is that both the generative and the auxiliary assumptions employed in a model be realistic. Yet the specification of appropriate assumptions -- whether generative or auxiliary -- must be predicated upon a conception of the consumer's decision process. On this logic, the multi-equation approach may be regarded as a tentative step in the direction of explaining consumer behavior.

Just as important, the multi-equation conception of the choice process is a catalyst to the formulation of questions that have heretofore received little, if any, attention. For example, explicit recognition that the consumer attaches differential significance to the various utility subfunctions leads to certain corollaries. It is, after all, clear that the consumer cannot be equally familiar with the qualitative properties of each of the n goods confronting him. Granting this, the likelihood is enhanced that he will undertake to distribute information acquisition or search effort. Professor Furubotn's assessment would seem to have basic relevance here [Furubotn 1974, p. 306]:

> Since only minor modification of the traditional theory of choice is needed to develop the new approach, close connections are maintained with marginal analysis. The differences in viewpoint introduced, however, are sufficient to permit a much more penetrating look into the internal structure of consumer preferences.[8]

On this logic, the multi-equation approach would seem to merit further attention.[9]

NOTES

[1]See Chapter 2, pp. 40-41.

[2]In a 1983 paper, Michael S. Miller posited a "satisfaction function" whose genesis is the utility tree. In his formulation "satisfaction" is "more encompassing than utility," including "the possibility that goods provide hedonic pleasures and fulfillment of status-striving desires" [Miller 1983, p. 48]. His "satisfaction function" is separable, with commodities categorized by type -- "necessities," "maintenance goods," and "luxuries and status goods." Moreover, he envisions a two-stage budgeting process, with money first allocated to "necessities" and then to "discretionary wants" [Miller 1983, pp. 49-50]. For more on the determination of budget shares see [Capps, Tedford and Havlicek 1985].

[3]See, for example [Furubotn 1967, pp. 55-61].

[4]Because the imposed satiety conditions do not rule out the possibility of boundary solutions at lower income levels, each of the L goods need not appear in the optimal consumption vector. At relatively low income levels, some of the L goods may not be consumed.

[5]The "missing money" problem to which I refer in Chapter IX has, in part, been a catalyst to the emergence of a literature which employs the logic of the utility tree. The literature envisions a two-stage constrained optimization problem in which, at stage one, "the intertemporal decision allocates total wealth over periods." Then, at stage two [Barnett, Fisher and Serletis 1992, p. 2111]:

> ... the total expenditure allocated in the first stage to the current period is then allocated over current period consumption of individual goods, asset services, and lesiure.

Proponents of this approach suggest, inter alia, that [Barnett, Fisher and Serletis 1992, p. 2115]:

> ... a good part of the [missing money] problem may be in the way money is measured -- both in the choice of component groupings and in the method of aggregating over those groups -- and in the way that the [money] demand model's capabilities relate to the generally nonlinear optimizing behavior of economic agents.

For an application of the two-stage approach to the generation of monetary aggregates, see [Anderson, Jones and Nesmith 1997b, esp. pp. 37-40]. See also [Anderson, Jones and Nesmith 1997a and 1997c]. I shall have more to say about this in Chapter IX, below.

[6]See, especially, Chapter 1, pp. 6-10 and 15-16. The point is that the definition of the commodity sets may be so general that virtually any observed consumption pattern may be reconcilable with the model. The interpretive rules are so broad as to accommodate whatever behavior is observed. To put the matter

differently, the model's designed classes of implications can be so broadly interpreted as to be essentially meaningless. And, finally, we may look at the matter in still another way. As we know, a model's interpretive rules identify the parameters of the system; they tell us what factors must be held constant if the model's predictions are to be testable (that is, if tests of the predictions are to be either confirmatory or disconfirmatory of the theory). On the other hand, a model's auxiliary assumptions assert that, as a matter of empirical reality, the parameters identified by the interpretive rules are, in fact, constant. The difficulty with the multi-equation formulation is that the number of independent variables is so large and the admissible consumption patterns so diverse that the parameters of the system are vague. It is not clear, therefore, what the parameters of the system should be, and what auxiliary assumptions should be, and indeed are, employed. It follows, pari passu, that the ambiguity of test results is enhanced, and the designed classes of implications are unclear. Moreover, any test results that are not reconcilable with the model's implications can, as in the traditional model, always be ascribed to "parametric change."

[7]Henry Aaron has recently observed that [Aaron 1994, p. 17]:

> ... the conventional [single equation utility function] framework fails to handle large classes of human behavior, which happen to include just about everything that is of concern to economists engaged in guiding social policy. In such cases, a good place to start would be to design utility models capable of RATIONALIZING the large chunks of behavior that current utility assumptions label as anomalous or irrational. [emphasis mine]

The approach he suggests contemplates a "utility representation in which each person consists of more than one, possibly many, utility functions" [Aaron 1994, p. 15]. I shall have more to say about this in Chapter VIII, below.

[8]It has been suggested, for example, that multiple preference systems [Hausman and McPherson 1993, p. 688]:

> ... very naturally model internal conflict concerning such personal choices as whether or not to smoke... as well as more clearly moral choices such as whether to contribute to charity....

I shall have more to say about this in Chapter VIII, below.

[9]For applications of the multi-equation approach, see [Roth 1975; Wolff 1985].

Chapter 5

The Household Production Function

> ... we are proposing the hypothesis that widespread and/or persistent human behavior can be explained by a gerneralized calculus of utility-maximizing behavior, without introducing the qualification 'tastes remaining the same.'
>
> George Stigler and Gary Becker

THE NEED FOR ADEQUATE EMPIRICAL INTERPRETATION, ONCE AGAIN

The multi-equation conception of the consumer's maximand involves a number of methodological difficulties. The key problem is the presence of an unidentified exogenous variable. Of particular interest here is the fact that unless the consumer's tastes and preferences are constant over the period during which his behavior is observed, test results are ambiguous. Evidence contradictory either of the model's predictions or of the rationality postulate can always be ascribed to "changes in taste." In short, the multi-equation formulation suffers from the same debility that plagues the orthodox ordinal utility formulation; namely, a lack of adequate empirical interpretation.

While recognition of the need for adequate empirical interpretation was not the only catalyst to his efforts, Gary Becker's household production function seeks to come to grips with this problem. On his view [Becker 1976b, p. 12], "Examples abound in the economic literature of changes in preferences conveniently introduced ad hoc to explain puzzling behavior." Indeed, in their treatment of the "Weaknesses in the Traditional Theory" [Michael and Becker 1973, p. 380], Professors Michael and Becker lay great emphasis upon the fact that:

> To whatever extent income and prices do not explain consumer behavior, the explanation rests with variations in taste since they are the portmanteau in the demand curve . . . For economists to rest a large part of their theory of choice on differences in tastes is disturbing since they admittedly have no useful theory of the formation of tastes from any discipline . . . The weakness in the received theory of choice, then, is the extent to which it relies on differences in tastes to 'explain' behavior when it can neither explain how tastes are formed nor predict their effects.

SOME INTRODUCTORY REMARKS

Presumably with empirical interpretation in mind, Professor Becker has proffered a "New Theory of Consumer Behavior"; an approach which is at once both novel and eclectic. In characterizing the consumer's decision process as a two-stage procedure [Michael and Becker 1973, pp. 381-382], Becker's "New Theory" has something in common with the multi-equation approach. In emphasizing the "technology of consumption" [Michael and Becker 1973, p. 394] he calls to mind the Lancastrian "New Approach."

While the "New Theory" has much in commmon with its intellectual precursors, there are substantive differences. Whereas in the models discussed thus far the decision unit is the "individual consumer," in the Becker formulation -- hereafter, the household production function approach, or HHPF -- the decision unit is the household. While it has intuitive appeal, focus on the household as the basic decision unit is a double-edged sword. On the one hand, the issue of aggregation must be faced. Unless all household members have homogeneous preference structures, analysis cannot proceed until it is known whose preferences guide the choice among comestibles. Short of assuming that the choices of the "head of the household" dominate, the presumption must be that the members of the household find some way of reconciling the claims of the household's members on its finite resources. Now, while solutions to this problem are conceivable [Samuelson 1965b], a general theoretical solution must be predicated upon an application of welfare theory [Graaff 1967, p. 52].[1]

If the HHPF approach forces consideration of some frequently intractable problems of aggregation, it is also congenial to the explicit treatment of nonmarket activities [Michael and Becker 1973, pp. 388-389 and 380-381] and of recognition of the value of time [Michael and Becker 1973, p. 388; Becker 1965] and of consumer knowledge [Michael and Becker 1973, p. 392]. Moreover, whereas the orthodox treatment ignores the application of human effort in the consumption process, the HHPF approach draws attention to the employment of household time and effort in the conversion of purchasable goods into "commodities."[2]

THE PRESUMED STABILITY OF PREFERENCE STRUCTURES

What distinguishes the HHPF approach from its precursors is not, however, the phenomena that come under its purview. Rather, it is the specification of the properties of the household's maximand that clearly distinguishes it:

> In the standard theory all consumers behave similarly in the sense that they all maximize the same thing -- utility or satisfaction. It is only a further extension then to argue that they all derive that utility from the same 'basic pleasures' or preference function, and differ only in their ability to produce these 'pleasures.' From this point of view, the Latin expression *de gustibus non est disputandum* suggests not so much that it is impossible to resolve disputes arising from differences in tastes but rather that in fact no such disputes arise! [Michael and Becker 1973, p. 392].[3]

There is no ambiguity here. What is asserted is homogeneity of tastes; a claim that is justified on the basis that it is "only a further extension" of the presumption that consumers seek to maximize consistently ordered utility functions. Moreover, the assertion is justified on the grounds that [Becker 1976b, p. 5]:

> Since economists generally have had little to contribute . . . to the understanding of how preferences are formed, preferences are assumed not to change substantially over time, nor to be very different between wealthy and poor persons, or even between persons in different societies and cultures.

Now it is not clear how one moves from the proposition that consumers (or households) maximize well-behaved utility functions to the propositions that: a) tastes are virtually constant over time, and that b) they can be treated as broadly similar across decision units.[4] It is even less clear how one can justify acceptance of these propositions based upon the fact that the formation of tastes is a black box into which the economist -- and everyone else -- sees darkly.

Assume for the moment that tastes are both broadly similar across decision units and stable over time. Having done this, one might plausibly ask what has been gained. Proponents of the HHPF approach argue that the gains are unambiguous [Michael and Becker 1973, p. 391]:

> The new approach is not in conflict with the traditional implications regarding household responses to changes in relative prices or real income. On the contrary, an important advantage of the new approach is its greater emphasis on income and price effects and, correspondingly, its reduced emphasis on the role of 'tastes' in INTERPRETING behavior. (emphasis mine)

It is the interpretation of behavior that is of interest to proponents of the HHPF approach. And so it must be. Each of the models discussed in earlier chapters suffers from a common debility; namely, the lack of adequate empirical interpretation. Each proceeds on the assumption that tastes are subject to change. Yet each recognizes that if test results are to be unambiguously interpretable, tastes must be constant. The presumed constancy of tastes is, therefore, an auxiliary assumption in these models; an assumption which may or may not be realistic.

The constancy of tastes is also a sine qua non for the unambiguous interpretation of HHPF test results. The difference is that the auxiliary assumption that tastes are constant is claimed to be redundant. It is asserted that, as a matter of empirical fact, tastes are constant. On this assumption, a degree of freedom is removed, and the interpretation of test results is unambiguous. In effect, ". . . the assumption of stable preferences provides a foundation for predicting the responses to various changes" [Becker 1976b, p. 7].

THE MODEL[5]

Whereas in the traditional model the objects of choice are presumed to be purchasable economic goods, the HHPF approach takes as the consumer's desiderata "commodities." Commodities are produced by the household under the technical restrictions imposed by a family of household production functions. While the nature of these production functions will be made clear below, for the moment our interest centers on a formal representation of the household's maximand. Let the household's utility function be

$$U = U(Z_1, Z_2, ..., Z_n) \qquad (5\text{-}1)$$

where the Z_i denote both the services derived from and the quantity of the commodity Z_i. The ith commodity is produced via the employment of a vector of purchasable market goods, x_i, and the application of a vector of quantities of the household's time. We have, then, as the family of household production functions

$$Z_i = Z_i(x_i, t_i \mid E) \qquad (5\text{-}2)$$

where E denotes a vector of "environmental" variables. E is a convenient means of summarizing the various technical parameters of the family of production functions; it is representative, in other words, of "the state of the art."[6]

The household's utility function (5-1) is presumed to be maximized subject to the technical constraints summarized by equation system (5-2) and a constraint on the household's time

$$T = t_w + \sum_{i=1}^{n} t_i, \qquad (5\text{-}3)$$

as well as the familiar income constraint

$$y = \sum_{i=1}^{n} p_i x_i, \qquad (5\text{-}4)$$

where t_w and t_i denote, respectively, the household's time spent in the labor market and in producing the Z_i. The p_i denote the market prices, and the x_i the utilization rates of the market goods employed in the production of the Z_i.

The time and income constraints can, however, be collapsed into a single resource constraint; a constraint on what is characterized as the household's "full income," S

$$S = wT + V = \sum_{i=1}^{n} (wt_i + p_i x_i) \qquad (5\text{-}5)$$

where the mnemonic notation w denotes the wage rate, assumed to be constant, and V is the household's nonwage income.

Taking the first derivative of the appropriate Lagrangian with respect to the commodities and setting the results equal to zero yields the following first order conditions for the optimal consumption rates of the commodities

$$\frac{MU_i}{MU_j} = \frac{w(dt_i/dZ_i) + p_i(dx_i/dZ_i)}{w(dt_j/dZ_j) + p_j(dx_j/dZ_j)} = \frac{\prod_i}{\prod_j} \qquad (5\text{-}6)$$

As (5-6) is written, the ratio of the marginal utilities of the two COMMODITIES, Z_i and Z_j , MU_i/MU_j must equal the ratio of their shadow prices, $\prod_i/\prod_j$.[7] If the household production functions are homogeneous of degree one in the goods and time, the marginal and average costs of producing the ith commodity would be equal [Stigler and Becker 1977, p. 77]. Granting this, in the absence of joint production, the new theory yields a "satisfactory model of the demand for commodities and the allocation of time as functions of 'commodity prices'" [Pollak and Wachter 1975, p. 256]. Of immediate interest, however, is that, from (5-6), the shadow prices of the commodities reflect their costs of household production, and that these costs, in turn, are determined by the prices of the purchasable goods, by time, and by the productivity of the goods and time in the production of the commodities.

Having secured the optimal consumption pattern of the commodities, the optimal utilization rates of the household's productive inputs is given by

$$\frac{(\partial U/\partial Z_i)\,(\partial Z_i/\partial f_{ik})}{(\partial U/\partial Z_j)\,(\partial Z_j/\partial f_{j\ell})} \equiv \frac{MU_i\,Mp_{ik}}{MU_j\,Mp_{j\ell}} = \frac{p_{fik}}{p_{fj\ell}} \quad (5\text{-}7)$$

where f_{ik} denotes the factor of commodity production k used in producing commodity Z_i, and f_ℓ is the factor ℓ employed in the production of Z_j. From (5-7) we know that when i=j, both factors of production (one of the purchasable goods and time) are used in the same household production function. In this event, the MUs in the middle term in (5-7) cancel, and the familiar first order condition for optimal input utilization emerges; namely, that the ratio of the marginal products must equal the ratio of the input prices. Alternatively, if k=ℓ the same input must be allocated among commodity production functions so as to equalize the utility value of its marginal product in the production of different commodities.[8]

The Implications for Consumer Behavior

Professor Becker's "New Theory of Consumer Behavior" is claimed to have a comparative advantage both in the interpretation of observed behavior, and in the extent of the array of observable phenomena that come under its purview. It is claimed, in particular, that [Michael and Becker 1973, p. 394]:

> . . . the household production function approach . . . systematically and symmetrically incorporates numerous constraints on the household's behavior, strengthens the reliance on changes in income and prices as explanations of observed behavior, and correspondingly reduces the reliance on differences in tastes and preferences. These alterations are desirable primarily because they yield a variety of additional behavioral predictions without heroic ingenuity or ad hoc theorizing. . . By reducing the role of tastes, WHICH HAVE DEFIED EFFECTIVE THEORETICAL ANALYSIS, the new approach expands the applicability of the economist's theory of choice into the nonmarket sector and hence makes the theory more useful in analyzing household behavior in its many dimensions. [emphasis mine][9]

While proponents of the HHPF approach recognize the theoretical (and, they might have said, empirical) intractability of the analysis of tastes and preferences, this much is clear: On the presumption that tastes are both broadly homogeneous and intertemporally stable, the simple expedient of incorporating production theoretic concepts into consumer theory yields important insights into household behavior. In the decision environment contemplated, households do not respond to changes in goods prices and real income in determining the composition of their optimal consumption bundles. Rather, they take account of changes in the prices and productivities of purchasable goods and of time, and of changes in the relative shadow prices of their ultimate desiderata, household-produced commodities. And, finally, it is not real income in the sense of nominal income adjusted for goods price changes that establishes the ultimate constraint on the household's behavior. Rather, full real income defines the household's opportunity set. On the presumption that full money income, S [see equation (5-5)] can be adjusted for changes in the COMMODITY price level, we have the result that [Michael and Becker 1973, p. 384]:

> The single constraint on the household's full real income indicates the limitation on its achievable basket of commodities. Forces which affect the market prices households pay and the productivity of the inputs they use alter their [relevant commodity price index] and thus change their full real income. Every household's [commodity price index] may differ just as its full money income may; more efficient household managers have larger real opportunity sets than less efficient ones with the same full money income, S.

In general, this approach admits of deliberate, systematic attempts to alter the productivity of the household's time. This, in turn, suggests that the approach is congenial to the analysis of the acquisition of human capital by household members. In short, the approach provides a more comprehensive and heuristic characterization of the elements involved in the consumer's (household's) decision process. Beyond this, the approach provides a useful interface between the theory of consumer behavior and an emerging literature on investment in human capital. The approach is not, however, without difficulty. Indeed, the empirical usefulness of the approach is severely encumbered by methodological and other difficulties. It is to these that I now turn.

METHODOLOGICAL AND OTHER DIFFICULTIES

Ignoring for the moment the problems attendant to the presumed constancy of tastes, the relevant question is whether the HHPF approach can properly be regarded as a theory of commodity demand. More precisely, can a model which employs commodity prices as arguments provide a satisfactory theory of commodity demand?

Unless each of the family of household production functions is homogeneous of degree one, and the various production processes involve no joint production, commodity prices cannot properly be employed as arguments of the commodity demand functions [Pollak and Wachter 1975]. This point is not lost on Professor Becker. He is careful always to specify that his model employs the "usual assumptions of homogeneity of the production function" [Michael and Becker 1973, p. 388].[10] What is not clear is that much can be said a priori about the degree of homogeneity of household production functions. On the other hand, we have reason to suppose that joint production is a relatively widespread phenomenon. Indeed,

> Commodities which involve time as an input are a particular problem, since their production often involves joint production. Jointness is pervasive because time spent in many productive activities is a DIRECT source of utility as well as an input into a commodity [Pollak and Wachter 1975, p. 256].

This is a particularly salient point. It is, moreover, a point of which Professor Becker has taken account.[11]

Having said this, it is important to recognize that violation of either or both of these two conditions does not, by itself, put the analytical integrity of the HHPF approach in jeopardy. When the technology exhibits nonconstant returns and/or joint production, the simple expedient of substituting goods prices, the wage rate, and nonlabor income for commodity prices will suffice. In effect, while commodity prices cannot be employed as arguments in the household's commodity demand functions, other arguments can be substituted. This result appears greatly to enhance the number of potential empirical applications of the model. The difficulty is that, while the number of potential empirical applications may be increased, a methodological problem remains; namely, the ambiguity of test results.

The Presence of an Unidentified Exogenous Variable

It is both useful and appropriate to begin with a quote that captures the essence of the HHPF approach:

. . . we are proposing the hypothesis that widespread and/or persistent human behavior can be explained by a generalized calculus of utility- maximizing behavior, without introducing the qualification 'tastes remaining the same' [Stigler and Becker 1977, p. 76].

As has been emphasized, the HHPF approach proffers an explicit interpretive rule. It tells us that, as a matter of empirical fact, tastes and preferences are intertemporally stable. On this view, it is redundant to include the presumed constancy of tastes in the ceteris paribus pound.

The problem is that it is not possible to secure independent evidence that, in fact, tastes are constant.[12] The HHPF approach suffers from the same debility to which every model of consumer behavior is subject; namely, the presence of an unidentified exogenous variable. The researcher cannot logically use one set of observational data to establish what the consumer's (household's) preference structure is and, at the same time, verify that the structure is constant. Unless we know what the preference structure is a priori, we cannot verify that it has been constant during the period of observation.[13]

If, in the spirit of the HHPF approach, we treat the assumption of the intertemporal stability of tastes as an interpretive rule, we are impelled, Professors Stigler and Becker notwithstanding, to treat it as an auxiliary assumption. Yet we know that we cannot secure independent evidence that the assumption is true. It follows that tests of its predictions can be neither confirmatory nor disconfirmatory of the model. If, on the other hand, we choose to treat the presumed constancy of tastes as a generative assumption, we are confronted with a different problem. Insofar as the assumption is not independently testable, it fails to satisfy one of the conditions for the realism of assumptions. It follows that one or more of the implications of the HHPF approach must be false.[14]

Whatever else is said, this much is clear: A theory which assumes stable preferences while at the same time relying on a non-market characterization of both the arguments of the maximand and of the consumer's income constraint cannot be empirically disconfirmed. This point has not been lost on others. Henry Aaron has noted, for example, that [Aaron 1994, p. 6]:

Becker ... notes that while preferences may be altered and formed, 'meta preferences' are stable. But if one can add 'meta preferences' whenever some observed behavior violates supposedly stable preferences, then fixed but invisible preferences are operationally indistinguishable   from values mutable with respect to any observable behavior and subject to evolution in response to time and experience.

On this logic, it is not clear "exactly what kinds of evidence would be inconsistent with the theory" [Hannan 1982, p. 71]. Indeed, in Hannan's view, it is not clear "whether ANY data could be shown convincingly to be inconsistent with the theory." As a result, Hannan is "not prepared to agree that the theory has already gained a high degree of empirical verification" [Hannan 1982, p. 71] (emphasis in original).[15]

While the HHPF approach does provide a convenient and heuristic means by which to rationalize observed consumer behavior, it raises more questions than it answers. So long as the approach is inexorably bound up with an untestable assertion about reality, its implications cannot be interpreted as explanations of observed consumer behavior. Worse still, because the stability of preferences cannot be independently tested, tests of the model's predictions must be recognized to be neither confirmatory nor discomfirmatory of the model. The ingenuity of its proponents and its intuitive plausibility notwithstanding, Professor Becker's "New Theory" stands four square in the same methodological quagmire as the other models of consumer behavior we have discussed.

NOTES

[1]If the household members have some common ethic which enables them to combine their preference scales into a household scale, the "private indifference curves" of the household give a consistent representation of the tastes of the household. On the other hand, if each household member acts independently, so that behavior fails to conform to a social welfare function, the choices of the household would appear irrational to the observer. For more on the social welfare function, see Chapter VIII, below.

[2]In this sense the HHPF approach has much in common with the utility tree approach or, more precisely, with some applications of the utility tree. See, for example [Muth 1966; Furubotn 1963].

[3]See also [Stigler and Becker 1977, especially p. 76].

[4]Indeed, Professors Stigler and Becker became, by 1977, somewhat tentative about the logical leap involved here [Stigler and Becker 1977, p. 76]:

> . . . we are proposing the hypothesis that widespread and/or persistent human behavior can be explained by a generalized calculus of utility- maximizing behavior without introducing the qualification 'tastes remaining the same.' IT IS A THESIS THAT DOES NOT PERMIT OF DIRECT PROOF BE- CAUSE IT IS AN ASSERTION ABOUT THE WORLD, NOT A PROPOSI- TION IN LOGIC. [emphasis mine].

For models which treat tastes as endogenously determined see [Frank 1987; Basmann, Molina and Slottje 1987]. See also Chapter VIII, below.

[5]For a more detailed formalization of the model, see [Becker 1965, pp. 495-500; Michael and Becker 1973, pp. 381-386].

[6]In their 1977 article, Professors Stigler and Becker write the household production functions somewhat more explicitly. In particular, they identify the parameters of the family of household production functions as the stocks of human capital possessed by the household's members and "all other inputs." What is envisioned is a very plausible state of affairs; namely, that the household's technology is determined, in part, by the character and content of its human capital. See [Stigler and Becker 1977, esp. p. 77].

[7]Note that the derivatives in (5-6) are marginal input-output coefficients.

[8]What is contemplated here is not a case of joint production. Joint production would mean that utilization of the same units of a given input results in the simultaneous emergence of different commodity outputs. Here we envision a different technical situation; one in which different units of a single input (either a good or time) are used in the production of different commodities. See, for example [Becker 1976b, p. 136, fn. 1].

[9]See also [Becker 1965, pp. 516-517; Becker 1976b, pp. 5 and 7; Stigler and Becker 1977, p. 89]. For a survey of the empirical applications of the approach, see [Michael and Becker 1973, pp. 386-391]. For other applications of the HHPF

approach see [Williams and Donath 1994; Corman 1986; Bivens and Volker 1986; Mendelsohn 1984; Graham and Green 1984; Rosenzweig and Schultz 1983; Sasaki 1983; Odland 1981; Blundell and Walker 1984; James 1983]. For an assessment of the problems associated with the measurement of household production see [Quah 1986]. See also [Quah 1987].

[10]See also [Becker 1965, p. 491; Stigler and Becker 1977, p. 77].

[11]In discussing the weak separability of the household's indirect utility function -- a function whose arguments are the inputs employed in the production of the commodities rather than the commodities themselves -- Professor Becker has this to say [Michael and Becker 1973, p. 387, fn. 3]:

> The existence of joint production . . . undermines the separability of the production processes. Some studies related to the use of time in many activities simultaneously are now underway.

For more on the weak separability of the household's indirect utility function, see [Becker 1965, p. 513; Michael and Becker 1973, pp. 385-386].

[12]West and McKee claim to have tested the Stigler-Becker theory that tastes and preferences are intertemporally stable. Their test focuses on the growth in private schooling in England during the first half of the 19th century. They assume that education is a normal good and observe that, over this period, the rise in real wages was modest. They conclude, therefore, that "Unless the income elasticity was VERY high, . . . the income effect alone could not explain the growth of schooling . . ." [West and McKee 1983, pp. 1118-1119] (emphasis in original). More heroically, they assert that the increase in schooling can be attributed to an "addiction effect." The logic here is that each increment to literacy adds to the stock of human capital which, in turn, reduces the marginal cost of incremental education. In effect, spreading literacy reduces the individual household's shadow price on education thereby inducing an increase in the quantity of education demanded [West and McKee 1983, p. 1119]. This logic is, of course, consistent with the HHPF approach. What is not at all clear is how one legitimately leaps from the assertion that the income effect could not plausibly have been large enough to account for the increase in education to the conclusion that, therefore, an addiction effect must have occurred AND that tastes are, therefore, intertemporally stable. There are simply too many unknowns. For an additional empirical test of the Stigler-Becker hypothesis see [Ben-Ner 1987].

[13]Going the other way, unless we have independent evidence that the preference structure was constant during the test period, it is not possible either to confirm or to discomfirm the rationality postulate (see Chapter II). The reference to the rationality postulate is particularly appropriate here because Professor Becker seems to argue that economic theory has basic relevance whether the decision unit is rational or not. On his view, "Not only utility maximization but also many other decision rules, incorporating a wide variety of irrational behavior, lead to negatively inclined demand curves because of the

effect of a change in prices on opportunities" [Becker 1962, p. 6]. Of basic relevance to our discussion is the fact that the definition of "irrationality" is taken to be "Any deviation from utility maximization . . ." [Becker 1962, p. 5, fn. 7].

The difficulty here is clear. If we have not established what the household's preference structure is, how are we to know what behavior is consistent with utility maximization? It follows that we cannot know what behavior is inconsistent with utility maximization. In Professor Pollak's words, "it is not clear what set of observations would cause economists to abandon . . . the version (of the neoclassical theory of consumer behavior) which assumes that preferences . . . are exogenous and identical over time and space" [Pollak 1985, fn. 8, pp. 584-585]. Interestingly, Professor Becker comes close to recognizing this, though he clearly means the remark to be supportive of the efficacy of the HHPF approach [Becker 1976b, p. 145]:

> . . . it is difficult to distinguish operationally between irrational choices and poorly informed ones, and the new approach to the theory of choice does give appropriate recognition to the investment in and costly accumulation of information.

[14]See, especially, Chapter 1, pp. 16-18.

[15]See also [Ben-Porath 1982, esp. p. 62] and [Furubotn 1994, pp. 31-34]. The essential point is that, in the HHPF approach, the objects of choice are not purchasable economic goods. Rather, they are produced via the employment of market goods, given the application of household time and the services of human capital. If preferences defined on the resulting "commodities" are to be stable then, *inter alia*, the decision makers in the sytem "must be 'completely rational'" [Furubotn 1994, p. 33]. In effect, "all of the innovations that lead to quality changes in consumption options have to be anticipated when the [preference] ordering is first formulated" [Furubotn 1994, p. 33]. Given what we know about agents' cognitive limitations, this is an implausible assumption. See, for example, Chapter VI, below.

Chapter 6

Procedural Rationality and the Technology of Choice

Economics, which has traditionally been concerned with what decisions are made rather than how they are made, has more and more reason to interest itself in the procedural aspects of decision

Herbert A. Simon

INTRODUCTION

A critical appraisal of received consumer theory has the character of an intellectual odyssey. Like Odysseus, we are tempted by the Sirens. At the most rudimentary level, we have the elegantly simple, highly stylized ordinal utility theory. Deceptively simply, it gives the appearance of generality; of wide application. Indeed, if he is not careful, the casual observer is likely to conclude that the limits to the model's applications are imposed by the ingenuity of the user, rather than by the intrinsic properties of the model. However, its "elegance" and simplicity notwithstanding, the elementary ordinal utility formulation cannot seriously be considered a part of the corpus of empirical science. Because the classical rationality postulate cannot be independently confirmed, tests of the model's predictions can be neither confirmatory nor discomfirmatory of the model [Chapter 2, pp. 35-37]. Worse still, a kind of intellectual inertia prevails; an inclination to "push the frontiers" of the ordinal utility formulation. There is a tendency to try to squeeze as much empirical content as is possible out of an irreducible minimum number of patently unrealistic generative assumptions. The presumption is that the correspondence of symbolism to reality can be enhanced via a modification of the mathematical structure of the ordinal utility formulation while, at the same time, retaining the orthodox construction of the consumer's maximand. The result has been the emergence of the Kuhn-Tucker variant of the ordinal utility model; a formulation which "solves" the problem of the emergence of optimal consumption bundles involving negative consumption rates of one or more goods, while at the same time generating a set of equally implausible implications [Chapter 2, p. 38]. Moreover, nothing useful is salvaged by technical virtuosity. The imposition of satiety conditions "loads" the model in favor of solutions involving positive consumption rates of all or most of the goods appearing in the utility function. The composite good theorem is of no help here. Appeal to this convention renders the truth value of the utility function independent of the truth value of its component parts; it imparts a tautological character to the utility function.

A balanced assessment of the ordinal utility formulation and of its technical extensions must conclude that it has contributed little to our understanding of consumer behavior. We are able, by appeal to any of these constructions, neither to explain consumer behavior nor to make unambiguously interpretable predictions.

The literature on the "New Approach" to consumer theory does, in a sense, represent a significant break with the orthodox tradition. At bottom, the break involves a new understanding of the arguments of the consumer's maximand, and an explicit characterization of the instantaneously prevailing "consumption technology."

Unfortunately, while Professor Lancaster's formulation has much to commend it, the weary traveler is ill-advised to take it to his bosom. While the formulation is heuristic, and while it does suggest several promising lines of inquiry, the predictive capabilities of the model are severely encumbered by the mathematical properties of the consumption technology. It is one thing to recognize -- quite plausibly -- that it is the qualitative properties of comestibles that constitute the consumer's desiderata. It is quite another to move from an optimal activities vector to a unique, optimal vector of purchasable economic goods. The presumption of a one-to-one correspondence between goods and activities is, under rather plausible conditions, of no help [see, esp., Chapter 3, pp. 56-58]. Neither is appeal to the pseudoinverse [Chapter 3, pp. 61-64], something which Professor Lancaster has evidently not considered. In short, the model is subject to goods indeterminacy; to an inability to predict which goods vector will be chosen at equilibrium.

Efforts to modify the basic structure of the consumer's maximand have not been limited to defining the utility function in characteristics space. Motivated by the need to resolve the problem of the number of goods chosen at equilibrium, Professor Furubotn has proffered a multi-equation formulation of the utility function [Chapter 4, pp. 76-82]. Following the organizational pattern of the utility tree [Chapter 4, pp. 73-76], the model has the singular advantage that its implications are reconcilable with observed consumer behavior.[1] In particular, the model does not yield the implication that all (or even most) of the goods appearing in the utility function will be chosen at equilibrium. Moreover, the model suggests that the consumer will choose among differentiates of given product types, and that the commodity composition of the optimal consumption bundle will not be invariant with respect to changes in real income.

While all of this represents a quantum intellectual leap (relative to the elementary ordinal utility formulation), the model must be recognized for what it is. It is, purely and simply, a convenient mnemonic representation of reality. Its forte is ex post rationalization rather than explanation or prediction [Chapter 4, pp. 84-85]. On the other hand, by focusing attention on the multi-staged nature of the consumer's decision process, the model is heuristic. It is suggestive of the direction in which the theory of consumer behavior might optimally move.[2]

The methodological difficulties associated with the multi-equation formulation center on the presence of an unidentified exogenous variable. In part because the consumer's preference structure is not known to be constant over the period during which his behavior is observed, and in part because it admits of so exhaustive an a priori listing of admissible commodity subsets, virtually any observed consumption pattern is reconcilable with predictions generated by the multi-equation model. Like its intellectual precursors, the model lacks adequate empirical interpretation.

The problem of inadequate empirical interpretation was one of the catalysts to the emergence of the household production function approach. The model's proponents set out, quite explicitly, to accomplish two things.

First, they seek, via the presumption of intertemporal stability of preferences to overcome the problem of inadequate empirical interpretation. Second, they seek to expand the set of designed implications of the theory of consumer behavior to include non-market phenomena. On their view, this second objective is accomplished by recognizing that households apply both time and effort in effecting the conversion of purchasable economic goods into "commodities." By taking explicit account of the consumer's "full income" and of the appropriate shadow price vector, one secures the (presumably desirable) result of reducing the role of tastes in the interpretation of observed consumer behavior [Chapter 5, p. 92].

While the specification of commodity demand functions does present certain technical difficulties, these are not intractable [Chapter 5, p. 97]. On the other hand, to say this is not to suggest that the model is more amenable to empirical interpretation than is any one of its intellectual precursors. The proponents of the household production function approach have simply assumed the problem of inadequate empirical interpretation away. Until they are able to secure independent evidence that tastes are intertemporally stable, the interpretation of empirical tests of the model will be ambiguous.

THE CLASSICAL RATIONALITY POSTULATE,
ONCE AGAIN

While much can be said about the body of received consumer theory, this much is clear: Each of its model variants suffers from the same debility; namely, the presence of an unidentified exogenous variable. It is precisely because the structure of the individual consumer's tastes is not known a priori that empirical disconfirmation of the models' predictions is not possible. Unless tastes are known before behavior is observed, it is a practical impossibility to establish the interpretive rules requisite to knowing the class of implications to which the model is supposed to give rise and, even more fundamentally, to know what behavior is consistent with the consumer's preference ordering. Reduced to its essentials, the problem is that a single set of data cannot be used to confirm both the rationality postulate and the predictive capabilities of the model.

The concept of rationality is central to the question of the empirical testability of consumer theory. Unfortunately, it is precisely the classical rationality postulate that encumbers the theory; that inveighs against its empirical testability [Ekelund, Furubotn, and Gramm 1972, p. 73]:

> Both utility theory and revealed-preference theory require that the consumer show highly consistent choice behavior. Thus, for example, if the consumer does not act in conformity with the strong axiom, he must be regarded as 'irrational' and the whole system of revealed preference effectively breaks down.

> This rather rigid position relative to consistent preferences is ill adapted to the needs of an empirical science. Before observed consumer choices can be interpreted confidently it would seem essential to learn more about individual decision- making behavior under the conditions actually operative in the real world. This means, <u>inter alia</u>, that the process of human decision-making itself and such factors as uncertainty, the cost of search, the social setting of choice, etc., must be taken into account by the demand model.

With this in mind, a number of avenues of research might reasonably be advocated. One might argue, for example, that the researcher must seek independent evidence that the consumer is, in fact, rational. Granting this, it does not seem unreasonable to broach a related question. Is there an alternative conception of rationality that is more amenable to direct (or indirect) empirical confirmation than is its classical counterpart? The answer to this question is emphatically yes. But adoption of the alternative view of rationality must be predicated upon a systematic consideration of the limits of human cognitive powers. The presumption is, in other words, that the technology of choice is inexorably bound up with -- indeed, it is partially defined by -- the problem solving skills of the human decision maker. On this view, explicit account must be taken of a critical interface between economics and psychology [Marschak 1978]. We must come to grips, in other words, with the question of how choices are made rather than which choices are made; we must, to borrow a phrase of Simon's, ask questions of a procedural rather than a substantive nature.

AN ALTERNATIVE TO THE CLASSICAL
RATIONALITY POSTULATE

More on the Concept of Rationality

Received consumer theory has centered on the question of what decisions are made rather than how they are made [Hogarth and Reder 1986]. Emphasis has traditionally been placed upon the explication and prescription of optimal solutions to constrained utility maximization problems, with little or no emphasis on the procedural aspects of the process by which a solution will have been secured. The emphasis has been upon what Simon has characterized as substantive rationality [Simon 1978a, p. 494]. Explicit account has not typically been taken of procedural rationality; that is, of "the rationality of a person for whom computation is the scarce resource -- whose ability to adapt successfully to the situations in which he finds himself is determined by the efficiency of his decision-making and problem-solving processes" [Simon 1978a, p. 504].

Emphasis upon the character and content of the individual consumer's decision-making process necessarily imparts a highly subjective character to the resulting model. This may be viewed as too high a cost. It is, after all, antithetical to the notion that there exists -- or that there can be developed -- a "general" theory of consumer behavior. There is, however, another view. One might plausibly argue that [Ekelund, Furubotn and Gramm 1972, p. 57]:

> In part, the unimpressive predictive record of demand theory reflects the fact that a substantial proportion of the literature . . . has been concerned with models having very limited empirical content. Interest has focused primarily on logical problems and on the formulation of a rigorous, compact, and highly general theory of consumer choice.

On this view, a theory may be so "general" as to be vacuous. Of course, one may plausibly ask by what expedient "more empirical content" may be introduced into the theory of consumer behavior. The answer is that we must take explicit account of the fact that the individual consumer's objective decision environment is one thing; his subjective perception of it may be -- and, I suspect, typically is -- quite another.[3] Granting this, we must contemplate [Simon 1966, p. 19]:

... modifications in the concept of economic man ... modifications in the direction of providing a fuller description of his characteristics ... We need a description of the choice process that recognizes that alternatives are not given but must be sought; and a description that takes into account the arduous task of determining what consequences will follow on each alternative.

In a word, emphasis must be placed upon a systematic characterization of the consumer's decision process; upon procedural rather than substantive rationality.

Normative and Positive Theories of Procedural Rationality

Procedural rationality is the rationality of a decision-maker for whom computation is the scarce resource. One might fruitfully think, therefore, of a theory of procedural rationality as a theory of computation. The position adopted here is that a theory of procedural rationality -- of computation -- is likely to prove useful in those "domains that are too complex, too full of uncertainty, or too rapidly changing to permit objectively optimal actions to be discovered and implemented" [Simon 1978a, p. 504]. This, in my judgment, is a sufficiently close characterization of the consumer's choice problem as to justify effecting a logical leap; namely, that the concept of procedural rationality might fruitfully be applied to consumer theory. There is, however, a complication. It is possible to make a formal distinction as between normative and positive theories of procedural rationality.

Normative theories of procedural rationality are prescriptive in nature; they are concerned with the problem of uncovering "good" or "best" methods by which to achieve some well-defined goal(s). Such theories have as their goal finding powerful problem-solving algorithms. An example of a normative science of procedural rationality is artificial intelligence; a discipline that is concerned "with programming computers to do clever, humanoid things -- but not necessarily to do them in a humanoid way" [Simon 1978a, p. 496].

Positive, or perhaps more appropriately, behavioral theories of procedural rationality are not concerned with the discovery of problem-solving algorithms. Rather, the objective is to construct operational counterparts for the decision processes actually employed by human decision-makers. The science of cognitive simulation, a discipline based principally on work that employs a computer to simulate human thought processes, is an example of a positive science of procedural rationality. The science of cognitive simulation has basic relevance to the problem of choice process simulation. Before taking up this problem, however, it is essential that we first attend to another matter.

Normative and Positive Theories of Consumer Behavior

While we have not heretofore had occasion to do so, it is useful to note the distinction between normative and positive theories of consumer behavior. Here we do not use the word "positive" in the instrumentalist's sense. Rather, the distinction is symmetrical to that which delineates normative and positive theories of procedural rationality. In this sense, normative or prescriptive theories of consumer behavior seek to prescribe optimal or "best" behavior. Descriptive or behavioral theories purport to characterize the actual decision-making behavior of consumers, with a view to explaining the choices actually made.

It is possible to argue that the development of the theory of choice has not evinced so powerful a dichotomy; that "behavioral and normative theories have developed as a dialectic rather than as separate domains" [March 1978, p. 588]. Prescriptive theories of choice have, for example, been influenced by efforts to apprehend the actual decision or choice process and, conversely, behavioral theories of choice have frequently taken as given some elementary notions about rational behavior.

Whether normative and positive theories of consumer behavior have been mutually affective or not, the position adopted here is straightforward. Insofar as the objective is to enhance the empirical testability of consumer theory, we must adopt the perspective of procedural rationality. We must explore and simulate the actual decision-making process of the individual consumer. Granting this, models of consumer behavior must take on a decidedly positive or behavioral character. At the risk of over- simplification, the position reduces to this: Before we can prescribe, we must first understand. Before we can understand why a consumer does what he does, we must know how he does it; we must possess a rudimentary understanding of the consumer's choice process.

The Problem of Rational Choice

The consumer's choice process involves two kinds of guesses. At one level, the consumer must make some assessment of the consequences of current actions and, at another level, he must assess his future preferences for those consequences.[4]

Even the most casual perusal of the literature reveals that the first guess has received wide attention. Broadly speaking, this literature emphasizes decision making under uncertainty. The relatively limited literature addressing the second guess -- that of assessing future preferences -- emphasizes choice under conflict or goal ambiguity.

That questions adhering to the second guess have not been widely explored is related to the propensity of economists to regard future preferences as exogenous and, or, stable, and as known with sufficient precision so as to render decisions unambiguous. While it is clear that this is a dubious position, our interest centers, for the moment, on the literature which addresses the first question; that of guesses about future consequences of current actions.

It is increasingly clear that orthodox demand formulations -- those considered in Chapters II through V -- are neither normative nor positive in many choice situations. Indeed, there is evidence that the maximization decision process is atypical [Simon 1966, pp. 4-8].[5] The net result has been that interdisciplinary studies have grown both in numbers and in importance [Suppes 1961], and attention has begun to focus on empirical investigations of consumer behavior in general, and on decision-making processes in particular. Indeed, it seems clear that [March 1978, p. 589]:

> As a result of these efforts, some of our ideas about how guesses about future consequences of current actions are made and how (they) ought to be made have changed. Since the early writings of Herbert A. Simon . . . bounded rationality has come to be recognized widely, though not universally, both as an accurate portrayal of much choice behavior and as a normatively sensible adjustment to the costs and character of information gathering and processing by human beings . . .[6]

Bounded Rationality

Bounded rationality contemplates a situation in which the technical constraints on choice include properties of human beings as processors of information and as problem solvers [Simon 1955, 1956, 1978b]. In effect, the technological constraints on choice include the consumer's cognitive attributes; in particular, the individual's computational ability, the nature and use of his memory, and so forth. The logic of the position is summarized by Professor Simon [Simon 1966, pp. 19-20]:

> Every human organism lives in an environment that generates millions of bits of new information every second, but the bottleneck of the perceptual apparatus certainly does not admit more than 1,000 bits per second, and probably much less . . . By the same token, there are hosts of inferences that might be drawn from the information stored in the brain that are not in fact drawn. The consequences implied by information in the memory become known only through active information processing, and hence through active selection of particular problem solving paths from the myriad that might have been followed.

The Treatment of Tastes

The problem of rational choice involves two judgments. The consumer must not only assess the consequences of current outcomes. He must, in addition, assess his future preferences for those consequences.

Our discussion to this point has emphasized the basic relevance of the concept of bounded rationality to the assessment of the consequences of current actions. Before proceeding, it would seem appropriate to comment on the second question; namely, how the consumer assesses his future preferences.

While some tentative efforts have been proffered [Basmann 1956], economists have not developed a theory of how preference structures change over time [Pollak 1978].[7] While this is perhaps attributable to the difficulty of the problem, there is an alternative explanation for the persistence of this theoretical lacuna. There is a tendency to rationalize the problem away; to assume that preference structures are intertemporally stable [Stigler and Becker 1977]. The presumption is that, given unchanging preferences, changes in the commodity composition of the consumer's consumption bundle are attributable to changes either in the consumer's full income, the prevailing vector of shadow prices, or both [see Chapter 5, esp. pp. 95-96]. In effect, the problem of explaining choice behavior is presumed to have nothing to do with explaining how the consumer assesses his future preferences. Rather, on the presumption that tastes are intertemporally stable, "explaining" behavior reduces to a definitional problem; a problem of finding operational counterparts for "full income" and the appropriate shadow price vector.

The difficulties here are obvious. At one level, a lack of correspondence between predicted and observed consumer behavior can always be ascribed to a failure to take account of the "right" level and composition of full income, or of the "right" shadow price vector, or both.[8] Reduced to its essentials, a theory that is based upon the presumption of stable preferences and that relies at the same time upon a non-market characterization of the consumer's income constraint cannot be empirically disconfirmed [Aaron 1994, p. 6]. It follows that such a theory cannot explain consumer behavior. Beyond this, it cannot be useful in a normative sense: "Prescriptions are useful only if we see a difference between observed procedures and desirable procedures" [March 1978, p. 597]. If we are ever to explain consumer behavior, we shall have to come to grips not only with the question of how consumers assess the present and the future consequences of their actions, but with how they assess their preferences for both present and future outcomes. What is required is an explicit characterization of the consumer's decision environment; a problem that is complicated by the fact that, given bounded rationality, there is no one-to-one correspondence between the consumer's objective and subjective decision environments [Morgan 1978; Chenault and Flueckiger 1983].

The C-D Gap

The lack of correspondence between the consumer's objective and subjective decision environments has been associated with a "competence-difficulty gap" [hereafter C-D gap].

Whereas standard choice theory assumes that there is no gap, Professor Ronald Heiner argues that decision makers "systematically restrict the use and acquisition of information compared to that potentially available" [Heiner 1983, p. 564]. That consumers do so should come as no surprise. As we have seen, the work of Professor Simon and his followers has long suggested this. Limited human information processing and perceptual abilities assure us that this must be so.

A corollary of the C-D gap is uncertainty about how to use information in selecting potential actions. The structure of the uncertainty is determined, in turn, by "environmental" and "perceptual" variables [Heiner 1983, pp. 564-565]. Broadly speaking, the environmental variables determine the complexity of the decision problem; the perceptual variables characterize the decision maker's "competence in deciphering relationships between [his] behavior and the environment" [Heiner 1983, p. 564].[9]

Given the C-D gap, Heiner argues that "observed regularities of behavior can be fruitfully understood as 'behavioral rules' that arise because of uncertainty in distinguishing preferred from less-preferred behavior" [Heiner 1983, p. 561]. This is the essence of Heiner's "reliability theory" which, in his view, "represents a general framework for analyzing behavior under all [different structures of uncertainty]" [Heiner 1983, p. 571]. In effect, "reliability theory" subsumes "standard economics" which [Heiner 1983, pp. 585-586]:

> . . . analyzes the special case of no uncertainty in selecting most preferred options. [Standard economics] forces the determinants of uncertainty into the residual 'error term' between observed behavior and the more systematic patterns claimed to result from optimization. I am thus suggesting a reversal of the explanation assumed in standard economics: the factors that standard theory places in the error term are, in fact, what is producing behavioral regularities, while optimizing will tend to produce sophisticated deviations from these patterns. Hence, the observed regularities that economics has tried to explain on the basis of optimization would disappear if agents could actually optimize.

While it is clear that "reliability theory" challenges the constrained optimization construct of standard choice theory this seems to me to be less important than the fact that "reliability theory" stands the received theory on its head.[10] Granting the logic of "reliability theory" if there were no uncertainty we should not be able to predict the behavior of consumers or other economic agents. In Professor Heiner's words [Heiner 1983, p. 569]:

> Predictable behavior is not an 'as if' simulation to optimizing, but rather will evolve only to the extent that agents are unable to maximize BECAUSE OF uncertainty. (emphasis mine)[11]

Reliability Theory and Experimental Economics

Professor Heiner's challenge to the classical rationality postulate extends to what has come to be called "experimental economics."[12] Heiner emphasizes that laboratory experiments in economics "depend on inducing agents to respond according to a prespecified value structure"

[Heiner 1985a, p. 260]. This, of course, is "the foundation from which our formal models are built" [Heiner 1985a, p. 261]. Yet Heiner wonders whether "agents in non-experimental markets behave according to well-defined, complete preference orderings" [Heiner 1985a, p. 260]. He therefore suggests that "a broadening of experimental design to allow for value uncertainty is necessary" [Heiner 1985a, p. 263].[13]

Whatever its implications for experimental economics, this much is clear: "Reliability theory" and the bounded rationality postulate have much in common. Both are less concerned with what decisions are made than with how they are made. Both would have us focus on the cognitive process and the inability of the decision-maker fully to process new information. Whether the basic postulate of "reliability theory" -- that predictable behavior is the result of behavioral rules adopted because of uncertainty -- is realistic or not, proponents of bounded rationality would certainly agree that [Wilde, LeBaron and Israelsen 1985, p. 407]:

> . . . the generation of knowledge is also the generation of ignorance. The capacity of our brains to process the information available to them is challenged by the very productivity of the brain itself . . .
>
> The difficulty of making intelligent decisions, whether personally or in an organization, has changed from ability to get information to one of processing a super abundance.[14]

THE REALISM OF ASSUMPTIONS, ONCE AGAIN

The Consumer's Objective Decision Environment and His Pereception of It

Both "reliability theory" and the concept of bounded rationality rest upon the notion that the consumer's subjective perception of his decision environment and its objective warp and woof are quite different things. This follows from the fact that the consumer's choice process is encumbered by the intervention of perception and cognition. This leads Professor Simon to suggest that "The (consumer's) information about his environment is much less than an approximation to the real environment" [Simon 1966, p. 19].[15] This has basic relevance to the question of how we might optimally structure our models of consumer choice. If our objective is to explain consumer behavior, there is no escape. Both the generative and the auxiliary assumptions upon which these models are constructed must be realistic.[16] In Professor March's words [March 1978, p. 588]:

> The engineering of choice depends on a relatively close articulation between choice as it is comprehended in the assumptions of the model and choice as it is made comprehensible to individual actors.

Models of consumer behavior must take explicit account of the fact that there is no one-to-one correspondence between the consumer's subjective and objective decision environments; that processes of perception and cognition are central to the question of how the consumer decides what bundle of comestibles is, at any cross-section of time, the "one to choose."[17] It follows that the assumptions through which we characterize the consumer's subjective decision environment -- the environment that is the only one immediately relevant to the ultimate choice of comestibles -- must be realistic. In effect, our various models' generative assumptions must be "realistic"; they must, so far as it is possible, accurately characterize the consumer's subjective decision environment.[18] Granting this, models of consumer behavior must take account of procedural rationality in general, and of bounded rationality in particular.[19]

The Human Problem Solver and the Science of Cognitive Simulation

It is possible to incorporate the concepts of procedural and bounded rationality in the theory of choice. Indeed, the machinery by which this result can be achieved already exists. I have in mind the Newell-Shaw-Simon conception of the Human Problem Solver (hereafter HPS) [Newell, Shaw and Simon 1958].[20]

The HPS is incorporated in a theory of human problem solving whose objective is to explain and predict the performance of a human problem solver handling specified, decision oriented tasks. The objective of the theory is to explain the process of human problem solving by identifying the types of decision processes actually employed. The essentials of these processes are captured by the theory's three generative assumptions; statements which assert that there exists for each HPS [Newell, Shaw and Simon 1958, p. 151]:

(1) A control system consisting of a number of memories which contain symbolized information and are interconnected by various ordering relations . .

(2) A number of primitive information processes, which operate on the information in the memories . . .

(3) A perfectly definite set of rules combining these processes into whole programs of processing . . .

Short and Long-Term Memory

While these postulates require clarification, a number of preliminary considerations call for immediate attention. First, the theory of human problem solving is part of the corpus of the positive science of procedural rationality. It is a theory belonging to the class of models employing the methods of cognitive simulation.[21] Second, explicit account is taken of the HPS's cognitive power at a number of different levels. Among these are the limits imposed by the varying capacities of decision makers' short and long-term memories. Information that is being processed by the HPS's central nervous system is stored in short-term memory (hereafter, STM). While the capacity of STM varies from individual to individual, research has shown that human performance on cognitive tasks is "dramatically sensitive to the limits of STM" [March 1978, p. 502].

Suppose, for example, that we confront an individual with a binary choice experiment on the presumption that the subject is a utility maximizer. Suppose that the experimenter rewards "plus" on one-third of the trials, and "minus" on the remaining two- thirds, and that the sequence is randomly determined. Now, provided that he perceived the sequence as random, the subject should always, rationally, choose minus.

Typically, the limits of the subject's STM impinge on his ability to perceive the pattern. Indeed, the most commonly observed behavior is event matching; a strategy whereby the subject chooses the two alternatives with relative frequencies roughly proportional to the relative frequency with which they are rewarded [Simon 1966, p. 8]. This behavior is largely attributable to attention to events in the recent past to the virtual exclusion of earlier events. Professor March has summarized the situation in this way [March 1978, p. 502]:

> . . . when a generalization is to be derived from a sequence of instances only a few of the most recent instances . . . can be held in (STM), with the result

that hypotheses are often entertained that contradict evidence that was available only a few minutes earlier.

While STM may be broadly characterized as having a small capacity, the HPS's information processing system is capable of storing large amounts of information in long-term memory (hereafter LTM). The information bits stored in LTM can, in time, be retrieved upon recognition of familiar patterns of stimuli. It is in this sense that we can perceive of the HPS as an "adaptive organism" [Simon 1966, p. 3]; as an organism whose decision-making is affected by accumulated experience and learning.[22] And it is precisely the accumulation of experience and of learning that [March 1978, p. 503]:

> may allow people to behave in ways that are very nearly optimal in situations to which their experience is pertinent, but be of little help when genuinely novel situations are presented.

Granting this, any theory which seeks to explain choice behavior must take explicit account of the limits imposed by the decision-maker's cognitive processes in general, and of learning and adaptation in particular. A theory which represents a tentative move is this direction is the theory of the trust investor.

The Trust Investor as a Human Problem Solver

The three basic postulates of the theory of the HPS may be clarified by appeal to a model whose purpose is to explain and predict the portfolio selection process of an individual trust investor [Clarkson 1962]. The basic postulates assert that for the trust investor there exist [Clarkson 1962, p. 27]:

> (1) A memory which contains lists of industries each of which has a list of companies associated to it. The memory also contains information associated with the general economy, industries and individual companies. [Investors categorize companies by industry. Not all investors may associate identical companies with a given industry, but the process of classification by industry remains invariant as the primary basis for listing companies in the memory. The information associated with each company also varies among investors, but each may be represented as having a list of attributes with their values stored in memory, e.g., growth rate, dividend rate, price earnings ratio, expected earnings, expected yield, etc.]

(2) Search and selection procedures which perform the task of searching the lists of information stored in memory, selecting those items that have the required attributes, regrouping the selected pieces of information into new lists, and performing algebraic operations when necessary. These procedures function in a manner similar to that of the traditional clerk who prepares lists of stocks suitable for current investment by scanning a master list.

(3) A set of rules or criteria which guide the decision-making process by stipulating when and how each process is to be used. The set of rules constitutes the structure of the decision process for an individual investor. It might be compared to the heuristics of the rational 'expert,' but . . . the set of rules must be defined unambiguously.

The point to be emphasized is that the theory of human problem solving presumes that decision processes can be both identified and isolated, and that they are representable, in the manner of cognitive simulation, by a series of "mechanical" processes. Assuming that these processes can be recorded in a set of statements that simulate the decision-making behavior of the HPS, this set of rules becomes the theory of the decision-making process. In this instance, the set of statements [(1), (2), and (3), above] constitute the generative assumptions of a theory of trust investment behavior. Of course, the theory of trust investment behavior, like any theory, also employs auxiliary assumptions. As always, these auxiliary assumptions must be realistic, whether the purpose of the model is prediction or explanation. It is, however, the realism of a model's generative assumptions that is a sine qua non for explanatory power, and it is for this reason that our interest centers now on the testability of the generative assumptions of the model of trust investment behavior.

On the Testability of the Generative Assumptions of the
    Theory of Trust Investment Behavior

The theory of trust investment behavior purports to explain the decision-making behavior of a particular HPS. If it is to have this capability, the generative (and the auxiliary) assumptions employed must satisfy two conditions: 1) they must not be known to be false a priori, and 2) they must be independently testable [See Chapter 1, pp. 18-20]. This requires that the generative assumptions of the model be empirically disconfirmable. As it happens, both the theory's assumptions and its predictions have been subjected to empirical test.

The test proceeded as follows. The data of the securities markets and of some specified trust accounts (all defined at a particular cross-section of time) were fed into the model. The model was then required to generate investment portfolios for the specified trust accounts. The portfolios so generated constituted the model's "predictions"; predictions that were then compared to the actual portfolios selected by the trust investor. However, because the testability and empirical confirmation of the model's generative assumptions constitute a prerequisite to explaining the trust investor's behavior, the behavior generated by the model's decision mechanisms (its generative assumptions) was compared with the observed behavior of the trust investor [Clarkson 1962, Chapters 5 and 6]. Comparisons were made on four separate occasions over a nine-month period, with the result that the model appeared to be employing many of the same decision procedures, and was selecting virtually the same portfolios, as was the trust investor.

While it is important that the model's predictions appear to have been confirmed, it is even more significant that the model's generative assumptions were empirically testable. To put the matter differently, what is at issue here is not the predictive capability of the model. Whether the generative assumptions of the model were empirically confirmed or not is not even at issue. What is important is that the generative assumptions of the model were both in principle and in fact subject to empirical disconfirmation. This suggests that a theory embodying the concepts of procedural and bounded rationality, a model of cognitive simulation is, at least in principle, capable of explaining the behavior of a particular HPS. That the HPS happens to be a trust investor is of little consequence [Clarkson 1962, p. 116]:

> . . . the theory of human problem solving contains three main postulates which assert the existence in a human decision-maker of a memory, some primitive information processes and a hierarchy of decision rules. The theory of trust investment turns these postulates into testable hypotheses by specifying in detail the content of the trust officer's memory and information processes, as well as the content and order of his decision rules . . .

> It should be noted . . . that the hypotheses of several theories of decision-making behavior are directly derived from the basic postulates of the theory of human problem solving. Consequently, it appears that the empirical truth value of postulates can be determined by a series of tests in a variety of empirical contexts.

THE THEORY OF CONSUMER BEHAVIOR, ONCE AGAIN

The basic relevance of the testability of the postulates of the theory of human problem solving "in a variety of empirical contexts" is immediately clear. Insofar as we seek to explain consumer behavior, and insofar as orthodox demand formulations are based upon non-testable generative (and auxiliary) assumptions, it is neither inappropriate nor rash to consider basing our models of consumer behavior upon the empirically testable postulates of the theory of human problem solving.

This suggestion is not new. Indeed, it was first broached in 1963 by Professor Clarkson [Clarkson 1963, esp. Chapters 7 and 8]. Though Clarkson's position is that the theory of consumer behavior might optimally be "reduced" to the theory of human problem solving, my recommendation is at once more circumspect and more eclectic.[23] The position adopted here is that the HPS formulation is a useful heuristic. It is suggestive of the direction in which the theory of consumer behavior must move. Just as there is much to be said for grounding production theory more firmly in the engineering sciences [Roth 1972, 1973, 1977], the empirical foundations of demand theory lie in what might broadly be characterized as the "engineering of choice." Insofar as the HPS approach takes explicit account of the limitations imposed by perception, memory, experience, and learning, it is a catalyst to thought; a convenient and mnemonic representation of reality. On this logic the HPS formulation can, <u>mutatis mutandis,</u> be used to simulate the decision processes that characterize the engineering of choice. It will enable us to come to grips with the sort of decision environment contemplated by Professor Shubik [Shubik 1970, p. 410]:

> Most of my friends (and I suspect most of Herb Simon's friends and Dick Cyert's friends) are rather poor models of utilitarian man . . . for the most part my friends are not technical experts on hi-fi sets or automobiles. To a great extent they are not always even sure of what they want; they are not particularly expert on judging quality; their decisions are made under uncertainty, and they regard the amount of time they spend making their decisions as often being a considerable cost to themselves.

Given such an enormously complex decision environment, it seems clear that the HPS formulation cannot be so accommodative as to yield "the" theory of consumer behavior. Rather, we shall have to reconcile ourselves to the development of a kind of patchwork quilt of theories, each of which may take as its point of departure the three basic postulates of the HPS construction. But, in each instance, before we are able to specify the precise content of the postulates -- for example, the character and content of the consumer's memories -- we must first determine the principal empirical statements that we seek to deduce from the theory. We shall have to define the class of implications to which a particular model will ideally give rise. Unless this is accomplished we shall not be able to specify the interpretive rules which will enable us unambiguously to determine whether a model has been empirically confirmed.

Suppose, for example, that a model has broadly to do with the consumer's income allocative procedure; with the question of how the consumer decides to allocate his current income among commodity categories.[24]   Given this problem, one of the information processes subsumed by the second postulate (p. 119, above) might involve the presumption that the proportion of his income that the consumer allocates to each consumption category -- housing, for example -- will reflect the proportions allocated by other consumers in the same "socioeconomic class". It might be assumed, in addition, that the proportion so allocated would not change over time so long as the consumer's real income does not vary "appreciably". On this logic, empirical confirmation (disconfirmation) of these generative assumptions would be predicated on an a priori specification of appropriate interpretive rules. Among these might be the explicit introduction of an adaptive mechanism; a mechanism that, for example, specifies how the category allocation would change if real income were to change.

The list of relevant decision processes can, of course, be expanded. Among other things, decision procedures that determine intra-category spending patterns would have to be specified, and appropriate interpretive rules promulgated.[25]

An explicit characterization of the consumer's decision processes, of the character and content of bounded rationality cannot, however, center exclusively upon the "engineering of choice." We must recognize also that the consumer's desideratum is not a matter of a priori logic; it is a matter of empirical investigation. There is some evidence, for example, that the HPS in general, and the consumer in particular, is a satisficer rather than a maximizer; that his decision-making is based on search activity designed to meet certain aspiration levels.[26]   Granting this, we may be well-advised to be somewhat more circumspect in imputing maximizing behavior to the individual consumer. In any case, it is sufficient to note that decision processes consonant with satisficing behavior can be modeled [Borch 1969; Roth 1975; Simon 1978b].

On balance, it appears we must be willing to substitute tedious, interdisciplinary study for the elegance, simplicity, and "generality" of the highly stylized models of received consumer theory. We must, I would argue, adopt the perspective of Professor Shubik:

> My objection to all of the [conventional] material is not that it does not represent a contribution to economic knowledge, but that it is presented to students of microeconomics as though it were THE RELEVANT way to study consumer behavior, rather than one partially explored path in almost virgin territory [Shubik 1970, p. 401].

We must abandon our proclivity to employ patently unrealistic assumptions in the construction of models of consumer behavior [Simon 1986]. Whether our emphasis be upon prediction, explanation, or both, we must recognize the basic relevance of realism of assumptions to the empirical interpretation of theories. And if this means we must be willing to absorb the costs implicit in exploring the interfaces among economics, psychology, the other social and, indeed, the physical sciences, then so be it.[27] If one accepts the notion that the development of science is a taxonomic process, and that consumer theory ought to be a part of the corpus of empirical science, there can be no turning back.[28]

A perusal of the literature suggests that this thinking is beginning to take hold. Indeed, it has been observed that [Conlisk 1996, p. 669]:

> Although the postulate of unbounded rationality has dominated economic modeling for several decades, the dominance is relaxing. Is this encouraging? Why bounded rationality?

Professor Conlisk provides an answer to his own rhetorical question -- an answer to which I fully subscribe [Conlisk 1996, p. 669]:

> ... four reasons are given for incorporating bounded rationality in economic models. First, there is abundant empirical evidence that it is important. Second, models of bounded rationality have proved themselves in a wide range of impressive work. Third, the standard justifications for assuming unbounded rationality are unconvincing; their logic cuts both ways. Fourth, deliberation about an economic decision is a costly activity, and good economics requires that we entertain all costs.

Granting this, my attention turns to a body of theory whose portmanteau includes bounded rationality and all that that implies, including information asymmetry, opportunism and, <u>pari passu</u>, positive transaction costs. We turn next to a consideration of what has come to be called the New Institutional Economics.

NOTES

[1]A comparatively recent development is the application of the utility tree approach to the theoretical and empirical analysis of money demand. See [Barnett, Fisher and Serletis 1992] and Chapter IX, below.

[2]The multi-equation utility function may be employed to incorporate the notion of distinct utility domains. See, for example [Aaron 1994, esp. pp. 14-16]. See also [Hausman and McPherson 1993, esp. p. 688] and Chapter VIII, below.

[3]The theory of cognitive dissonance represents one attempt to come to grips with the lack of correspondence between the objective decision environment and the decision-maker's perception of it. See for example [Gilad, Kaish and Loeb 1987]. For present purposes, the theory of cognitive dissonance can be understood to involve the following propositions: (1) Persons not only have preferences over states of the world, but also over their BELIEFS about the state of the world. (2) Persons have some control over their beliefs, and (3) beliefs, once formed, "persist over time" [Akerloff and Dickens 1982, p.307]. For an application of cognitive dissonance theory to development policy issues see [James and Gutkind 1985].

[4]Of course, in the view of Professors Stigler and Becker, the second "guess" is not a guess at all. On their view, the individual's preference structure is intertemporally stable; it is only the vector of relevant shadow prices and the consumer's "full" income that change [Stigler and Becker 1977]. See also Chapter V, above. If one adopts the Stigler-Becker view, the choice process involves only the first kind of guess. In any case, I shall momentarily have more to say about the Stigler-Becker hypothesis.

[5]There is, moreover, a logical difficulty with the orthodox maximization formulation: All decisions involve the absorption of "optimization costs"; of decision-method, data and selection costs. Granting this, a "circularity problem" arises [Pingle 1992, p. 10]:

... [The] difficulty with strict optimization theory has become known as the 'circularity problem' -- there does not exist an optimization problem which can be solved that fully incorporates the cost of decision making.

See also [Furubotn 1997, pp. 15-17] and Chapter VII, below.

[6]In general, Professor March regards preferences as neither absolute, stable, consistent, precise nor exogenous. He urges that economists (and others) adopt a conception of preferences which respects what he characterizes as the "intelligence of ambiguity." See, for example [March 1982].

[7]If economists have not developed a theory of preference formation, they increasingly recognize the endogeneity of preference structures. See, for example [Buchanan 1994b, p. 76; Furubotn and Richter 1994, p. 12; Williamson 1993, p. 104 and Stiglitz 1993, pp. 111-112].

[8]See page 98, above. See also [Ben-Porath 1982; Hannan 1982]. The problem extends to the transaction cost approach to the analysis of family decision-making. In Professor Pollak's view, "the transaction cost approach generalizes the new home economics by recognizing that internal structure and organization matter" [Pollak 1985, p. 584]. The "new home economics" is, of course, a euphemism for Becker's Household Production Function approach. Pollak concludes, however, that "A principal defect of the transaction cost approach is its failure to provide a structure for rigorous econometric investigation" [Pollak 1985, p. 606].

[9]Heiner suggests that, in economics, the environmental variables subsume such things as "the complexity and volatility of both present and future exchange, legal and political conditions." The perceptual variables "describe mistaken perceptions about what is more preferred, information processing errors, unreliable probability information, etc." [Heiner 1983, p. 564, fn. 16].

This view is broadly consistent with the position adopted by Professor Michael Miller. In his view [Miller 1983, p. 45]:

> The world is characterized by too many interconnecting economic and noneconomic variables and commodities for the flawless preference ordering of economic rationality to be generally true. These conditions and uncertainties . . . overwhelm the actor's limited computational ability.

See also [March 1978, p. 598] and [Furubotn 1997].

[10]Heiner evidently believes that "reliability theory" represents a challenge to the received approach generally and to the classical rationality postulate in particular. Apparently believing that the classical rationality postulate implies optimizing behavior, he argues that [Heiner 1983, p. 562]:

> . . . allegiance to [conventional models] is not grounded in the claim of empirical fruitfulness, despite the usual rhetoric that this is the case. Rather, it is based on a deeper methodological issue about the effect of dropping the basic rationality assumption.

A rough paraphrase of Professor Heiner's position would, therefore, be that: a) the classical rationality postulate implies optimizing behavior; b) because of uncertainty economic agents cannot optimize; therefore, c) the classical rationality assumption should be dropped. See also [Wilde, LeBaron and Israelsen 1985, esp. p. 404 and Heiner 1985b]. See [Plott 1986; Tversky and Kahneman 1986; Etzioni 1987] for opposing views. See also [Bös 1986; Leibenstein 1986; Bös 1987].

[11]For an application of Professor Heiner's C-D gap analysis, see [Kaen and Rosenman 1986]. Professors Kaen and Rosenman conclude that:

> The postulated C-D gap not only explains the presence of nonperiodic regularities in price changes [in financial markets], but also elucidates the

always recognized possibility for superior fundamental analysts to consistently outperform the market. These analysts simply have a relatively smaller C-D gap! [Kaen and Rosenman 1986, p.219].

For comments on Professor Heiner's approach see [Bookstaber and Langsam 1985; Garrison 1985]. See also [Heiner 1985c]. For additional applications of Professor Heiner's analysis, see [Buchanan 1994a, p. 127] and [North 1994, p. 363].

[12]For more on experimental economics, see the section entitled Tests of the Postulates, Chapter 2, p. 34 and [Roth 1986; Binmore 1987; Butler and Hey 1987]. For some applications of the experimental approach see [Harrison and McKee 1985; Battalio, Kagel and MacDonald 1985; Miller and Plott 1985; Thistle 1985; Dejong, Forsythe and Lundholm 1985; Battalio, Kagel and Phillips 1986; Coursey and Schulze 1986; Berg et al. 1986; Guttman 1986; Brookshire, Coursey and Schulze 1987; Benson and Feinberg 1988; Kroll, Levy and Rapaport 1988; Banks, Plott and Porter 1988; Grether, Schwartz and Wilde 1988; Kotlikoff, Samuelson and Johnson 1988].

[13]See also [Friedman 1985, p. 264]. Professor Vernon Smith, one of the chief practitioners of experimental economics, agrees with Heiner's assessment. Smith suggests that [Smith 1985, p. 266]:

> . . . both the animal and especially the human preference studies of Kagel et al exhibit 'dynamic' effects or lagged responses that are not even supposed to exist in received preference theory, and which may reflect the 'insecure preference beliefs' suggested by Heiner.

In general, Smith has "no disagreement with Heiner's critique of classical preference theory . . ." [Smith 1985, p. 271] and warns us that [Smith 1985, pp. 265-266]:

> When testing formal market theories [experimentally], we should always be aware that WE ARE STUDYING BEHAVIOR WITHIN THE CONTEXT OF OUR REPRESENTATIONS OF THE ECONOMIC ENVIRONMENT. If any of these representations is wrong, then our studies have only increased our self-knowledge, not our knowledge of things (natural economic processes) . . .

> If we are to increase our knowledge of things, then our ultimate aim should aspire to more than discovering that the behavioral properties of our own creations are consistent with controlled experimental evidence . . . (emphasis mine)

See also [Smith 1982, pp. 931 and 952].

[14]Professors Slovic and Lichtenstein have suggested that limited cognitive capacity may account for the phenomenon of "preference reversals." In their view, preferences are "neither absolute, stable, consistent, precise or exogenous (unaffected by the choices they control)" [Slovic and Lichtenstein 1983, p. 599]. Preference reversal occurs when individuals choose a bet carrying a high probability of winning a modest sum [the "P bet"] rather than another bet carrying a low probability of winning a large amount of money [the "$ bet"]: "The typical finding is that people choose the P bet, but assign a larger monetary value to the $ bet. This behavior is of interest because it violates all theories of preference, including expected utility theory" [Slovic and Lichtenstein 1983, p. 596]. See also [Holt 1986].

     Whether the preference reversal phenomenon can be accounted for by the C-D gap remains to be seen. What is clear is that [Slovic and Lichtenstein 1983, p. 603]:

> . . . anything less than a radical modification of traditional theories is unlikely to accommodate these phenomena . . . economists [are urged] not to resist these developments but, instead, [should] examine them for insights into the WAYS THAT DECISIONS ARE MADE and the ways that the practice of decision making can be improved. (emphasis mine)

"Experimental" economists are aware of the issues raised by preference reversal. Professor Vernon Smith has, for example, noted that [Smith 1985, p. 268]:

> The wide variety of different experimental studies of decision making under uncertainty yielding results inconsistent with [the expected utility hypothesis], are subject to different interpretations in terms of the damage they inflict on EUH. I think a key element in these interpretations is what Jacob Marschak . . . long ago called the cost of thinking, calculating, deciding, and acting, which are all part of what I have called the subjective cost of transacting . . .

See also [Knez, Smith and Williams 1985, esp. p. 401; Segal 1988; Karni and Safra 1987].
     [15]With the Lancastrian and HHPF models as their points of departure, Ruth Mack and T. James Leigland argue that "real man perceives the world selectively" [Mack and Leigland 1982, p. 104]. In their view, "net cognitive evaluation -- conscious or covert" -- includes household production activity, evaluative activity [which involves judging "the mix of valued qualities (arguments of the qualitatively differentiated utility vector) which the characteristics of the commodities are expected (uncertainly and sometimes ambiguously) to yield"] and "an additional process which converts information to feeling" [Mack and

Leigland 1982, p. 105]. The evaluative process is complicated by the fact that "In the case of evaluative activity -- the expectation and definition of utility -- there is no objective referent for the household" [Mack and Leigland 1982, p. 106].

[16]See Chapter 1, esp. pp. 18-20.

[17]The need to understand the cognitive process extends to the question of how individuals decide whether or not to undertake protective action. The purchase of flood and earthquake insurance is an example [Kunreuther and Slovic 1978]. The approach also has basic relevance to the question of expectations formation [Haltiwanger and Waldman 1985]. In general, while it seems appropriate to conclude that "research on individual decision making is highly relevant to economics whenever predicting ... behavior is the goal" [Russell and Thaler 1985, pp. 1080-81] some authors disagree. See for example [Miller 1986].

[18]The same is true of the models' auxiliary assumptions. But this is true of any model, whether its purpose is explanation or prediction. See Chapter 1, esp. pp. 15-16. In any case, our interest centers here upon the generative assumptions, the realism of which is a sine qua non for explanatory power. See Chapter 1, esp. pp. 16-18.

[19]The presumption must be that this suggestion will be greeted with some resistance. As Professor Williamson has emphasized, bounded rationality is one of the cognitive assumptions on which the transactions cost literature relies [Williamson 1981, p. 1545]. Elsewhere Williamson observes that [Williamson 1985, p. 45]:

Economists object to [bounded rationality] because limits on rationality are mistakenly interpreted in nonrationality or irrationality terms .... Other social scientists demur because reference to intended rationality makes too great a concession to the economists' maximizing mode of inquiry.

There is evidence, however, that resistance is beginning to erode. See, for example [Conlisk 1996].

[20]See also [Simon 1966, pp. 24-25; March 1978, pp. 590-591].

[21]See pages 109-110, above.

[22]There is evidence, for example, that the expert chess player does not "search out" the correct move; he "recognizes it". More precisely, a skilled chess player holds in LTM as many as 50,000 different patterns of pieces. He has the capacity, moreover, to recognize when they are present in a chess position, and he is able to retrieve from LTM the array of possible moves that are relevant, given those patterns [Chase and Simon 1973]. For more on the impact on consumer choice of product learning and of memory see [Meyer and Sathi 1985; Hoch and Ha 1986; Biehal and Chakravarti 1986].

[23]"Theory reduction" within a branch of science -- be it physics or economics -- occurs when a theory (call it T_2) is replaced by a new theory (T_1) that explains all the phenomena covered by T_2, as well as a further set not covered by it [Clarkson 1963, p. 105]. For theory reduction in this sense to occur, two

conditions must be met [Clarkson 1963, pp. 107-108]:

> . . . a necessary condition for the reduction of T_2 to T_1 is that suitable relations be constructed so that the terms and expressions contained in T_2 are derivable from the basic postulates and concepts of T_1. Another condition . . . is that the basic postulates or principal hypotheses of T_1 must be empirically testable as well as being reasonably well confirmed by the available evidence.

[24]I have in mind, for example, the sort of problem contemplated by Strotz, Kraft and Kraft and others. See Chapter 4, esp. p. 75.

[25]There is evidence that this problem may not be so complex as it may at first appear. In particular, there is evidence of a certain homogeneity in the decision processes employed in quite different contexts [Newell, Shaw and Simon 1960; Newell and Simon 1961]. Granting this, the similarity among decision processes may facilitate simulation.

[26]See, for example [Kapteyn et al 1979; Crain et al 1984; Simon 1957, 1966; Edwards 1954; Davidson and Suppes 1957; Bush and Mostelle 1955; Papandreou et al 1957; Luce 1957; Rose 1957]. See also [Furubotn 1997].

[27]A number of authors have set out to do precisely this. See, for example [Alhadeff 1982; Baum 1985; Blair and Burton 1987]. What is in any case clear is that a literature is beginning to develop around the notion that the interfaces among economics and other disciplines are, and should be, explored. See, for example [Frank 1992], [Baron and Hannan 1994], [Lewin 1996] and [Hausman and McPherson 1993].

[28]Interestingly, one of the chief proponents of the view, roughly paraphrased, that the limits of the applicability of the classical rationality postulate to an ever-wider class of phenomena are imposed only by the model builder's ingenuity, appears to be rethinking his position. In his Nobel lecture Professor Becker observed that [Becker 1993, p. 386]:

> Actions are constrained by income, time, imperfect memory and calculating capacities, and other limited resources.

He concludes that "My work may have sometimes assumed too much rationality" [Becker 1993, p. 402].

Chapter 7

Bounded Rationality and the New Institutional Economics

Non-zero transaction costs and bounded rationality constitute fundamental features of reality that must be accounted for in economic theory

E.G. Furubotn

INTRODUCTION

Granting the logic of what has been said, the development of economics as an empirical science hinges importantly on the employment of realistic auxiliary and generative assumptions. This presumes, of course, that the essence of an empirical science is the generation of confirmable (disconfirmable) hypotheses. The implication for consumer theory is that emphasis must be placed upon how decisions are made rather than which decisions are made. In short, the behavioral assumptions which underlie our models of consumer behavior must take explicit account of the cognitive processes actually employed. Particular attention must center on the agent's cognitive attributes. This is a logical corollary of the fact that "every human organism lives in an environment that generates millions of bits of new information every second" [Simon

1966, p. 19]. Yet we know that the consumer's perceptual apparatus cannot process all of the available information. Moreover, we know that "the consequences implied by information in the memory become known only through active information processing" [Simon 1966, p. 20]. Given the volume of extant and incremental, newly available information it should come as no surprise that, in most cases of practical importance, there is no one-to-one correspondence between the consumer's objective and subjective decision environments; that consumers -- and decision makers generally -- "systematically restrict the use and acquisition of information compared to that potentially available" [Heiner 1983, p. 564]. This logic leads inexorably to the conclusion that economic agents are "intendedly rational, but only limitedly so" [Williamson 1985, p. 45]. It follows that the cognitive assumption which most appropriately underlies consumer theory is bounded rationality.

Not surprisingly, many economists have resisted this idea. As Professor Williamson has emphasized, "Economists object to it because limits on rationality are mistakenly interpreted in nonrationality or irrationality terms" [Williamson 1985, p.45].

THE NEW INSTITUTIONAL ECONOMICS AND THE CONSUMER'S DECISION ENVIRONMENT

This resistance notwithstanding, there is a rapidly developing literature which makes explicit use of bounded rationality [Williamson 1981, p. 1545].[1] The point of departure of the New Institutional Economics [hereafter NIE] is that the decision maker's choice set is both broader and narrower than traditionally envisioned.[2] The set is narrower because [North 1986, p. 230]:

> ... institutions define a limited set of alternatives available at any moment in a society. This limited set of alternatives is shaped by the structure of political decision rules and property rights, as well as by the norms of behavior that limit the alternatives available to people.[3]

On the other hand, the choice set is broader "... because it includes the multiple dimensions that characterize goods and services and the performance of agents...." [North 1986, p. 230].

The "multiple dimensions" to which the literature refers contemplate both the vector of technologically determined characteristics subsumed by the Lancastrian or New Approach [Chapter III] and the bundle of property rights which are attached to each good or service [and are therefore transferred in any exchange]:

> At any moment of time, there is a legally sanctioned structure of property rights in existence, and each individual in the system possesses definite property rights over certain economic goods and services. In other words, each individual has an initial endowment composed of quantities of 'effective commodities' (specific commodities plus associated property rights) [Furubotn and Pejovich 1974, p.5].[4]

"Property rights", in turn, are understood to be "sanctioned behavioral relations among men that arise from the existence of things and pertain to their use" [Furubotn and Pejovich 1972, p. 1139]. Of particular interest is the right of ownership, a subcategory of the general concept of property rights. The right of ownership is comprised of three elements: (a) the right to use an asset, (b) the right to appropriate returns from the asset, and (c) the right to change the asset's form and/or substance [Furubotn and Pejovich 1974, p. 4]. The essential point is that different property rights assignments imply different penalty-reward structures and, pari passu, "decide the choices that are open to decision makers" [Furubotn and Pejovich 1972, p. 1138]. The choice set confronting decision makers is therefore partially dependent upon the prevailing property rights structure, the structure of political decision rules, and the norms of behavior that delimit the alternatives actually available.[5] It follows that the opportunity set is manifestly more complicated than the one envisioned by traditional theory. The same is true of the economic agent's objective function: "effective commodities" rather than consumption rates of unidimensional goods and services enter as arguments of the utility function [Furubotn and Pejovich 1972, p. 1139]. The NIE therefore "encompasses a concept of utility functions broader than the traditional neoclassical utility function" [North 1986, p. 230].

PRODUCTION, EXCHANGE AND THE ROLE OF BOUNDED RATIONALITY

The essence of an economic system is production and exchange. Both activities involve transactions and the contracts which specify the terms of exchange. It is for this reason that the NIE "is at base a study of contracting" [North 1986, p. 231]. Explicit account is taken of the fact that, in a world of "effective commodities" exchange is not costless. Positive transaction costs arise both because of the costliness of measuring the multiple attributes of goods and services [North 1986, p. 232] and because of the "opportunism" that characterizes market participants.[6] "Opportunism" is understood to be "self-interest seeking with guile" [Williamson 1981, p. 1545]. More precisely, opportunism "refers to the incomplete or distorted disclosure of information, especially to calculated efforts to mislead, distort, disguise, obfuscate, or otherwise confuse" [Williamson 1985, p. 47]. The juxtaposition of multi-dimensional "effective commodities" and opportunism implies: (a) that exchange is both costly and complex, and (b) that the costs of contract enforcement "become a critical factor in the degree to which transaction costs in society are lowered and hence exchange made possible" [North 1986, p. 232].[7]

All of this has basic relevance to the notion that consumers [and economic agents generally] are, at best, "intendedly rational, but only limitedly so"; that cognitive processes are characterized by bounded rationality. In a world of "effective commodities" and opportunism the "ranges of possible messages, offers, threats, etc. which can be given during the [exchange or contracting] process, including the timing of moves, are hard to delimit" [Johansen 1979, p. 511]. In short, in a world of attribute and/or performance ambiguities "[b]ounded rationality limits are quickly reached" [Williamson 1985, p. 59].[8]

THE NEW INSTITUTIONAL ECONOMICS AND NEOCLASSICAL THEORY

Initially, proponents of the NIE did not seek to displace received microeconomic theory. As Professor North has observed [North 1986, p. 230]:

Modern institutional economics begins with two premises: 1) that the theoretical framework should be capable of INTEGRATING neoclassical theory with an analysis of the way institutions modify the choice set available to human beings; and 2) that this framework must build upon the basic determinants of institutions, so that we can not only define the choice set really available to people at any time, but also analyze the way ... institutions change and therefore alter the available choice set over time. [emphasis mine].[9]

As originally envisioned, the intent of the NIE was to deepen our understanding of the processes of production and exchange and, pari passu, to broaden the reach of standard neoclassical theory [Furubotn and Pejovich 1974, p. 1]:

According to proponents of the new approach .... individuals respond to economic incentives, and the pattern of incentives present at any time is influenced by the prevailing property rights structure. On this logic, it is clear that careful specification of the institutional setting of an economic problem is essential . . . . it also follows that GENERALIZATION OF TRADITIONAL MICROECONOMIC THEORY IS BOTH FEASIBLE AND NECESSARY; by making appropriate adjustments for different property rights configurations, THE APPLICABILITY OF CLASSICAL MARGINALISM CAN BE EXTENDED GREATLY. [emphasis mine].[10]

The deus ex machina by which neoclassical theory was to be generalized is a careful, systematic explication of the character and content of economic agents' decision environments. Central to this is recognition of the implications for decision makers' objective functions and opportunity sets of the interplay of multi-dimensional effective commodities and opportunism [Furubotn and Pejovich 1972, pp. 1137-38]:

The `property rights' literature begins with the presumption that modifications must be made in the conventional analytical framework if economic models having WIDER APPLICABILITY are to be developed ... it is necessary to define the particular utility function that reflects the decision maker's preferences, and to determine the actual set of options ... that is attainable ... the usefulness of any such model depends on how skillfully the specification is made of the objective function and opportunity set. [emphasis mine].[11]

In recent years its proponents have become somewhat more circumspect about the reconcilability of neoclassical theory with the behavioral and other postulates which characterize the NIE. The views of Professor Furubotn are suggestive of the new thinking [Furubotn 1994, p. 8]:

... it is the position of the present paper that there must be a jump to a fundamentally different type of analysis.... in models where incomplete information and bounded rationality play key roles, the very process by which economic solutions are generated is quite different from that envisioned in the neoclassical case.

The genesis of the new thinking is the realization that the "hybrid models" to which the NIE appealed led, inter alia, to logical inconsistencies [Furubotn 1994, p. 10]:

In the so-called 'hybrid' models that are found so widely in the [NIE] literature, a consistent point of view is not maintained. Inter alia, decision makers are taken to have split economic personalities. They are perfectly informed about some matters yet completely ignorant about others. Or, alternatively, different economic actors in the same model show different motivations and capabilities.

Reduced to its essentials, internal inconsistencies arise when assumptions are drawn from "two disparate universes -- the neoinstitutionalist and the neoclassical" [Furubotn 1997, p. 4]. Fundamentally, an environment characterized by positive transaction costs and bounded rationality [and all that it implies] is irreconcilable with the behavioral, technical and other postulates which underlie received, neoclassical theory. The problem is that, characteristically, [Furubotn 1997, p. 9]:

... hybrid neoinstitutional models.... presuppose the simultaneous existence of: (I) bounded rationality,(ii) positive transaction costs, (iii) complete knowledge of essential data, and (iv) rational-choice decision making.

Consider, for example, that in a representative, hybrid NIE model the producer is presumed to absorb costs in learning about input prices and input quality, yet the same producer is implicitly assumed to produce subject to the technical restrictions imposed by a neoclassical flow-flow production function [Furubotn 1997, p. 11]. As is well known, the latter is presumed to be the only efficient -- in the sense of output maximizing -- technical alternative available to the firm. In effect, a logical corollary of a decision environment characterized by bounded rationality and positive transaction costs is denied: A boundedly rational actor cannot be assumed to possess exhaustive knowledge of the technical alternatives confronting him. Yet, to assume that a single equation flow-flow production function exhaustively represents the available technical options is, mutatis mutandis, to assert that the firm possesses exhaustive technical knowledge. In fact, of course, the boundedly rational firm must "discover" its technical options. Yet, "When discovery is necessary, the production function is attenuated and appears merely in partial form" [Furubotn 1997, p. 11].[12] Such a construct cannot meaningfully be represented by a single equation, flow-flow production function.

Granting the logic of what has been said, it seems clear that the NIE cannot rely on "hybrid" models. Account cannot be taken of some informational needs while other needs are ignored. Broadly speaking, the explicit recognition of bounded rationality has a logical corollary: Exhaustive knowledge of anything is beyond the decision maker's capability. This brute fact is irreconcilable with the behavioral, technical and other postulates of neoclassical theory. On this logic, explicit account must be taken of a panoply of costs which are not internalized in the stylized neoclassical decision environment. These costs -- styled "optimization" costs -- subsume decision-method, data, and selection costs [Furubotn 1997, p. 14]. The problem is that once such costs are internalized -- as they must be in a world characterized by bounded rationality -- a point of no return is reached: The basic postulates of the NIE cannot be reconciled with those employed in the received, neoclassical theory.

While much can be said about the NIE this much is clear: Proponents of the NIE seek to employ generative assumptions which take explicit account of the limits imposed by prevailing property rights and political structures, by behavioral norms and, pari passu, by multi-dimensional effective commodities. A corollary of this enormously complex decision environment is that the behavioral assumptions which underlie the analysis must recognize the limits imposed by decision makers' cognitive abilities. The presumption is, therefore, that decision makers are "intendedly rational, but only limitedly so"; that economic agents are subject to bounded rationality. What is equally clear is that bounded rationality implies neither nonrationality nor irrationality. Proponents of the NIE understand this. The evolution of economics as an empirical science hinges importantly on a broader acceptance of this powerful insight.

Finally, the new thinking embodied in the NIE has powerful implications for social welfare theory. Inter alia, once explicit account is taken of cognitive limitations, of information asymmetries and of opportunistic behavior, the logical foundations of the efficiency frontier and of the social welfare function are called into question. This is the subject matter of Chapter VIII.

NOTES

[1]Writing in 1991 Professors Furubotn and Richter elucidated the view that the New Institutional Economics "seeks to extend the range of applicability of neoclassical theory" [Furubotn and Richter 1991, p. 1]. The deus ex machina by which this was to be accomplished was the introduction of "several crucial changes... [in] the orthodox theory of production and exchange" [Furubotn and Richter 1991, p. 4]. Without explication the changes contemplated were [and are]: (1) methodological individualism; (2) utility maximization; (3) bounded rationality, and (4) opportunistic behavior. See also [Furubotn 1994, p. 23].

[2]For a critical review of the NIE see [Carter 1985].

[3]"Institutions" are "regularities in repetitive interactions among individuals .... Institutions are not persons, they are customs and rules that provide a set of incentives and disincentives for individuals" [North 1986, p. 231].

[4]See also [Furubotn and Richter 1991, pp. 5-8].

[5]To this list of exogenous and endogenous constraints might be added moral constraints which, for some individuals, further limit the choice set. See, for example [Buchanan 1994a, esp. p. 133]. I shall have more to say about this in Chapter VIII, below.

[6]For more on the concept of transaction costs see [Furubotn and Richter 1991, esp. pp. 8-11]. See also [Furubotn 1994, esp. p. 15]. An essential point is that a decision environment characterized by bounded rationality and increasing complexity is, pari passu, an environment characterized by information asymmetry. This, in turn, means that opportunistic behavior is likely to emerge. It follows that transaction costs must be positive. Finally, it is clear that economists of all persuasions have paid scant attention to the notion that ethical behavior can, inter alia, contribute to the minimization of transaction costs. An exception is Professor Buchanan who has argued that if "the necessary personal constraints are not present, or if they have been and are eroding", then "investment in both policing and preaching becomes more productive" [Buchanan 1994a, p. 125]. I shall have more to say about this in Chapter VIII, below.

[7]Recognition that exchange, policing and enforcement costs are generally positive has led, inter alia, to the development of transaction cost economics [Williamson 1985, esp. Chapter 1]. Moreover, the property rights literature takes as one of its points of departure the notion that transaction costs tend to be positive [Furubotn and Pejovich 1972, p. 1141]. This is significant precisely because the NIE builds on the transaction costs, property rights [and public choice] literature [North 1986, p. 235]. See also [Williamson 1985, p.16].

[8]For a critical view of Williamson's approach see [Hill 1985]. See also [Dow 1987]. For an opposing view see [Alchian and Woodward 1988]. For a response to Dow see [Williamson 1987]. Finally, for an application of Heiner's C-D Gap approach to the problem of the firm's internal structure see [Heiner 1988].

[9]The essential point is that, at one time, new institutional economists emphasized the need to retain the basic analytical structure of neoclassical theory [Furubotn and Pejovich 1972, p. 1138]:

... each decision maker is assumed to be motivated by self-interest and to move efficiently toward the most preferred operating position open. It follows, therefore, that under the conditions envisioned, MARGINALISM IS NOT REJECTED; THE TECHNIQUES ARE MERELY EXTENDED TO NEW APPLICATIONS. [emphasis mine].

[10]See also [Furubotn and Richter 1991, p. 1].

[11]This theme is explored more fully in [Furubotn and Richter 1991, esp. pp. 1-5].

[12]For more on what might be characterized as the "subjective" production function, see [Roth 1972] and [Roth 1977].

Chapter 8

The Implications for Social Welfare Theory

Quite a lot of high-brow economics... accepts the appropriateness of the standard general equilibrium model, with everyone pursuing their self-interest, given tastes and technology.... But the high ground is not secure at all. The most basic element of such modeling, namely the motivation of human beings, is not well addressed.

Amartya Sen

INTRODUCTION

The classically rational decision maker -- homo economicus -- does not simply possess exogenously determined, consistently ordered and intertemporally stable preferences.[1] He affects narrowly self-interested,[2] utility maximizing decisions in a frictionless world; a decision environment in which well-defined property rights are unattenuated, and transactions are costless. Significantly, this institutionless and intendedly value-free decision environment is the foundation upon which the orthodox theory of consumer behavior and, mutatis mutandis, the new social welfare theory are built.

While Professor Becker has recently acknowledged that "My work may have sometimes assumed too much rationality" [Becker 1993, p. 402] it is clear that he and others have been effective proponents of the view that, with minor adaptation, this characterization of economic man's decision environment can be employed to predict or, more heroically, explain, virtually all observed human behavior.[3] Interestingly, while this view has gained some currency among sociologists and other social scientists, many New Institutional, experimental and other economists have become skeptical about the behavioral postulates which underlie the received theory.[4] At issue are the implications for the new social welfare theory of the literature which questions the empirical content and internal consistency of the received, neoclassical theory's behavioral postulates.

MORE ON HOMO ECONOMICUS

The essential features of economic man's decision environment are easily characterized: He is an atomistic, autonomous optimizer possessed of a well-behaved objective function and subject to one or more exogenously determined constraints. The central property of his objective function is captured by classical rationality, while the latter includes exogenously determined, stable preferences. Significantly, in contemporary usage, "rationality" has been taken to mean that economic man acts in his narrow self-interest [Persky 1995, p. 223]. Equally important, the desiderata are taken to be goods whose physical and technical characteristics are known with certainty, and whose associated property rights are well-defined and unattenuated. In this environment transaction costs are zero, information asymmetries are absent and, pari passu, opportunistic behavior is not observed.

Reduced to its essentials, whether the desideratum is single- or multi-period utility maximization, there is a one-to-one correspondence between economic man's objective and subjectively perceived decision environments. Inter alia, the presumption that tastes are both exogenously determined and intertemporally stable assures us that evolutionary phenomena are either ruled out, or that such phenomena leave unchanged [Becker 1976b, p. 5]

> [those] underlying preferences [which are] defined over fundamental aspects
> of life, such as health, prestige, sensual pleasure, benevolence or envy.

While various elements of this characterization of economic man's decision environment have been subject to critical assessment, my interest centers, initially, on the presumed stability of preferences.[5]

"Stable" Preferences, Once Again

As we have seen, assumptions may be classified as generative or auxiliary. From the instrumentalist perspective the test of a model is the correspondence of predictions with observable reality. On this view, the empirical content of a model's generative assumptions is a matter of no consequence. In contrast, the empirical confirmability (disconfirmability) of a model hinges upon the realism of its auxiliary assumptions. It follows that, (a) because it is a generative assumption, classical rationality need not be realistic, and (b) because it is an auxiliary assumption, stability of preferences must be empirically confirmed; it must be realistic.

Difficulties arise precisely because the stability of preferences assumption cannot be tested independently of the classical rationality postulate. The literature typically characterizes this problem as reflecting the presence of an unidentified exogenous variable; economic man's tastes and preferences. While it is analytically convenient to regard tastes as exogenously determined and "beyond analysis" the assumption leads to a logical conundrum: Absent independent confirmation that economic man is classically rational, the key auxiliary assumption of the model cannot be empirically confirmed. It follows, inter alia, that the model can be neither confirmed nor disconfirmed.

The root cause of the inability to confirm (disconfirm) the received model is the presumed exogeneity of economic man's preference structure. Yet the assumption is retained -- in spite of the methodological difficulties to which it gives rise, and in spite of a panoply of evolutionary and other phenomena which appear to influence tastes. Indeed, it can be argued that sensitivity to the potential role of evolutionary phenomena was the catalyst to the Stigler/Becker effort to show that such phenomena as addiction and habit formation are consistent with the stability of "underlying preferences" defined over "fundamental aspects of life". Unfortunately, these -- presumably stable -- metapreferences do not govern choices among anything that is observable; they can only be inferred. In effect, the "underlying preferences" to which the Stigler/Becker approach appeals are [Aaron 1994, p. 6]:

> ... operationally indistinguishable from values mutable with respect to any observable behavior and subject to evolution in response to time and experience.[6]

It seems clear that efforts to shore up the stability of tastes assumption by appeal to underlying metapreferences are complicated by two irremediable facts: (1) Virtually any observed behavior can be rationalized ex post by appeal to "underlying preferences". It follows, mutatis mutandis, that models which appeal to "underlying preferences" cannot be disconfirmed [Pollak 1985, fn. 9, pp. 584-585]. (2) There is a growing body of evidence that evolutionary phenomena do affect preference structures. There is evidence, in short, that preferences are neither constant nor exogenously determined.[7]   For example, the "anomalous behavior" literature[8] may find its genesis in the path dependency of preference structures. Preferences may, in fact, be shaped by experience, by learning, and by the intervention of higher-order preferences [North 1994, p. 365]. The latter may affect an individual's preferences in one of two ways. First, it seems clear that because some persons have preferences for preferences they seek to alter others' preferences. Second, decisions may be complicated by internal conflict. For example, the decision to smoke (not to smoke) may be complicated by growing awareness that second-hand smoke may harm others.[9] If one grants both the existence and the potential affective power of such transparently evolutionary phenomena it is not implausible to conclude that "To assert that preferences are stable is ... a palpable absurdity" [Aaron 1994, p. 17].

Bounded Rationality, Information Asymmetries and Transaction Costs

Economic man's decision environment is decidedly uncomplicated: He knows what he prefers, he is not other-regarding, and he maximizes utility, given his internally consistent, stable preference structure and one or more [typically exogenously determined] economic constraints. Notably absent in this account is the possible intervention of other, endogenously determined constraints. Perhaps chief among these is the decision-maker's cognitive limitations. This omission is particularly troubling, given that there is a discrepancy [Egidi and Marris 1992, p. 3]:

... between the perfect rationality that is assumed in classical and neoclassical economic theory and the reality of human behavior as it is observed in economic life. The point [is] not   that people are consciously and deliberately irrational ... but that neither their knowledge nor their power of calculation allow them to achieve the high level of optimal adaptation of means to ends that is posited in economics.

In short, as was emphasized in Chapters VI and VII, decision-makers are both boundedly rational and subject to a growing competence-difficulty gap.[10] Roughly paraphrased, the essential idea is that the explosive growth of knowledge and the increasing complexity of interpersonal relationships imply a growing gap between decision makers' competence and the difficulty of the choice [and other] problems which confront them. Granting this, it seems clear that decision makers' limited information processing abilities constitute an endogenous constraint on choice - and other -- behavior.[11]

Decision makers' limited cognitive abilities have numerous implications. Among these are the fact that limited information processing abilities militate against the emergence of optimizing solutions. Equally important, a decision environment characterized by bounded rationality is, pari passu, one in which information asymmetries are pervasive. These asymmetries contemplate differing stocks of knowledge, differing abilities to process extant and new knowledge, and an inability always to disentangle the effects of random events from those effects which obtain because of opportunistic behavior. The existence of relational contracts is prima facie evidence that decision makers are aware of the potential for opportunistic behavior.[12] In effect, the presence of information asymmetries is congenial to the emergence of opportunistic behavior; to [Williamson 1985, p. 47]:

> ... the incomplete or distorted disclosure of information, especially to calculated efforts to mislead, distort, disguise, obfuscate, or otherwise confuse.

A corollary of this is that, even in the presence of relational contracts between principals and agents, "completely accurate monitoring and full enforcement of property rights are impossible" [Furubotn 1994, p. 25]. Roughly paraphrased, a world characterized by limited information processing abilities is, mutatis mutandis, a world in which the rights to use, to appropriate returns, and to change the form of assets may be systematically and surreptitiously attenuated.[13] Granting this, principals have incentive to absorb the ex ante and ex post costs associated with establishing and monitoring relational contracts. It follows, therefore, that one of the implications of bounded rationality is positive transaction costs.

ETHICS AND THE UTILITY FUNCTION

The case for the explicit incorporation in economic models of bounded rationality appears compelling. As John Conlisk has argued [Conlisk 1996, p. 669]:

> First, there is abundant empirical evidence that [bounded rationality] is important. Second, models of bounded rationality have proved themselves in a wide range of impressive work. Third, the standard justifications for assuming unbounded rationality are unconvincing; their logic cuts both ways. Fourth, deliberation about an economic decision is a costly activity, and good economics requires that we entertain all costs.

Transparently, bounded rationality implies positive decision costs. But, as has been emphasized, it is also conducive to opportunistic behavior and, pari passu, to positive transaction costs. This, in turn, suggests that economists -- and others -- must place greater emphasis on the value and importance of ethical norms. Inter alia, explicit account must be taken of the actual and potential role of ethical norms, both as arguments of utility functions and as endogenously determined constraints on behavior.

Economists' resistance to this notion is animated, in part, by their commitment to "positive", intendedly value-free analysis. Indeed, whereas many sociologists regard preferences and values as "results of enduring exchanges and social contracts" [Baron and Hannan 1994, p. 1117], the inclination of economists is to adopt the convention employed by Kenneth Arrow in his 1951 classic [Arrow 1951, p. 7]:

> ... we will ... assume ... that individual values are taken as data and are not capable of being altered by the nature of the decision process itself.

While his motivation was clearly to simplify the analysis of social choice, Arrow acknowledges that "the unreality of this assumption has been asserted by such writers as Veblen, Professor J. M. Clark, and Knight [Arrow 1951, p. 8]. To that list could be added, among others, John Stuart Mill [Persky 1995, p. 226], James Buchanan, and Amartya Sen. Indeed, in rejecting both "the assumption of given preferences ... and ... the presumption that people are narrowly self-interested homo economicus...." Sen observes that "... we do have the capacity -- and often the inclination -- to understand and respond to the predicament of others" [Sen 1995, p. 17]. On this logic, Sen argues that

... the practical reach of social choice theory ... is considerably reduced by its tendency to ignore value formation through social interactions.[14]

For his part, Professor Buchanan lays great emphasis upon the endogeniety of preferences and values [or ethical norms], and upon the efficacy of "preaching" or "investment in ethical persuasion" [Buchanan 1994b, p. 62]. On his view [Buchanan 1991, p. 186]:

The methodological individualist must ... acknowledge the relationships between individual utility functions and the socioeconomic-legal-political-cultural setting within which evaluations are made. But [this] carries with it... the possible productivity of investment in the promulgation of moral norms.

Buchanan's point is "not [to] deny the existence of noneconomic origins of morals" [Buchanan 1994b, p. 80]. Rather, the point is that the efficacy of "preaching" or "constructing" ethical norms flows from the fact that opportunistic behavior imposes costs on society; costs of which economists must take account.[15]

The potential role of ethical norms as constraints on opportunism -- and as catalysts to other-regarding behavior -- is, it seems to me, self-evident. It is, moreover, a role which may become increasingly important. The growth of knowledge and the growing complexity of relationships mean that we know less and less about each other, and about the objective properties of our decision environments. Professor Buchanan summarizes the situation in this way [Alchian et al 1996, p. 417]:

... there is cause for concern, or at least for further inquiry, as technology develops so as to create further erosion in the continuity of buyer-seller relationships and to replace personal by impersonal dealings.

While it is possible under such conditions partially to rely on contractually derived legal rules, the instrumental role of ethical norms cannot be denied: Inter alia, endogenously generated ethical constraints tend both to discourage opportunistic behavior and to engender trust.[16]

Incorporating Ethical Norms

Granting the logic of what has been said, it seems reasonable to conclude that [Hausman and McPherson 1993, p. 673]:

> The morality of economic agents influences their behavior and hence influences economic outcomes.

That said, the question which confronts us is, How might ethical norms and moral tastes be incorporated in economic models?

While other approaches are possible, empirical findings in evolutionary and other branches of contemporary psychology may be helpful. Roughly paraphrased, these findings suggest that utility does, in fact, derive from the consumption of goods and services. But utility also derives from self-reference, from helping [hurting] others, from caring about others as "ends", from interpersonal relationships, and from setting goals and achieving them [Aaron 1994, p. 15].

The essential point is that each of these desiderata may be understood to contemplate a utility domain. While these distinct domains cannot be captured by a single-equation, intertemporally stable utility function, they may be represented by multiple preference systems; by an array of utility subfunctions defined for one individual. Inter alia, appeal to a multi-equation utility function facilitates the formal modeling of such "internal conflicts" as whether or not to purchase a good whose moral attributes -- whether in acquisition or in use -- may be in question.[17] The essential point is that ethical considerations can be explicitly introduced into the decision process, either as arguments of one or more of the decision makers' utility subfunctions, or as constraints on behavior.[18]

THE IMPLICATIONS FOR THE NEW SOCIAL WELFARE THEORY

As is well known, classical rationality, stability of tastes, and constant technology are the key generative and auxiliary assumptions of the new social welfare theory. While logical and other difficulties attach to the specification and presumed stability of the commodity production functions,[19] our interest centers on the implications for social welfare theory of bounded rationality, information asymmetry and the incentive to engage in opportunistic behavior. It seems clear that, once account is taken of these phenomena, an a priori case can be made for the formal modeling of ethical norms. This is true for the received theory of consumer behavior and, pari passu, for the new social welfare theory.

Some Preliminaries

The conventional view is that welfare theory is value-free in orientation and in execution. Yet it is clear that the core ideas of the theory -- classical rationality, efficiency (in the sense of Pareto optimality) and the Bergsonian social welfare function -- are value loaded [Hausman and McPherson 1993,p. 675]:

> ... the standard definition of a social optimum compares social alternatives exclusively in terms of the goodness of their outcomes (rather than the rightness of their procedures) and identifies the goodness of outcomes with satisfaction of individual preferences. These commitments to value only outcomes and to measure outcomes only in terms of individual utilities are neither [value] neutral nor uncontroversial.[20]

Moreover, it is relatively easy to show that, because of the structure of the model, the new social welfare theory endorses an implicit "windfall ethic." Reduced to its essentials, the model does not admit of endogenously generated technological change. This is a necessary correlative of the perfect knowledge assumption: Because it is not possible to appropriate the benefits associated with the generation of new knowledge, technological change is introduced "like manna from heaven". Yet exogenously generated technical change results, necessarily, in windfall changes in the distribution of welfare [Furubotn 1971, p. 412]:

> By its nature, any social welfare function establishes a set of ethical standards and, in effect, specifies the relative 'deservingness' of the individuals within the system.... The welfare 'rule' here implies that particular individuals OUGHT to benefit or to lose from exogenous change in the technical data.

Whatever else is said, it is clear that, contrary to the traditional view, the new social welfare theory is implicitly value-laden. It follows that resistance to the notion that ethical considerations ought explicitly to be introduced cannot be sustained by appeal to the theory's value-free nature.

While it may be intendedly value-free it is, in fact, a part of the corpus of ethical theory.

If resistance to the incorporation of ethical norms is animated by commitment to "positive" analysis, the disinclination to incorporate bounded rationality, information asymmetry and opportunism is reflective of attachment to the admittedly convenient analytical fiction of zero transaction costs. It is after all clear that the path to first-best Paretian optima is [apparently] facilitated by frictionless transactions. Yet, while it is not generally recognized, the zero transaction cost assumption leads to a logical conundrum [Furubotn 1991, p. 664]:

> On the one hand, costless transactions are essential to ensure the existence of basic structural conditions that are needed for the operation of an efficient atomistic system.... On the other hand, costless transactions serve to ... permit the formation of stable collusive agreements among decision makers and, thus, encourage behavior that effectively rules out perfect competition (and optimality).

In effect, the "analytically convenient" zero transaction cost assumption rules out the satisfaction of the conditions for the General Pareto Optimum.

Granting the logic of what has been said, there is reason to question both the behavioral postulates and the internal consistency of the new social welfare theory. At the most rudimentary level, the claim that social welfare theory is value-free cannot be sustained. It is, in fact, a part of the corpus of ethical theory. Once this has been said, there is no compelling methodological reason to resist the explicit incorporation of bounded rationality, information asymmetries and opportunistic behavior. Incorporation of these broadly descriptive features of observable reality does, indeed, imply that transaction costs are positive. But, as we have seen, the analytical fiction of zero transaction costs leads to a logical conundrum. In contrast, recognition of the interrelationships among limited cognitive abilities, information asymmetries and opportunism serves to underscore the role of ethical norms in the minimization of transaction [and other] costs. It is difficult to see how economists concerned with the "minimization of costs" can reconcile themselves to the persistence of what is, effectively, a theoretical lacuna.

Some Thoughts on the Efficiency Frontier

It seems clear that the representative agent's preference structure cannot adequately be represented by an intertemporally stable, single-equation utility function. Inter alia, each agent's preference system contemplates a number of preference domains, with each domain representable by a utility subfunction. Presumably, the arguments of one or more of the subfunctions includes goods and services. But the presumption is that one or more of the subfunctions must include arguments which are broadly reflective of society's view of acceptable behavior; of how the individual "ought" to behave. On this view [Buchanan 1994a, p. 128]:

> Economics models persons as maximizers of utility, but arguments in utility functions include rules that restrict the choices that are made.

In effect, individuals' utility domains incorporate both tastes and values (or moral tastes). While the formal modeling of such phenomena may, in principle, be accomplished in a number of ways, a sine qua non would appear to be a broader understanding of the defining characteristics of goods and services. Included among the vector of characteristics of any good or service would be its qualitative and technical properties, its associated property rights bundle, and its moral attributes. The latter would contemplate both the moral attributes of the good in use and the "moral attributes of the processes of [the good's] acquisition" [Buchanan 1994a, p. 134].

The logic of the approach suggests that each of the goods and services contemplated by one or more of an individual's utility subfunctions may be understood to be a differentiate of a particular product type. Given this understanding, each product type, x_T, $T = 1,2,..., $ m occurs in differentiated forms, with each differentiate distinguished, inter alia, by the n individuals' subjective perceptions of its qualitative, technical, property rights and ethical attributes.[21]

Given the complexity of this decision environment little can be said a priori about the arguments of any individual's multi-equation utility function. This much is clear: As the argument developed in Chapter IV suggests, no one can plausibly be supposed to possess exhaustive knowledge of the array of objectively and subjectively distinguishable differentiates of the indefinitely large number of product types which confront him. In short, because of the intervention of cognitive and information processing limitations, there can be no one-to-one correspondence between the objective and the subjectively perceived choice space. This, in turn, has a number of implications. First, the "goods" which appear as arguments of any one individual's utility subfunctions must be understood to comprise a subset of the goods extant at any cross-section of time.[22] Second, there can be no presumption that the same subset of "goods" will appear in any two individuals' utility subfunctions.

These considerations suggest that the choice space in which individuals' preference structures are defined is itself subjectively determined. Indeed, the subjective nature of the space is underscored by another consideration: Each of the n individual's preference structures is defined on distinct utility domains. While one individual may be narrowly self-interested another may be other-regarding, with the latter understood, for example, to contemplate meddlesome or meta-preferences or both. Once this has been said it is clear that no two individuals can plausibly be assumed to possess utility functions defined in the same space.

If one grants the logic of what has been said the implications for the efficiency frontier are clear. Once allowance is made for the complex nature of decision makers' disparate desiderata and, at the same time, for ethically -- and otherwise --motivated internal conflict, it is not possible to determine the space in which an efficiency frontier might be derived.

It should be emphasized that the problem goes beyond the of-cited nirvana fallacy. As is well known, the fallacy obtains when the efficiency frontier is held up as a benchmark without taking explicit account of one or more real and unavoidable constraints [Furubotn 1994, p. 12]. Reduced to its essentials, the complexities outlined here suggest that the efficiency frontier cannot meaningfully be defined. This is true at a cross-section of time and, mutatis mutandis, at different points in time. Path dependencies including such observable phenomena as learning,   the emergence of new goods, cultural effects and habit formation serve only to underscore the essential point: The efficiency frontier appears not to have an operational counterpart.[23]

Some Thoughts on the Social Welfare Function

If the complexities outlined above militate against the specification of an efficiency or welfare frontier it seems clear that the same can be said of the Bergsonian Social Welfare Function.

It is well known that the General Possibility Theorem establishes that, if interpersonal utility comparisons are excluded, there is no possible method of aggregating individual rankings of social alternatives which meets five ostensibly innocuous criteria [Arrow 1951, pp. 24-31]. Absent interpersonal utility comparisons [IUCs] [Arrow 1951, p. 59]:

> ... the only methods of passing from individual tastes to social preferences which will be satisfactory and which will be defined for a wide range of sets of individual orderings, are either imposed or dictatorial.

While it is known that the impossibility result may not hold if IUCs are permitted [Sen 1970, Chapters 7 and 8], the basic problem is "the heterogeneity of men, the variance of their preferences and capacities for satisfaction" [Rothschild 1993, p. 89]. While strategies may be conceived which allow for some generalizations regarding IUCs, each is subject to daunting problems.[24] In any case, each of the available strategies makes the implicit assumption that preference structures are constant. This, as we have seen, is difficult to reconcile with the growing body of evidence that preferences are path-dependent. This suggests, inter alia, that intertemporal phenomena such as learning, habit formation, the appearance of new products and even public discourse imply an IUC problem for the same individual.[25] These and other technical difficulties -- including the inability to test the classical rationality and stability of preference assumptions independently -- suggest that Arrow's impossibility result will retain its basic relevance.

Some Thoughts on Freedom and Rights

Economists who are intellectually committed to consequentialist theory -- including the body of social welfare theory -- generally regard freedom as instrumentally or intrinsically valuable (or both). It is clear, for example, that the path to first-best Paretian optima contemplates the free exchange of goods and services [and productive inputs] whose associated property rights bundles are both fully understood and unattenuated. Characteristically, when these -- usually implicit -- assumptions have been relaxed, attention has centered on one particular rights construal; namely, property or, more particularly, ownership rights. Broadly speaking, analysis has proceeded on the assumption that exchange rights are unattenuated, with interest centering on the implications for economic outcomes of the attenuation of ownership rights. In the event, broader understandings of "freedom" and "rights" have gone largely unattended. As Hausman and McPherson have observed [1993, p. 693]:

> It is ironic that welfare economics focuses almost exclusively on the Pareto efficiency concepts. For economists typically value individual freedom, and much of the traditional case for capitalism was not so much in terms of its capacity to 'deliver the goods' as in terms of the protection that the separation of economic and political power offers to individual liberty....

Given economists' intellectual commitment to the instrumental and/or intrinsic value of freedom and, pari passu, of rights, it is surprising that relatively little attention has been paid to careful explications of their role in theory generally, and in social welfare theory particularly. Yet when such efforts have been made they have served, generally, to underscore the indeterminacy of consequentialist social welfare theory. Sen and Gibbard have shown, for example, that in the presence of "meddlesome" or "nosy" preferences, respect for individual liberty may rule out the possibility of any social choice.[26] The essential point is that, if just one person cares about just one other person's consumption pattern -- and both persons can be decisive over their own choices -- "every possible [social] outcome will be vetoed by somebody" [Hausman and McPherson 1993, p. 716].

While it is possible to argue -- in the manner of Nozick and others -- that "liberty" in the sense of privacy rights does not convey the right to be decisive with respect to social choices, the essential question appears to be the motivation behind the "meddlesome" preferences. Thus, if "A" prefers on moral grounds that "B" not engage in a particular private activity, "A's" preferences may, legitimately, play a role in social decisions. Yet, if meddlesome preferences do have a legitimate role, then [Hausman and McPherson 1993, p. 717]:

> ... the axiomatic approach which has characterized most work on social choice theory leaves us more ambivalent.

The essential point is that, whether economists regard it as intrinsically valuable or not, freedom is instrumentally important to the attainment of first-best Paretian optima. Yet, as we have seen, in the presence of meddlesome [and other] preferences, respect for privacy rights may be irreconcilable with the attainment of Paretian optima. That said, the corollary is clearly not that freedom and rights should, in the explication of social welfare theory, be ignored. Given their instrumental role in the theory, social welfare theorists have no choice: An explicit analysis of the implications for social welfare theory of various freedom and rights construals is a logical necessity.

Once this has been said, it is tautological that social welfare theory is not "value free". The irremediable fact is that "freedom" or "liberty" and "rights" are dimensions of moral evaluation [Hausman and McPherson 1993, esp. pp. 693-696]. Whether regarded as morally exigent in themselves [Singer 1993, p. 265], or merely as instrumental to the promotion of welfare -- as in the case of consequentialist social welfare theory -- the implicit or explicit invocation of rights implicates moral theory. It follows, pari passu, that neither the efficiency frontier nor the Social Welfare Function can be explicated by appeal to orthodox, single-equation utility functions. Insofar as freedom and rights -- which, by definition, determine the distribution of freedom [Hausman and McPherson 1993, p. 696] -- are regarded as instrumentally or intrinsically valuable, agents' utility functions must be understood to consist in families of utility subfunctions or "domains". Each subfunction, in turn, contemplates arguments whose defining characteristics include, inter alia, ethical attributes. Yet, as we have seen, the explicit incorporation of utility domains has an unintended consequence: Inter alia, the space in which the efficiency frontier is to be defined becomes indeterminate, and Arrow's impossibility result is reinforced.

PUBLIC POLICY IMPLICATIONS

Whether casually or "scientifically" invoked, the new social welfare theory is the deus ex machina by which economists shape public policy recommendations. The confidence with which this is frequently done reflects many, perhaps most, economists' view that the theory and its component parts are both empirically confirmable and "value free." The problem, as we have seen, is that the theory is neither confirmable [disconfirmable], nor "value free". Moreover, when systematic attempts are made to incorporate phenomena which are reflective of decision environments as they are actually configured, the theory is rendered indeterminate. Reduced to its essentials, the root cause of the indeterminacy is that social welfare theory is consequentialist in orientation.[27] It places emphasis upon outcomes; on the implications for individuals' well-being of changes in discretionary policies. Yet, given the presence of unidentified preferences and values, "There is no criterion through which policy may be directly evaluated" [Buchanan 1987, p. 247].[28]

In the face of this theoretical and empirical lacuna, the question becomes, What should be the focus of economic analysis? An alternative proffered, among others, by Professor Buchanan, is to focus evaluative attention on the institutions -- the "rules of the game" -- which, in part, shape agents' decision environments.[29] As we saw in Chapter VII [North 1994, p. 360]:

> Institutions are the humanly devised constraints that structure human interaction. They are made up of formal constraints (rules, laws, constitutions), informal constraints (norms of behavior, conventions and self-imposed codes of conduct), and their enforcement characteristics. Together they define the incentive structure of societies and specifically economies.

One of the implications of a shift from a consequentialist to a constitutional or "procedural" perspective is that economists' attention will center less on prediction and on "getting the prices right," and more on "getting the institutions right" [Williamson 1994 p. 321].

Inter alia, this approach contemplates an explicit accounting of "codes of conduct", including ethical norms. Given a decision environment characterized by limited cognitive abilities, information asymmetries and opportunism this seems appropriate. Indeed, it seems plausible to argue that, in the face of an increasingly complex decision environment [Wilde, LeBaron and Israelson 1985, p. 406]:

> ... institutions must evolve which enable each agent in the society to know less and less about the behavior of other agents and about the complex interdependencies generated by their interaction.[30]

Granting the logic of what has been said it appears that economists may properly have a role to play in crafting an institutional structure consonant with (a) the minimization of the deleterious effects of a growing competence- difficulty gap, and (b) the maximization of ethical behavior.[31] It seems clear, in short, that economists [Buchanan 1994a, p.125]

... should recognize that the efficacy of any market order depends critically on ... endogenous behavioral constraints... and, further, that, to an extent, these constraints may, themselves, be 'constructed' .... If the necessary personal constraints are not present, or if they have been eroding ... increased resource investment in both policing and preaching becomes more productive.

A shift to a constitutional or procedural approach seems justified on methodological grounds. Indeed, attention to the "rules of the game" may, indirectly, address a fundamental problem attaching to the received theory of consumer behavior [and, *pari* passu, the new social welfare theory]. As was suggested in Chapter VI, observed regularities in consumer [and other] behavior may find their genesis in the employment of behavioral rules that arise because of uncertainty. Professor Heiner has argued that, in the face of a growing competence-difficulty gap [Heiner 1983, p. 570]:

> ... greater uncertainty will cause rule-governed behavior to exhibit increasingly predictable regularities, so that uncertainty becomes the basic source of predictable behavior.

If Professor Heiner's view is broadly reflective of reality, the growth of knowledge and the increasing complexity of social, intrafirm, and market relationships will result, given agents' cognitive and information processing limitations, in increased appeal to rule-governed behavior or decision heuristics [Heiner 1983, p. 561].[32] If this view is correct, agents can be expected to "systematically restrict the use of and acquisition of information compared to that potentially available" [Heiner 1983, p. 564]. A corollary of this is that "optimization" becomes a [presumably rarely observed] special case.

The essential point is this: A recurring theme of this book has been the inability to confirm (disconfirm) the received theory of consumer behavior. The problem arises because of the inability to test the classical rationality postulate without independent evidence that preference structures are, in fact, stable. If, as Professor Heiner suggests, agents do employ decision rules or heuristics, a shift to a constitutional or procedural orientation may enhance the empirical confirmability (disconfirmability) of economists' models of consumer behavior. Here, confirmability (disconfirmability) would not depend upon securing independent evidence that endogenously determined preference and value structures were constant during a given trial or test. Indeed, if the argument developed above is correct, preference and value structures are path-dependent and, therefore, not intertemporally stable. Instead, the empirical confirmability (disconfirmability) of "procedural" models would depend upon securing independent evidence that the "rules of the game" -- including ethical and other behavioral norms -- were constant. Given these (potentially) empirically confirmable (disconfirmable) auxiliary assumptions, the behavioral postulates or generative assumptions would consist in the specification of the decision rules -- including habits, rules of thumb, or routines -- which appear to be operative.

Whether a shift to a constitutional or procedural approach enhances the empirical confirmability (disconfirmability) of economists' models is, however, in a sense, irrelevant. At issue is the apparently irremediable fact that the "usefulness" of consquentialist models -- notably the received theory of consumer behavior and the New Social Welfare Theory -- is encumbered by the complexity of agent's desiderata and by the growing disparity between subjectively perceived and objectively determined decision environments. The singular advantage of a constitutional or procedural orientation is that it forces attention to issues which naturally attend such an environment. Among these are cognitive limitations, information asymmetries, opportunism and, pari passu, the role of ethical norms in determining economic outcomes.

I have suggested that adoption of this perspective will likely be resisted. Most economists are, after all, intellectually committed to the institutionless, intendedly value-free decision environment of. an atomistic, autonomous, narrowly self-interested "economic man." On the assumption that resistance will be encountered it seems reasonable to offer some final observations: On the one hand, there is some evidence that economics students are less other-regarding than students of other disciplines.[33] On the other hand, as was suggested above, there is a growing body of evidence in social and evolutionary psychology which suggests that a moral sense may be endogenously determined [Kuran 1996, pp. 440-441; Frank 1996, p. 117]. This suggests, inter alia, that, value [and, presumably, preference] structures are path-dependent. This is significant for its own sake. But it is also important because it appears to vindicate Adam Smith's view, paraphrased by Muller, that [Muller 1993, pp 102-103]:

Moral consciousness... is a process of internal conversation, of talking to ourselves. In that process, our natural egoism is partially restrained by our awareness of an external standard, the standard which we would use to judge our actions if we were a spectator who was biased neither toward ourselves nor toward those affected by our actions. This is the standard of what Smith calls 'the impartial spectator.'[34]

In effect, morality grows "out of the process of growing up and living in the company of others" [Wilson 1989, p. 65]. This suggests that the atomistic, narrowly self-interested economic man of "positive" economics is not the decision maker that Adam Smith had in mind. Indeed, [Wilson 1989, p.66]:

... the Adam Smith who invented capitalism, described the useful effects of the invisible hand, and showed how the free pursuit of self-interest would lead to greater prosperity than any system of state-controlled exchanges was also the Adam Smith who, more deeply than anyone since, has explored the sources and power of human sympathy and the relationship between sympathy and justice.

Transparently, Adam Smith envisioned a world in which decisions were not taken in "the uncompromising pursuit of narrowly defined self-interest" [Sen 1995, p. 15]. Equally important, the decision environment in which Smith's impartial spectator functions is not institution-free. Quite the contrary: Smith sought to "bring about improvement ... through designing institutions which would strengthen the incentive to act in a socially beneficial way" [Muller 1993, pp. 197-198].

In short, Adam Smith's political economy was neither value- nor institution-free. The reluctance of "positive" economists to embrace an explicitly normative procedural approach to economics may be partially attributable to a misreading of The Wealth of Nations. Or it may be attributable to their failure to remember that the author of The Wealth of Nations was also the author of The Theory of Moral Sentiments.[35] Whatever the cause(s) of their attachment to the received theory of consumer behavior and, pari passu, to the New Social Welfare Theory, they do so at considerable cost.

NOTES

[1]For more on the definitions of rationality typically encountered in the literature, see [Klamer 1989, p. 141]. See also Chapters II and IV, above.

[2]The notion that individuals act in their narrow self-interest is sometimes used to rationalize patently unethical behavior. Cheung [1996, p. 1] has asserted, for example, that:

> ... all individuals, government officials and politicians without exception, are constrained self-maximizers.... each and every politician and government official has only one priority in mind. Just like you and me, they get up in the morning and think about how to produce more income for themselves, and under the usual social and political constraints corruption is generally the most convenient avenue to achieve the goal.

Continuing, Cheung insists that [1996, p. 3]:

> Any other way of thinking is inconsistent with the postulate of constrained maximization. In other words, any other argument shows no faith in mankind.

Other economists have argued that "corruption is an optimal response to market distortions and may improve allocative efficiency" [Lui 1996, p. 26], and that [Tullock 1996, p. 7]:

> Most people who object to corruption probably do so on moral grounds without considering the practical effects.

In Tullock's view [Tullock 1996, p. 6]:

> ... corruption ... may have some redeeming features. It may make possible smaller or no salary payments to officials who, if carefully supervised, will still carry out their functions on a fee-for-service basis.

For his part, Serguey Braguinsky argues that whether corruption is conducive or detrimental to economic growth depends upon the prevailing institutional structure [Braguinsky 1996].

Suffice it to say that: (1) Corruption is not necessarily congruent with self-interest; (2) efficiency is a peculiar standard by which to assess unethical behavior, and (3) as we shall see, the efficiency standard is severely encumbered by the complexity of decision makers' desiderata.

[3]For an example of this literature, see [Demsetz 1997].

[4]See, for example, [Furubotn 1994] and [Williamson 1993, esp. p. 107]. As Conlisk has observed [1996, p. 669]:

Although the postulate of unbounded rationality has dominated economic models for several decades,the dominance is relaxing.

Conlisk proffers four reasons for incorporating bounded rationality in economic models and concludes that [Conlisk 1996, p. 692]:

The evidence and models surveyed suggest that a sensible rationality assumption will vary by context, depending on such conditions as deliberation cost, complexity, incentives, experience, and market discipline.

[5]For representative critiques of economic man, see [Cox and Epstein 1989], [Elster 1989], [Furubotn 1994], [Nelson 1995], [North 1994], [Sen 1995], and [Tversky and Thaler 1990].

[6]For a critique of the Stigler/Becker approach, see [Furubotn 1994, pp. 31-34]. See also Chapter V, above.

It is at least arguable that Professor Becker has begun to rethink his position. Indeed, in his 1993 Nobel lecture he observed that [Becker 1993, p. 386]:

Actions are constrained by income, time, imperfect memory and calculating capacities, and other limited resources.

He concluded that "My work may have sometimes assumed too much rationality" [Becker 1993, p.402].

[7]See, for example, [Aaron 1994, p. 17] and [Sen 1995, pp. 17-18]. See also [Smith 1994, esp.p. 120] and [Bowles and Gintis 1993, p. 100].

[8]See, for example, [Tversky and Thaler 1990].

[9]See, for example, [Hausman and McPherson 1993, p. 688].

[10]See, for example, pp. 113-114, above. See also [Conlisk 1996].

[11]For a discussion of cognitive limitations as an endogenous constraint on choice, see [Buchanan 1994a, p. 133].

[12]See, for example, [Furubotn and Richter 1991, pp. 18-24].

[13]For a discussion of the implications of such a decision environment for federal on-, off-, and off-off-budget activity, see [Roth 1994].

[14]See [Sen 1995, p. 18] and [Hausman and McPherson 1993, p. 683].

[15]For a discussion of the origins of ethics see [Singer 1993, esp. Chapter 1].

[16]See, for example, [Buchanan 1991, p. 179] and [Wilde, Le Baron and Israelsen 1985, p. 407]. In attempting to "unravel [Alchian's] survivalist criterion in terms of its implied behavioral limits" Professor Buchanan lays great emphasis on the role of ethical norms [Alchian et al 1996, p. 417]:

... the normative status of this criterion may be quite different in differing institutional settings. Patterns of behavior that ensure survival in the technological complexity of today's extended, but highly politicized, markets may not, independently of some ethical reinforcement, carry with them the normative implications that emerged so clearly in the stylized textbook constructions.

[17]See, for example, [Klamer 1989, p. 144] and [Hausman and McPherson 1993, p. 688].

[18]While the technical difficulties associated with this approach are manifest, they are not insurmountable. And, while it might be argued that such an approach might, at best, enable economists and others to rationalize observed behavior ex post, that may be the price which has to be paid [Aaron 1994, p. 17]. The logic of methodological pluralism argues that prediction and explanation are, after all, not the only legitimate goals of science. Moreover, as we have seen, there are profound methodological problems associated with the empirical confirmability (disconfirmability) of models which assume classical rationality and stable preferences. For more on methodological pluralism, see [Caldwell 1991, p. 24].

[19]See, for example, [Roth 1979].

[20]The essential point is that the new social welfare theory is an example of a "consequentialist [moral] theory ... of what justifies an option over alternatives ... not an account of how agents ought to deliberate in selecting the option" [Singer 1993, p. 235]. Moreover, as a form of utilitarianism, consequentialist welfare theory is [Singer 1993, p. 245]:

first and foremost, a standard for judging public action --action which, whether performed by private individuals or public officials, affects various people besides just yourself.

While the new social welfare theory does not implicate the question of what procedures ought to be employed in promoting good consequences, it must, necessarily, implicate the question of what "good" ought to be promoted. It follows, pari passu, that the new social welfare theory is an ethical theory; one which argues that the "good" which ought to be promoted is the maximization of utility. See, for example, [Singer 1993, Chapters 19 and 20].

[21]See, for example, [Furubotn and Pejovich 1974, pp. 4-5], [Buchanan 1994a, p. 134] and [Roth 1975].

[22]See, for example, [Furubotn 1994, p. 34] and [Roth 1975].

[23]Robert Frank has observed that it is not clear "... how even to DEFINE an efficiency standard when individual preferences are highly malleable" [Frank 1996, p. 119] (emphasis in original).

[24]See, for example, [Rothschild 1993, pp. 91-96]. Inter alia, "welfare" utilitarians argue that it is possible to know 'what is in people's interests, ..., without knowing what is inside their heads" [Singer 1993, p. 246]. This approach appears, at least in part, to rely on the notion of "primary social goods"; of things "which it is supposed a rational man wants whatever else he wants" [Rawls 1971, p. 92]. The "primary social goods" convention may, in turn, share some common

ground with Professor Becker's notion of "basic pleasures" or "underlying preferences" defined over "fundamental aspects of life." See, for example, [Becker 1976b, pp. 5 and 145]. Suffice it to say that such "metapreferences" are "operationally indistinguishable from values... subject to evolution in response to time and experience" [Aaron 1994, p. 6].

[25]See, for example, [Furubotn 1994, pp. 34-35] on the process of information diffusion.

[26]See, for example, [Sen 1995, p. 13] and [Hausman and McPherson 1993, pp. 715-716].

[27]See, for example, [Singer 1993, Chapters 19 and 20].

[28]See also [Sen 1995, p. 2] and [Sandmo 1990, p. 51].

[29]Professor Buchanan argues that [Alchian et al 1996, p. 418]:

> As political economists we should pay more attention to what the appropriately defined institutional setting is and must be.

See also [Buchanan 1991, p. 40], and [Buchanan 1987, p. 247]. For more on institutions as "rules of the game" see [North 1994, p. 361]. See also [Sen 1995, p. 2] and [Sandmo 1990].

[30]See also [Heiner 1983, p. 580] and [North 1994, p. 363].

[31]For more on why economists should be interested in moral questions, see [Hausman and McPherson 1993, esp. pp. 673-674]. For an application of these concepts, see [Roth 1994].

[32]The behavioral rules to which individuals appeal may themselves be path-dependent, and conditioned by evolving cultural settings. As DeVany has observed [DeVany 1996, p. 442]:

> Cultural evolution is a means of arriving at viable solutions to recurrent situations without each generation paying the costs of trial and error learning. High decision costs - obtaining the information, computing the decision, evaluating the outcomes - can lead to reliance on cultural transmission of decision.

[33]See, for example, [Yezer, Goldfarb and Poppen 1996] and [Frank, Gilovich and Regan 1996].

[34]See also [Frank 1992, esp. p. 148].

[35]Professor Demsetz acknowledges the "two Adam Smiths". In Demsetz' view, however, the Adam Smith who "characterizes behavior as often sympathetic to the feelings of others" had in mind "persons who are related to each other or who are close friends" [Demsetz 1997, p. 6]. In Demetz' view, these "sympathetic" impulses are not relevant to, presumably impersonal, "commercial activity."

Chapter 9

A Postscript on Empirical Demand Estimation

> . . . it is true that [economists] have only limited success in dealing with many practical problems. But if anyone tries to attribute this to economists having second-rate minds, we can refer with pride to the imposing intellectual structure that we call economic theory.
>
> Thomas Mayer

INTRODUCTION

The problems with consumer theory reduce in their essentials to the inability to provide adequate interpretive rules. As we have seen, the problem is pervasive, associated as it is with ordinal utility theory and its various technical extensions, with the Lancastrian or "New Approach," with the multi-equation utility function, and with the household production function.

While appeal to procedural rationality suggests an avenue of escape from this methodological quagmire, this frontier has yet to be fully explored. For the present it is indisputable that most empirical demand analyses take as their point of departure an orthodox conception of the consumer's decision environment. Whether static or intertemporal, the decision environment contemplates, <u>inter alia</u>, an objective function firmly grounded in classical rationality, with stability of preferences assumed.

Practitioners of the science-art of econometrics seem implicitly to recognize the limitations of this approach. Recent discussion centering on the proper specification of the money demand equation is heuristic.

MONEY DEMAND ESTIMATION

Until the emergence of the "missing money" problem [Goldfeld 1976; Cooley and LeRoy 1981, p. 831], many considered the question of the appropriate specification of the money demand equation to be settled. As Hafer and Hein have suggested, the basic Goldfeld equation had become "the standard of comparison for alternative money demand specifications" [Hafer and Hein 1979; Cooley and LeRoy 1981, p. 995].

After 1973 the perception began to grow that something had gone awry. Money demand equations seemed systematically to overpredict the quantity of cash balances demanded. One response was to reopen what Judd and Scadding call the "pre-1973 agenda of empirical issues -- how to define money; which interest rate(s) measured the opportunity cost of holding money, and whether a measure of transactions or wealth was the correct scale variable" [Judd and Scadding 1982, p. 1006].

A balanced assessment of the post-1973 work concluded, however, that [Judd and Scadding 1982, p. 1014]:

> . . . reopening the pre-1973 agenda did not help to clarify the issues that it had posed. None of the traditional alternative empirical specifications appeared to be superior to the conventional Goldfeld equation in the sense of reducing materially the latter's post-1973 overpredictions.

With this [and other] empirical problems in mind, a literature has begun to emerge which is intended, <u>inter alia</u>, to "offer a solution to the long-running money demand puzzle" [Barnett, Fisher and Serletis 1992, p. 2115]. Reduced to its essentials, this new literature contemplates research in two areas: (1) the construction of non-simple-sum monetary aggregates, and (2) the estimation of systems of financial asset-demand equations.

Research under the first rubric takes as its point of departure the notion that simple-sum money aggregates -- currently, M1, M2, M3 and L -- imply that each of the various aggregates' components are perfect substitutes. This, it is clear, is difficult to reconcile with the proliferation of apparently imperfectly substitutable financial assets [Barnett, Fisher and Serletis 1992, p.2108]. Moreover, the relative prices of financial assets change over time. Unless they are compensated price changes, such changes result in both substitution and income effects. Granting this, the problem with simple-sum monetary aggregates is that [Barnett, Fisher and Serletis 1992, p. 2093]:

> ... in aggregation theory a quantity index should measure the income effects... of a relative price change but should be unresponsive to pure substitution effects.... [Yet] The simple-sum index cannot untangle income from substitution effects if its components are not perfect substitutes.

With these considerations in mind, the new literature proffers Divisia monetary aggregates which, in turn, can be entered as dependent variables in systems of financial asset-demand equations. The literature suggests that [Barnett, Fisher and Serletis 1992, p. 2115]:

> Unlike conventional linear money demand equations, a system of demand equations derived from a flexible functional form with data produced from the Divisia index can be expected to capture those movements in money holding that are due to changes in the relative prices among [imperfectly substitutable] assets.... the approach offers a solution to the long-running money-demand puzzle.

Whether or not the new approach resolves the aggregation problem, it is clear that fundamental methodological problems attach to the estimation of "systems of financial asset-demand equations." The essential point is that the new approach follows the organizational pattern of the utility tree.[1] On this view, the representative consumer-labor supplier-asset portfolio manager is confronted with a two-stage optimization problem. At stage one he affects an expenditure allocation among broad categories. Here, the categories contemplate consumption goods, leisure and the services of monetary assets. At the second stage, the representative agent allocates expenditures within each category.

There are, broadly speaking, two problems with this characterization of the agent's decision environment. First, as was shown in Chapter IV, taxonomic problems result in a level of commodity [and service] aggregation that renders the model's predictions vacuous.[2] Second, and more generally, the utility tree formulation and, pari passu, the aggregation-theoretic literature on money demand, lacks interpretive rules. In effect, the lack of adequate empirical interpretation increases the ambiguity of test results. Because of the presence of an unidentified exogenous variable -- the consumer-labor supplier-asset portfolio manager's preference structure -- a comparison of observed consumption, leisure and money holding patterns with the model's predictions can never be disconfirmatory. On the one hand, given the generality of its predictions, virtually all observed behavior can be claimed to fall within the model's designed classes of implications. On the other hand, given the presence of an unidentified exogenous variable, test results which appear to be irreconcilable with the model's predictions can always be ascribed to "changes in tastes and preferences."

All of this has basic relevance to the methodological issues which have been a recurring theme of this book. Precisely because they assume classical rationality and the stability of preferences, neither transactions nor portfolio, or the newer "aggregation-theoretic" approaches to money demand are capable of specifying adequate interpretive rules. As Professors Cooley and LeRoy have noted [Cooley and LeRoy 1981, p. 825]:

> ... in economics, particularly macroeconomics, the theory used to derive tests ordinarily does not generate a complete specification of which variables are to be held constant when statistical tests are performed on the relation between the dependent variable and the independent variables of primary interest.

In short, the theory which underlies money demand estimation does not adequately specify the auxiliary assumptions; the givens upon which the empirical confirmation (disconfirmation) of the theory depends. This, as we have seen, has two corollaries. First, theories of money demand can neither be confirmed nor disconfirmed. Second, because the givens are not adequately specified, determination of the proper vector of independent variables becomes, in part, a matter of prior beliefs [Cooley and LeRoy 1981, p. 830].[3] In the case of money demand estimation, the result has been that [Cooley and LeRoy 1981, p. 832]:

> ... the presence of specification uncertainty has induced analysts of money demand to make extensive but completely informal use of prior information.[4]

The problem of specification uncertainty has led Cooley and LeRoy to conclude that [Cooley and LeRoy 1981, p. 832]:

... what is required is a more formal and explicit means of representing prior information, or the lack of it, about model specification. Leamer's analytical procedure and reporting style are one way of fulfilling this requirement.

EXTREME BOUNDS ANALYSIS

The analytical procedure to which Cooley and LeRoy refer is Edward Leamer's Extreme Bounds Analysis (EBA).[5] Reduced to its essentials, EBA proposes to deal with the problem of specification uncertainty by dividing the "explanatory" variables in a regression equation into two classes: the "free variable(s)" and the "doubtful variable(s)." The purpose, in Leamer's words, is to take the con out of econometrics [Leamer 1983]. The vehicle by which this is to be accomplished is, in effect, a variant of what we have come to characterize as sensitivity analysis. Indeed, whereas the convention seems to be to refer to his approach as EBA, Leamer prefers the characterization Global Sensitivity Analysis (GSA) [Leamer 1985, p. 311].

The mechanics of the approach are, in principle, straightforward. At stage one, the researcher must adduce at least one implication of the relevant theory. An implication of the theory of money demand might, for example, be that the demand for money depends on "the" interest rate (as a measure of the opportunity cost of holding real money balances), and that the coefficient linking "the" interest rate to real cash balances is negative, "no matter what measure of transactions is used, and no matter what other variables are included in the regression" [Cooley and LeRoy 1981, p. 827]. Granting this, EBA suggests that the researcher perform tests on the "fragility of the inference" that changes in real money balances are inversely related to changes in "the" interest rate. The researcher is encouraged to determine the sensitivity of the estimated interest rate coefficient to the inclusion (noninclusion) of "doubtful" variables in the regression equation. Presumably, the researcher will, <u>inter alia</u>, report the extreme values of the "free" interest rate coefficient which emerge according as "doubtful" variables are (are not) included in the regression equation. This reporting procedure would replace the prevailing practice of selective reporting of the results of specification searches, and would enable the researcher to demonstrate the robustness of his inferences, given a clearly defined set of specifications.[6]   In Professor Leamer's words [Leamer 1983, p. 38]:

> What I propose to do is to develop a correspondence between regions in the assumption space and regions in the inference space. I will report that all assumptions in a certain set lead to essentially the same inference. Or I will report that there are assumptions within the set under consideration that lead to radically different inferences. In the latter case, I will suspend inference and decision, or I will work harder to narrow the set of assumptions.

MONEY DEMAND, AGAIN

Using Leamer's suggested approach, Cooley and LeRoy set out to test the inference that the interest elasticity of the demand for money is both negative and statistically significant.[7] They take as "free" variables the Treasury bill rate and the savings and loan passbook rate. Their "doubtful" variables consist of a "variety of other variables frequently appearing in estimated money demand models in the reported literature" [Cooley and LeRoy 1981, p. 828]. Their results indicate that

> ... the estimated interest elasticity is extremely sensitive to the inclusion or noninclusion of the doubtful variables, is not clearly negative, and is in any case much closer to zero than is indicated in much of the reported literature. It follows that the results reported in the literature are not in fact robust, reflecting instead highly selective reporting of a specification search that converges toward regions of the parameter space that contain 'significant' negative estimated interest elasticities. [Cooley and LeRoy 1981, p. 828].

Based on these results Cooley and LeRoy conclude that "we are unable to devise a statistical procedure that will identify a demand relation" [Cooley and LeRoy 1981, p. 828].

This, it is clear, is an unhappy state of affairs. Yet, given the recurring theme of this book it should come as no surprise that empirical demand estimation should run afoul of the underlying theory's inability adequately to specify interpretive rules. There is, it seems, no escape: Technical virtuosity -- "'data mining,' 'fishing,' 'grubbing,' 'number crunching'" to use Leamer's characterizations [Leamer 1983, p. 37] -- is unavailing. Moreover, appeal to the use of proxy variables serves to complicate the specification problem [Garrod and Roberts 1986]. Absent the ability to specify what is held constant, the underlying utility theory simply cannot specify which variables appropriately appear in a demand equation.

Perhaps unwittingly, in their paper entitled "What WILL Take the Con Out of Econometrics?" (emphasis mine) McAleer et al make the same point. In their view, EBA "is most emphatically NOT the medicine to cure an ailing patient" [McAleer, Pagan and Volker 1985, p. 305]. And to what do they attribute this failure? In their view [McAleer, Pagan and Volker 1985, p. 297]:

> ... the conclusions drawn from EBA are intimately bound up with the classification of variables as doubtful and free.

This, it seems to me, is just another way of saying that the underlying theory is unable systematically to specify "which variables are to be held constant when statistical tests are performed on the relation between the dependent variable and the independent variables of primary interest" [Cooley and LeRoy 1981, p. 825].

McAleer et al proffer their own "solution" to the model specification problem. Their "three-stage approach to modeling" involves the "selection and subsequent simplification of a general model and a rigorous evaluation of any preferred model" [McAleer, Pagan and Volker 1985, p. 306].

While this is fine in principle, McAleer et al give no guidance as to how the underlying theory is to be constructed [Cooley and LeRoy 1986]. When they apply their approach to a re-specification of the Cooley-LeRoy money demand equation they seek to determine "what type of model would have eventuated, GIVEN ONLY THE DATA SERIES USED BY COOLEY AND LeROY AS INPUT, if a proper modeling strategy had been followed" [McAleer, Pagan and Volker 1985, pp. 301-302] (emphasis mine). They conclude -- quite arbitrarily -- that "Under the restrictions on the universe of available variables, the main direction in which generalization of Cooley and LeRoy's model can take place is in the order of dynamics" [McAleer, Pagan and Volker 1985, p. 302].

Using the same variables as Cooley and LeRoy, but introducing a lag structure, McAleer et al insist that Cooley and LeRoy were wrong to conclude that the interest elasticity of money demand is zero:

> we can say that all variables in the estimated relationship (including BOTH interest rates) are highly significant, and to adopt [the Cooley- LeRoy]

hypothesis of a zero interest rate effect . . . would be totally inappropriate. [McAleer, Pagan and Volker 1985, p. 305].

This is very curious. McAleer et al contend that "extreme bounds are generated by the imposition of highly arbitrary, and generally unknown, restrictions between the parameters of a model" [McAleer, Pagan and Volker 1985, pp. 305-306]. I quite agree. Indeed, I agree with the corollary they deduce, namely that what is required is

> a general, adequate model from which the bounds may be derived, AND A CONSENSUS OVER WHICH VARIABLES ARE CRITICAL TO A RELATIONSHIP [McAleer, Pagan and Volker 1985, p. 306]. (emphasis mine)

Yet it is precisely their arbitrary decision to add a lag structure to the Cooley-LeRoy variables which renders the McAleer-Pagan-Volker analysis vacuous. In Professor Leamer's words [Leamer 1985, p. 308]:

> [McAleer et al] propose to deal with specification ambiguity by charting one possible ad hoc route through the thicket of possible models. Complicated ad hoc searches like the one they suggest have no support in statistical decision theory, and virtually none in classical sampling theory. What is to be made of a procedure that sets scores of parameters to zero if they are not 'statistically significant' at arbitrarily chosen levels of significance?

What, indeed, is to be made of ad hoc model specification? Perhaps Professor Leamer elsewhere answers his own rhetorical question. At one level a certain amount of "ad hocery" is to be expected, given the proclivity of applied researchers to invoke prior beliefs.[8] In Professor Leamer's words [Leamer 1983, p. 38]:

> In some areas of study, the list of variables is partially conventional, often based on whatever list the first researcher happened to select.

While Professor Leamer may or may not have had it in mind, I would add simply that this tendency is most in evidence in empirical demand estimation.[9] Small wonder! Empirical demand estimation is predicated on a theory of demand which is simply incapable of specifying which variables are appropriately held constant when statistical tests are performed. Lacking adequate interpretive rules empirical demand estimation suffers from the worst possible debility: Test results are not unambiguously interpretable -- the results of t and F tests and Durbin-Watson statistics notwithstanding.[10] Perhaps Professor Leamer says it best [Leamer 1983, p. 34]:

> If utility seems not to have been maximized, it is only that the econometrician has misspecified the utility function. The misspecification matrix M thus forms Imre Lakatos' 'protective belt' which protects certain hard core propositions from falsification.

WHAT THE BOSS WANTS TO HEAR

The "'protective belt' which protects certain hard core propositions from falsification" is wrapped most tightly around the corpus of utility and, <u>mutatis mutandis</u>, consumer theory. The juxtaposition of the classical rationality postulate and the assumption of stable preferences assures us that theories of consumer behavior can be neither confirmed nor disconfirmed. While the model builder cannot -- legitimately -- have the satisfaction of asserting that his model is confirmed, neither can the critic -- legitimately -- assert that it has been disconfirmed.

As in all things, this state of affairs bestows benefits and imposes costs. From the model builder's perspective the chief benefit must be that he can never unambiguously be shown to have been wrong. Bad predictions can always be attributed, <u>inter alia</u>, to "changes in taste." In effect, the only operative constraint confronting the model builder is the tolerance level of his models' users. Consistently bad predictions are, after all, likely to impose pecuniary and, or, non-pecuniary costs on the customer.[11] In any case, there is a sense in which the model builder is insulated from effective criticism: If he can never be sure why his predictions were wrong (right), neither can the customer.

The costs are, of course, non-trivial. Given the lack of interpretive rules the model builder can never know with precision which variables are appropriately included in his model. The current disarray in the money demand literature is, as we have seen, heuristic. This is surely an inefficient way to conduct scientific analysis. Worse still, when a model appears in some sense to have failed, the researcher cannot know why. If he does not know what was (was not) held constant during the period of analysis -- let alone what should have been held constant -- he has no hope of knowing how best to modify the model. If, as we argued in

Chapter I, the evolution of science is an iterative process, this does not bode well for economics.

Beyond this, the inability to specify adequate interpretive rules carries with it the potential for all manner of mischief. Arguably, the most troublesome implication of all of this is the latent potential always to "give the boss what he wants to hear."

As we have seen, prior beliefs about the effects of interest rate changes on money demand have heavily influenced the "specification searches" so prevalent in the money demand literature. Yet, if this is true of money demand, it is also true of the whole panoply of empirical demand analyses. Does anyone seriously doubt, for example, that a researcher would continue his "specification search" if he secured a positive own price elasticity coefficient, a negative interest elasticity coefficient on personal saving or a positive coefficient linking imports to the ratio of foreign to domestic prices?

The point here is not so much that the researcher has prior beliefs, though this is clearly both relevant and important. Rather, it is that the model builder's customer may have prior beliefs. Does it seem implausible, for example, that a defendant in antitrust litigation may have the prior belief that the Herfindahl-Hirschman Index number at issue is too narrowly construed; that there are substitutes for his product of which account has not been taken and that, therefore, cross price elasticities linking demand for his product(s) to the prices of other products MUST BE positive? And is it possible that, given the lack of adequate interpretive rules, a sufficiently exhaustive "specification search" just might turn up one or more positive cross price elasticity coefficients?

If all of this is true at the microeconomic level it is most assuredly true at the macroeconomic policy level. Presumably without realizing it, Members of Congress have been arguing for years about the sign of the coefficient linking uncompensated changes in marginal tax rates to work effort.[12] Broadly speaking, Members opposed to supply-side economics have adopted the view that uncompensated reductions in marginal tax rates will result in less rather than more work effort.[13] On the other hand, Members sympathetic to supply-side economics have adopted the prior belief that uncompensated cuts in marginal tax rates "must" result in more rather than less work effort.[14]

The effect on labor supply of an uncompensated change in marginal tax rates is not a matter which can be settled a priori. It is an empirical question.[15] Yet the resolution of this issue depends ultimately upon the specification of a labor supply function. This, in turn, is predicated on a familiar understanding of the labor supplier-consumer's decision environment: He is rational in the classical sense, his preference structure is stable, and he seeks to maximize utility subject to an appropriately defined constraint.

Given the inability of such models to specify adequate interpretive rules, is it any wonder that model builders employed by politicians on both sides of the issue should engage in "specification searches"? Does it come as a surprise that the results of these searches seem unerringly to turn up results consistent with the customers' (model builders'?) prior beliefs? I think not.

PRIOR BELIEFS, VALUE JUDGMENTS AND PUBLIC POLICY

If this line of reasoning suggests that demand models can be made to yield theoretical and empirical results consistent with prior beliefs it also suggests that they cannot impart an "objective" or "positive" character to public policy decisions. Given the ambiguity of test results economic policy decisions based upon such models must be partially driven by sociopolitical value judgments. This is true in the conventional sense that public policy goals are normative. But it is also true that the choice of policy instruments must, ultimately, be value-loaded. Lacking adequate interpretive rules, the researcher cannot unambiguously interpret test results. Because he cannot "prove" the superiority of one policy menu over another, it follows that the researcher's recommendations will, necessarily, reflect his prior beliefs. These prior beliefs, in turn, must have been at least partially shaped by the researcher's value system. Professor Nabers' elegant statement has basic relevance [Nabers 1966, p. 73]:

> . . . the development of economics involves à process which makes value judgments inevitable. The selection of the problems to be analyzed presumes an ability to discriminate between the important and the unimportant. The acceptance of procedural method involves a similar type of value judgment. It is necessary to determine standards of factual relevance in the absence of the unlikely possibility that all facts may be considered. From a given theoretical analysis the content of the results may be presented differently, even though each possible presentation is in accordance with the accepted rules of logic. THE SELECTION OF THE CONTENTS OF THE CONCLUSIONS IS DEPENDENT ULTIMATELY

UPON THE VALUES OF THE THEORIST. FINALLY, OF COURSE, THE ASSESSMENT OF THE IMPORTANCE OR SIGNIFICANCE OF THE RESULTS IS BASED UPON A KIND OF DISCRIMINATION WHICH HAS ITS ROOTS IN THE VALUE POSITION OF THE THEORIST. (emphasis mine)

Nabers' remarks are clearly intended to apply to the development of economics generally. I do not disagree. I would add simply that it is consumer theory which is, at every stage of analysis, most amenable to the injection of sociopolitical value judgments. Technical virtuosity cannot compensate for the lack of adequate empirical interpretation any more than invocations of statistical significance can reduce the ambiguity of test results. Policy recommendations based on ambiguous test results must, inevitably, reflect the researcher's prior beliefs and the value judgments on which they are anchored.

Ambiguity of test results is not, however, the only means by which value judgments inhere in economic analysis. Value judgments are, in fact, endemic to economics and the other sciences. As Professor McCloskey has observed [McCloskey 1983, p. 488]:

Modernism promises knowledge free from doubt, metaphysics, and personal conviction; what it delivers merely renames as Scientific Method the scientist's metaphysics, moral and personal convictions.[16]

It is indisputable that, in developing theories, in testing hypotheses and in interpreting results, economists draw on "metaphor, case study, upbringing, authority, introspection, simplicity, symmetry, fashion, theology and politics" [McCloskey 1983, p. 511].[17] Yet all of these factors are conventionally regarded as falling under the rubric of the "context of discovery." Presumably, the "context of discovery" -- the way economists [and scientists generally] develop hypotheses -- is somehow different from the "context of justification" or empirical confirmation [McCloskey 1983, p. 511]. Whether or not this distinction can legitimately be made is not the point. The point is that the process of model building and hypothesis testing is inexorably bound up with value judgments.[18] This suggests that there is a sense in which all economic inquiry is subject to what is derisively referred to as "ad hocery." The solution to ad hoc model specification is, of course, appeal to "a theory"; a construct which, inter alia, points unambiguously to the inclusion (exclusion) of particular variables in a regression equation. In the case of standard demand theory, this is a practical impossibility. The presence of an unidentified exogenous variable -- the consumer's tastes and preferences -- militates against this. Beyond this, "'having a theory' is not so open and shut as it might seem," precisely because the theory one "has" at a cross section of time is partly dependent upon "what reasoning is prestigious at the moment" [McCloskey 1983, p. 502].[19]

The corollary of all of this is not that economists should stop building and testing models of consumer behavior. It is that they should seek systematically to provide adequate interpretive rules. If this requires that economists abandon classical rationality and embrace "something like" procedural rationality, this seems to me to be a price worth paying. Just as important, because they play so crucial a role both in model specification and in the interpretation of test results, we would be well-advised to make our implicit value judgments explicit.[20] Having done so, we can fairly say to our model-consuming public: "<u>Caveat emptor</u>."

NOTES

[1]See Chapter 4, above, esp. pp. 73-76. For an application of this approach, see [Anderson, Jones and Nesmith 1997b, esp. pp. 37-40]. See also [Anderson, Jones and Nesmith 1997a and 1997b].

[2]See Chapter 4 above, especially pp. 75-76.

[3]See also [Judd and Scadding 1982, pp. 1014-1015]. For more on the appropriate specification of the money demand equation see [Roley 1985].

[4]As Cooley and LeRoy have noted [Cooley and LeRoy 1981, p. 830]:

in the money demand literature the practice is to conduct hundreds of regressions in batches of several dozen regressions each. At each stage the regressions with wrong signs are discarded, and those most consistent with the researcher's preferences are interpreted and used as the basis for the next series of regressions.

The result has been a marked propensity to report positive income (wealth) elasticity coefficients, negative interest rate elasticities, and unit price level elasticities of money demand. See, for example [Laidler 1980, p. 221]. These results are, of course, consistent with what might appropriately be characterized as "prior beliefs."

[5]See, for example [Leamer 1978, 1983 and 1985 and McAleer, Pagan and Volker 1985]. See also [Mayer 1993, p. 143].

[6]Professor Leamer stresses both the need "to focus on the problem for which the 'extreme bounds analysis' is intended, namely the choice of variables" [Leamer 1985, p. 312], and the fact that "we ought to be demanding much more complete and more honest reporting of the fragility of claimed inferences" [Leamer 1983, p. 38]. See also [Cooley and LeRoy 1986] and [Mayer 1993, pp. 140-142].

[7]For an additional example of EBA "in action" see [Polasek 1984].

[8]Professor Vernon Smith emphasizes the role of prior beliefs in the "specification search" process [Smith 1982, p. 929]:

Based on introspection, some casual observations of some process, and a contextual interpretation of the self-interest postulate, a model is specified and then 'tested' by estimation using the only body of field data that exists. The results turn out to be ambiguous or call for 'improvements' (some coefficients - for example, income - have the 'wrong' sign or are embarrassingly close to zero), and now one is tempted to modify the model in ways suggested by these results to improve the fit with 'reasonable expectations.'

In Professor Smith's view, this scenario puts "the econometric methodology . . . on particularly thin ice . . ." [Smith 1982, p. 929] precisely because [Smith 1982, p. 929, fn. 8]:

. . . the whole process becomes an exercise in fitting a particular belief system to field data by manipulating model specification and perhaps estimation methods.

Finally, Professor Smith emphasizes that "There is nothing to prevent exactly the same procedure from being applied to experimental data" [Smith 1982, p. 929, fn. 8].

[9]While prior beliefs and subjective knowledge play a central role in the empirical analysis of demand, the same can be said of applied economics generally. In his review of Professor Leamer's 1978 book, Christopher Sims makes precisely this point [Sims 1979, p. 567]:

The sooner Leamer's cogent writings can lead us ... to recognize that all applied work is shot through with applications of uncertain, subjective knowledge, and to make the role of such knowledge more explicit and more effective, the better.

See also [McCloskey 1983] and pp. 176-178.

[10]For more on empirical testing, see [Mayer 1993, esp. Chapter 10].

[11]This assumes, of course, that the customer remembers the predictions, and that he will have taken actions predicated upon them.

[12]"Uncompensated" in the sense of incorporating both an income and a substitution effect.

[13]Their logic suggests that a cut in marginal tax rates would generate both a substitution and an income effect. The pure substitution effect would, because of the increase in the after-tax price of leisure, result in more work effort. The pure income effect would, in their view, result in less work effort, because the utility maximizing labor supplier could earn the same after tax income while working less. On this view, the income effect would overwhelm the substitution effect, so that a cut in marginal tax rates would result in less rather than more work effort.

[14]These Members would argue that the substitution and income effects to which the marginal tax rate reduction gives rise would "work in the same direction."

[15]For a collection of papers on this general issue, see [Aaron and Pechman 1981]. See also [Feldstein 1995].

[16]"Modernism" is "an amalgam of logical positivism, behaviorism, operationalism, and the hypothetico-deductive model of science" [McCloskey 1983, p. 484]. See Chapter I for a discussion of instrumentalism or logical positivism.

[17]The fact that economists generally believe more than their "evidence of a suitably modernist and objective sort implies" is evidence of this [McCloskey 1983, p. 493].

[18]See [McCloskey 1983, pp. 482 and 493]. See also Chapter VIII, above.

[19]Professor McCloskey cites, for example, the use of accumulated output in equations intended to account for changes in productivity. Prior to 1962 the use of such a proxy for experience or learning would have exposed the model builder to the charge of "ad hocery." Arrow's 1962 essay on "Learning by Doing" made the procedure acceptable [McCloskey 1983, p. 502]. Other examples abound: The use of accumulated output as a proxy for "demonstration effects" in the theory of demand; the use of the "degree of urbanness" as a proxy for the stigma discount rate associated with receipt of transfer payments, etc.

[20]This logic extends to economists' use of language. As Professor McCloskey has observed, the metaphors of economics convey both the authority of Science and the claim of Science to ethical neutrality. In his view, even the phrase "marginal productivity" "encapsulates a most powerful piece of social description." He suggests that the phrase [McCloskey 1983, p. 508]:

... brings with it an air of having solved the moral problem of distribution .. . It is irritating that it carries this message, because it may be far from the purpose of the economist who uses it to show approval for the distribution arising from competition.

Granting this, McCloskey admonishes us that "It is better . . . to admit that metaphors in economics can contain such a political message than to use the jargon innocent of its potential" [McCloskey 1983, p. 508]. See also [Sims 1979, p. 567]. For more on the "rhetoric of economics" see [Mäki 1988] and [McCloskey 1988].

Bibliography

Aaron, H. J. and Pechman, J. A. (eds.). 1981. How Taxes Affect Economic Behavior. Washington, DC: The Brookings Institution.

Aaron, H. J. 1994. "Public Policy, Values, and Consciousness." Journal of Economic Perspectives, Vol. VIII (Spring).

Abelson, P. W. and Markandya, A. 1985. "The Interpretation of Capitalized Hedonic Prices in a Dynamic Environment." Journal of Environmental Economics and Management, Vol. XII (September).

Agarwal, M. K. and Ratchford, B. T. 1980. "Estimating Demand Functions for Product Characteristics: The Use of Automobiles." Journal of Consumer Research, Vol. VII (December).

Akerloff, G. A. and Dickens, W. T. 1982. "The Economic Consequences of Cognitive Dissonance." American Economic Review, Vol. LXXII (June).

Akerloff, G. A. and Yellen, J. L. 1985. "Can Small Deviations from Rationality Make Significant Differences to Economic Equilibria?" American Economic Review, Vol. LXXV (September).

Alcaly, R .E. and Klevorick, A. K. 1970. "Judging Quality by Price, Snob Appeal, and the New Consumer Theory." Zeitschrift für Nationalökonomie, Vol. XXX.

Alchian, A. A., Buchanan, J. M., Demsetz, H., Leijonhufvud, A., Lott, Jr., J. R., Sharpe, W. F. and Topel, R. H. 1996. "In Celebration of Armen Alchian's 80th Birthday: Living and Breathing Economics." Economic Inquiry , Vol. XXXIV (July).

Alchian, A. A. and Woodward, S. L. 1988. "The Firm is Dead: Long Live the Firm: A Review of Oliver E. Williamson's The Economic Institutions of Capitalism." Journal of Economic Literature, Vol. XXVI (March).

Alhadeff, D. A. 1982. Microeconomics and Human Behavior: Toward a New Synthesis of Economics and Psychology. Berkeley and London: University of California Press.

Anderson, J. E. 1985. "On Testing the Convexity of Hedonic Price Functions." Journal of Urban Economics, Vol. XVIII (November).

Anderson, R. G., Jones, B. E. and Nesmith, T. D. 1997a. "Introduction to the St. Louis Monetary Services Index Project." Federal Reserve Bank of St. Louis Review, Vol. LXXIX, January/February.

Anderson, R. G., Jones, B. E. and Nesmith, T. D. 1997b. "Monetary Aggregation Theory and Statistical Index Numbers." Federal Reserve Bank of St. Louis Review, Vol. LXXIX, January/February.

Anderson, R. G., Jones, B. E. and Nesmith, T. D. 1997c. "Building New Monetary Services Indexes: Concepts, Data and Methods." Federal Reserve Bank of St. Louis Review, Vol. LXXIX, January/February.

Atkinson, S. E. and Crocker, T. D. 1987. "A Bayesian Approach to Assessing the Robustness of Hedonic Property Value Studies." Journal of Applied Econometrics Vol. II (January).

Atkinson, S. E. and Halvorsen, R. 1984. "A New Hedonic Technique for Estimating Attribute Demand: An Application to the Demand for Automobile Fuel Efficiency." Review of Economics and Statistics, Vol. LXVI (August).

Arrow, K. J. 1951. Social Choice and Individual Values. New Haven and London: Yale University Press.

Asher, C. C. 1992. "Hedonic Analysis of Reliability and Safety for New Automobiles." Journal of Consumer Affairs, Vol. XXVI (Winter).

Bajic, V. 1984. "Housing-Market Segmentation and Demand for Housing Attributes: Some Empirical Findings." American Real Estate and Urban Economics Association Journal, Vol. XIII (Spring).

Bandyopadhyay, T. 1988. "Revealed Preference Theory, Ordering and the Axiom of Sequential Path Independence." Review of Economic Studies, Vol. LV (April).

Banks, J. S., Plott, R. and Porter, D. P. 1988. "An Experimental Analysis of Unanimity in Public Goods Provision Mechanisms." Review of Economic Studies, Vol. LV (April).

Barmish, B. R. 1984. "A New Approach to the Incorporation of Attributes into Consumer Theory." Journal of Economic Theory, Vol. XXXII (February).

Barnett, C. J. 1985. "An Application of the Hedonic Price Model to the Perth Residential Land Model." Economic Record, Vol. LXI (March).

Barnett, W. A., Fisher, D. and Serletis, A. 1992. "Consumer Theory and the Demand for Money." Journal of Economic Literature, Vol. XXX (December).

Baron, J. N. and Hannan, M. T. 1994. "The Impact of Economics on Contemporary Sociology." Journal of Economic Literature, Vol. XXXII (September).

Bartik, T. J. 1987. "Estimating Hedonic Demand Parameters with Single Market Data: The Problems Caused by Unobserved Tastes." Review of Economics and Statistics, Vol. LXIX (February).

Bartik, T. J. 1988. "Measuring the Benefits of Amenity Improvements in Hedonic Price Models." Land Economics, Vol. LXIV (May).

Basmann, R. L. 1956. "A Theory of Demand with Variable Consumer Preferences." Econometrica, Vol. XXIV (January).

Basmann, R. L., Molina, D. J. and Slottje, D. J. 1987. "Price-Dependent Preferences and the Fechner-Thurstone Direct Utility Function: An Exposition." Journal of Institutional and Theoretical Economics, Vol. CXLIII (December).

Basu, K. 1984. "Fuzzy Revealed Preference Theory." Journal of Economic Theory, Vol. XXXII (April).

Battalio, R. C., Kagel, J. H. and MacDonald, D. N. 1985. "Animals' Choices over Uncertain Outcomes: Some Initial Experimental Results." American Economic Review, Vol. LXXV (September).

Battalio, R. C., Kagel, J. H., and Phillips, O. R. 1986. "Optimal Prices and Animal Consumers in Congested Markets." Economic Inquiry, Vol. XXIV (April).

Baum, S. R. 1985. "Moral Philosophy, Cognitive Psychology and Economic Theory." Eastern Economic Journal, Vol. XI (October-December).

Becker, G. S. 1976a. "Altruism, Egoism, and Genetic Fitness: Economics and Sociobiology." Journal of Economic Literature, Vol. XIV (September).

Becker, G. S. 1976b. The Economic Approach to Human Behavior. Chicago: The University of Chicago Press.

Becker, G. S. 1962. "Irrational Behavior and Economic Theory." Journal of Political Economy, Vol. LXX (February).

Becker, G. S. 1993. "Nobel Lecture: The Economic Way of Looking at Behavior." Journal of Political Economy, Vol. CI (June).

Becker, G. S. 1965. "A Theory of the Allocation of Time." Economic Journal, Vol. LXXV (September).

Ben-Ner, A. 1987. "Preferences in a Communal Economic System" Economica, Vol. LIV (May)

Ben-Porath, Y. 1982. "Economics and the Family - Match or Mismatch? A Review of Becker's Treatise on the Family." Journal of Economic Literature, Vol. XX (March).

Benson, B. L. and Feinberg, R. M. 1988. "An Experimental Investigation of Equilibria Impacts of Information." Southern Economic Journal, Vol. LIV (January).

Berg, J. E., et al. 1986. "Controlling Preferences for Lotteries on Units of Experimental Exchange." Quarterly Journal of Economics, Vol. CI (May).

Biehal, G. and Chakravarti, D. 1986. "Consumer's Use of Memory and External Information in Choice: Macro and Micro Perspectives." Journal of Consumer Research, Vol. XII (March).

Binmore, K. 1987. "Experimental Economics." European Economic Review, Vol. XXXI (February/March).

Bitros, G. C. And Panas, E. E. 1990. "Demand for Product Attributes: The Case of Automobiles in Greece." International Journal of Transport Economics, Vol. XVII (October).

Bivens, G. E. and Volker, C. B. 1986. "A Value-Added Approach to Household Production: The Special Case of Meal Preparation." Journal of Consumer Research, Vol. XIII (September).

Blair, E. and Burton, S. 1987. "Cognitive Processes Used by Survey Respondents to Answer Behavioral Frequency Questions." Journal of Consumer Research, Vol. XIV (September).

Blundell, R. and Walker, I. 1984. "A Household Production Specification of Demographic Variables in Demand Analysis." Economic Journal, Vol. XCIV, 1984 Supplement.

Boland, L. A. 1979. "A Critique of Friedman's Critics." Journal of Economic Literature, Vol. XVII (June).

Boland, L. A. 1981. "On the Futility of Criticizing the Neoclassical Maximization Hypothesis." American Economic Review, Vol. LXXI (December).

Bookstaber, R. and Langsam, J. 1985. "Predictable Behavior: Comment." American Economic Review, Vol. LXXV (June).

Borch, K. 1969. The Economics of Uncertainty. Princeton: Princeton University Press.

Bös, D. 1986. "On Supporting the Maximization Postulate." Journal of Behavioral Economics, Vol. XV (Winter).

Bös, D. 1987. "On Supporting the Maximization Postulate." Journal of Behavioral Economics, Vol. XVI (Summer).

Bowles, S. and Gintis, H. 1993. "The Revenge of Homo Economicus." Journal of Economic Perspectives, Vol. VII (Winter).

Braguinsky, S. 1996. "Corruption and Schumpeterian Growth in Different Economic Environments." Contemporary Economic Policy, Vol. XXIV (July).

Brookshire, D. S., Coursey, D. L. And Schulze, W. D. 1987. "The External Validity of Experimental Techniques: Analysis of Demand Behavior." Economic Inquiry, Vol. XXV (April).

Brucks, M. and Schurr, P. H. 1990. "The Effects of Bargainable Attributes and Attribute Range Knowledge on Consumer Choice Processes." Journal of Consumer Research, Vol. XVI (March).

Brumat, C. M. and Tomasini, L. M. 1979. "A Probabilistic Extension of Lancaster's Approach to Consumer Theory." Zeitschrift für Nationalökonomie, Vol. XXXIX (3-4).

Buchanan, J. M. 1994a. "Choosing What to Choose." Journal of Institutional and Theoretical Economics, Vol. CL (March).

Buchanan, J. M. 1987. "The Constitution of Economic Policy." American Economic Review, Vol. LXXVII (June).

Buchanan, J. M. 1991. The Economics and the Ethics of Constitutional Order. Ann Arbor: The University of Michigan Press.

Buchanan, J. M. 1994b. Ethics and Economic Progress. Norman and London: University of Oklahoma Press.

Burton, P. S. 1994. "Support for a Characteristics Approach: Evidence from the Market for Insecticides." Canadian Journal of Economics, Vol. XXVII (February).

Bush, R., and Mostelle, F. 1955. Stochastic Models for Learning. New York: Wiley.

Bushaw, D. W. and Clower, R. W. 1957. Introduction to Mathematical Economics. Homewood, IL: Richard D. Irwin.

Butler, D. J. and Hey, J. D. 1987. "Experimental Economics: An Introduction." Empirical Economics, Vol. XII, No. 2.

Caldwell, B. J. 1991. "Clarifying Popper." Journal of Economic Literature, Vol. XXIX (March).

Caldwell, B. J. 1983. "The Neoclassical Maximization Hypothesis: Comment." American Economic Review, Vol. LXXIII (September).

Capps, O., Jr., Tedford, J. R. and Havlicek, J., Jr. 1985. "Household Demand for Convenience and Non-convenience Foods." American Journal of Agricultural Economics. Vol. LXXVII (November).

Carter, M. R. 1985. "A Wisconsin Institutionalist Perspective on Microeconomic Theory of Institutions: The Insufficiency of Pareto Efficiency." Journal of Economic Issues, Vol. XIX (September).

Caves, R. E. and Williamson, P. J. 1985. "What is Product Differentiation, Really?" Journal of Industrial Economics, Vol. XXXIV (December).

Chalfant, J. A. and Alston, J. M. 1988. "Accounting for Changes in Taste." Journal of Political Economy, Vol. XCVI (April).

Chase, W. G. and Simon, H.A. 1973. "Skill in Chess." American Scientist, Vol. LXI (July-August).

Chenault, L. A. and Flueckiger, G. E. 1983. "An Information Theoretic Model of Bounded Rationality." Mathematical Social Sciences, Vol. VI (November).

Chern, W. S., Lochman, E. T. and Yen, S. T. 1995. "Information, Health Risk Beliefs, and the Demand for Fats and Oils." Review of Economics and Statistics, Vol. LXXVII (August).

Chernichovsky, D. and Zmora, I. 1986. "A Hedonic Prices Approach to Hospitalization Costs: The Case of Israel." Journal of Health Economics, Vol. V (June).

Cheung, S. N. S. 1996. " A Simplistic General Equilibrium Theory of Corruption." Contemporary Economic Policy, Vol. XIV (July).

Clarkson, G. P. E. 1962. Portfolio Selection: A Simulation of Trust Investment. Englewood Cliffs: Prentice-Hall.

Clarkson, G. P. E. 1963. The Theory of Consumer Demand: A Critical Appraisal. Englewood Cliffs: Prentice-Hall.

Cohen, M. D. and Axelrod, R. 1984. "Coping with Complexity: The Adaptive Value of Changing Utility." American Economic Review, Vol. LXXIV (March).

Conlisk, J. 1996. "Why Bounded Rationality?" Journal of Economic Literature, Vol. XXXIV (June).

Cooley, T. F. and LeRoy, S. F. 1981. "Identification and Estimation of Money Demand." American Economic Review, Vol. LXXI (December).

Cooley, T. F. and LeRoy, S. F. 1986. "What will Take the Con Out of Econometrics? A Reply." American Economic Review, Vol. LXXVI (June).

Corman, H. 1986. "The Demand for Education for Home Production." Economic Inquiry, Vol. XXIV (April).

Cosmides, L. and Tooby, J. 1994. "Better than Rational: Evolutionary Psychology and the Invisible Hand." American Economic Association Papers and Proceedings, Vol. LXXXIV (May).

Coursey, D. L. and Schulze, W. D. 1986. "The Application of Laboratory Experimental Economics to the Contingent Valuation of Public Goods." Public Choice, Vol. XLIX, No. 1.

Cox, J. C. and Epstein, S. 1989. "Preference Reversals Without the Independence Axiom." American Economic Review, Vol. LXXIX (June).

Crain, W. M., Shugart, W. F. II and Tollison, R. D. 1984. "The Convergence of Satisficing to Marginalism: An Empirical Test." Journal of Economic Behavior and Organization, Vol. V (September-December).

Cropper, M. L. et al. 1993. "Valuing Product Attributes Using Single Market Data: A Comparison of Hedonic and Discrete Choice Approaches." Review of Economics and Statistics, Vol. LXXV (May).

Custer, W. S. 1986. "Hospital Attributes and Physician Prices." Southern Economic Journal, Vol. LII (April).

Davidson, D., and Suppes, P. 1957. Decision Making: An Experimental Approach. Stanford: Stanford University Press.

DeBoer, L. 1985. "Resident Age and Housing Search: Evidence From Hedonic Residuals." Urban Studies, Vol. XXII (October).

DeBorger, B. 1986. "Household Attributes and the Demand for Housing Characteristics." Tidschrift Vor Economie en Management, Vol. XXXI, No. 2.

DeJong, D. V., Forsythe, R. and Lundholm, R. J. 1985. "Ripoffs, Lemons, and Reputation Formation in Agency Relationships: A Laboratory Market Study." Journal of Finance, Vol. III (July).

Debreu, G. 1959. Theory of Value. New York: Wiley.

Demsetz, H. 1997. " The Primacy of Economics: An Explanation of the Comparative Success of Economics in Social Science." Economic Inquiry, Vol. XXXV (January).

DePalma, A., Myers, G. M. and Papageorgiou, Y. Y. 1994. "Rational Choice Under an Imperfect Ability to Choose." American Economic Review, Vol. LXXXIV (June).

DeVany, A. 1996. "Information, Chance, and Evolution: Alchian and the Economics of Self-Organization." Economic Inquiry, Vol. XXXIV (July).

Dow, G. K. 1987. "The Function of Authority in Transaction Cost Economics." Journal of Economic Behavior and Organization, Vol. VIII (March).

Duesenberry, J. S. 1952. Income, Saving and the Theory of Consumer Behavior. Cambridge: Harvard University Press.

Eastwood, D. B., Brooker, J. R. and Terry, D. E. 1986. "Household Nutrient Demand: Use of Characteristics Theory and a Common Attribute Model." Southern Journal of Agricultural Economics, Vol. XIX (December).

Edmonds, R. G., Jr. 1985. "Some Evidence on the Intertemporal Stability of Hedonic Price Functions." Land Economics, Vol. LXI (November).

Edwards, W. 1954. "The Theory of Decision Making." Psychological Bulletin, Vol. LI (September).

Egidi, M. and Marris, R. (eds.) 1992. Economics, Bounded Rationality and the Cognitive Revolution. Aldershot, England: Edward Elgar Publishing Limited.

Ekelund, R. B., Furubotn, E.G., and Gramm, W. P. 1972. The Evolution of Modern Demand Theory. Lexington, MA: D.C. Heath and Company.

Elster, J. 1989. "Social Norms and Economic Theory." Journal of Economic Perspectives, Vol. III (Fall).

Encarnacion, J. Jr. 1990. "Consumer Choice of Quality." Economica, Vol. LVII (February).

Etzioni, A. 1987. "On Thoughtless Rationality (Rules-of-Thumb)." Kyklos, Vol. XL, No. 4.

Fallis, G. and Smith, L. B. 1985. "Price Effects of Rent Control on Controlled and Uncontrolled Rental Housing in Toronto: A Hedonic Index Approach." Canadian Journal of Economics, Vol. XVIII (August).

Feenstra, R. C. 1995. "Exact Hedonic Price Indexes." Review of Economics and Statistics, Vol. LXXVII (November).

Feldstein, M. 1995. "Behavorial Responses to Tax Rates: Evidence from the Tax Reform Act of 1986." American Economic Association Papers and Proceedings, Vol. LXXXV (May).

Ferguson, C. E. 1972. Microeconomic Theory. 3rd edition. Homewood, IL: Richard D. Irwin, Inc.

Fisher, I. 1927. "A Statistical Method for Measuring 'Marginal Utility' and Testing the Justice of a Progressive Income Tax." In Economic Essays in Honor of John Bates Clark. New Haven: Yale University Press.

Fleming, M. C. and Nellis, J. G. 1985. "The Application of Hedonic Indexing Methods: A Study of House Prices in the United Kingdom." Statistical Journal, Vol. III (September).

Follain, J. R. and Jimenez, E. 1985. "The Demand for Housing Characteristics in Developing Countries." Urban Studies, Vol. XXII (October).

Frank, R. H. 1987. "If Homo Economicus Could Choose His Own Utility Function, Would He Want One With a Conscience?" American Economic Review, Vol. LXXVII (September).

Frank, R. H. 1992. "Melding Sociology and Economics: James Coleman's Foundations of Social Theory." Journal of Economic Literature, Vol. XXX (March).

Frank, R. H. 1996. "The Political Economy of Preference Falsification: Timur Kuran's Private Truths, Public Lies." Journal of Economic Literature, Vol. XXXIV (March).

Frank, R. H., Gilovich, T. D. and Regan, D. T. 1996. "Do Economists Make Bad Citizens?" Journal of Economic Perspectives, Vol. X (Winter).

Friedman, D. 1985. "Experimental Economics: Comment." American Economic Review, Vol. LXXV (March).

Friedman, M. 1949. "The Marshallian Demand Curve." Journal of Political Economy. Vol. LVII (December).

Friedman, M. 1953. "The Methodology of Positive Economics." In Essays in Positive Economics. Chicago: University of Chicago Press.

Friedman, M. and Savage, L. J. 1948. "The Utility Analysis of Choices Involving Risk." Journal of Political Economy. Vol. LVI (August).

Fuchs-Seliger, S. 1980. "On the Continuity of Utility Functions in the Theory of Revealed Preference." International Economic Review, Vol. XXI (October).

Furubotn, E. G. 1971. "Economic Organization and Welfare Distribution." Swedish Journal of Economics, Vol. IV.

Furubotn, E. G. 1994. Future Development of the New Institutional Economics: Extension of the Neoclassical Model or New Construct? Jena: Max-Planck Institute for Research into Economic Systems.

Furubotn, E. G. 1991. "General Equilibrium Models, Transaction Costs, and the Concept of Efficient Allocation in a Capitalist Economy." Journal of Institutional and Theoretical Economics, Vol. XLVII (December).

Furubotn, E. G. 1997. "The Old and the New Institutionalism in Economics." In Economics and Ethics in the Historical School of Economics: Achievements and Present Relevance. Springer Verlag.

Furubotn, E. G. 1967. "Observed Consumption Patterns and the Utility Function." Metroeconomica, Vol. XIX (January-April).

Furubotn, E. G. 1963. "On Some Applications of the Utility Tree." Southern Economic Journal. Vol. XXX (October).

Furubotn, E. G. 1969. "Quality Control, Expected Utility, and Product Equilibrium." Western Economic Journal, Vol. VII (March).

Furubotn, E. G. 1974. "The Quasi-Concave Utility Function and the Number of Distinct Commodities Chosen at Equilibrium." Weltwirtschaftliches Archiv, Vol. CX, Number 2.

Furubotn, E. G. and Pejovich, S. 1974. The Economics of Property Rights. Cambridge, Mass.: Ballinger Publishing Company.

Furubotn, E. G. and Richter, R. 1991. "The New Institutional Economics: An Assessment." In The New Institutional Economics. Tübingen: J. C. B. Mohr (Paul Siebeck).

Furubotn, E. G. and Richter, R. 1994. "The New Institutional Economics: Bounded Rationality and the Analysis of State and Society." Journal of Institutional and Theoretical Economics, Vol. CL (March).

Furubotn, E. G. and Pejovich, S. 1972. "Property Rights and Economic Theory: A Survey of Recent Literature." Journal of Economic Literature, Vol. X (December).

Gabriel, S. A. 1987. "Economic Effects of Racial Integration: An Analysis of Hedonic Housing Prices and the Willingness to Pay." American Real Estate and Urban Economics Association Journal, Vol. XV (Fall).

Garrison, R. W. 1985. "Predictable Behavior: Comment." American Economic Review, Vol. LXXV (June).

Garrod, P. V. and Roberts, R. K. 1986. "Prices as Proxies for Prices." American Journal of Agricultural Economics, Vol. LXVIII (August).

Georgescu-Roegen, N. 1970. "The Economics of Production." American Economic Association Papers and Proceedings, Vol. LX (May).

Giannias, D. A. 1990. "Quantity and Quality Variations in a Class of Hedonic Equilibrium Models." Economic Notes.

Gilad, B., Kaish, S. and Loeb, P. D. 1987. "Cognitive Dissonance and Utility Maximization: General Framework." Journal of Economic Behavior and Organization, Vol. VIII (March).

Goldfeld, S. F. 1976. "The Case of the Missing Money." Brookings Papers on Economic Activity, 3, pp. 683-730.

Goodman, A. C. 1983. "Willingness to Pay for Car Efficiency: A Hedonic Price Approach." Journal of Transport Economics and Policy, Vol. XVII (September).

Gorman, W. M. 1957. "Convex Indifference Curves and Diminishing Marginal Utility." Journal of Political Economy, Vol. LXVI (February).

Graaff, J. De V. 1967. Theoretical Welfare Economics. Cambridge: Cambridge University Press.

Graham, J. W. and Green, C. A. 1984. "Estimating the Parameters of a Household Production Function with Joint Products." Review of Economics and Statistics, Vol. LXVI (May).

Graves, P. E. and Knapp. T. A. 1985. "Hedonic Analysis in a Spatial Context: Theoretical Problems in Valuing Location-Specific Amenities." Economic Record, Vol. LXI (December).

Green, H. A. J. 1964. Aggregation in Economic Analysis. Princeton: Princeton University Press.

Grether, D. M., Schwartz, A. and Wilde, L. L. 1988. "Uncertainty and Shopping Behavior; An Experimental Analysis." Review of Economic Studies, Vol. LV (April).

Greville, T. N. E. 1959. "The Pseudoinverse of a Rectangular or Singular Matrix and Its Application to the Solution of Systems of Linear Equations." SIAM Review, Vol. I (January).

Grunert, K. G. 1989. "Attributes, Attribute Values and Their Characteristics: A Unifying Approach and an Example Involving a Complex Household Investment." Journal of Economics and Psychology, Vol. X (June).

Grunewald, O., Faulds, D. J. and McNulty, M. S. 1993. "Evidence on Agglomeration in Quality Space - Revisited." Journal of Industrial Economics, Vol. XL (June).

Guttman, J. M. 1986. "Matching Behavior and Collective Action: Some Experimental Evidence." Journal of Economic Behavior and Organization, Vol. VII (June).

Hadar, J. 1965. "A Note on Stock-Flow Models of Consumer Behavior." Quarterly Journal of Economics, Vol. LXXIX (May).

Hafer, R. W. and Hein, S. E. 1979. "Evidence on the Temporal Stability of the Demand for Money Relationship in the United States." Federal Reserve Bank of St. Louis Review, Vol. LXI (December).

Haltiwanger, J. C. and Waldman, M. 1985. "Rational Expectations and the Limits of Rationality: An Analysis of Heterogeneity." American Economic Review, Vol. LXXV (June).

Hannan, M. T. 1982. "Families, Markets, and Social Structures: An Essay on Becker's A Treatise on the Family." Journal of Economic Literature, Vol. XX (March).

Harrison, G. W. and McKee, M. 1985. "Experimental Evaluation of the Coase Theorem," Journal of Law and Economics, Vol. XXVIII (October).

Hausman, D. M. and McPherson, M. S. 1993. "Taking Ethics Seriously: Economics and Contemporary Moral Philosophy." Journal of Economic Literature, Vol. XXXI (June).

Heiner, R. A. 1985a. "Experimental Economics: Comment." American Economic Review, Vol. LXXV (March).

Heiner, R. A. 1988. "Imperfect Decisions in Organizations: Toward a Theory of Internal Structure." Journal of Economic Behavior and Organization, Vol. IX (January).

Heiner, R. A. 1983. "The Origin of Predictable Behavior." American Economic Review, Vol. LXXIII (September).

Heiner, R. A. 1985b. "Origin of Predictable Behavior: Further Modeling and Applications." American Economic Association Papers and Proceedings, Vol. LXXV (May).

Heiner, R. A. 1985c. "Predictable Behavior: Reply." American Economic Review, Vol. LXXV (June).

Henderson, J. E. and Quandt, R. E. 1971. Microeconomic Theory: A Mathematical Approach. 2nd edition. New York: McGraw-Hill Book Company.

Hendler, R. 1975. "Lancaster's New Approach to Consumer Demand and Its Limitations." American Economic Review, Vol. LXV (March).

Hicks, J. R. 1958. "The Measurement of Real Income." Oxford Economic Papers, Vol. X (June).

Hicks, J. R. 1956. A Revision of Demand Theory. Oxford: Oxford University Press.

Hicks, J. R. 1939. Value and Capital. 1st edition. Oxford: Oxford University Press.

Hicks, J. R. and Allen, R. G. D. 1934. "A Reconsideration of the Theory of Values." Economica, Vol. I (February and May).

Hill, C. W. L. 1985. "Oliver Williamson and the M-Form Firm: A Critical Review." Journal of Economic Issues, Vol. XIX (September).

Hoch, S. J. and Ha, Y. W. 1986. "Consumer Learning: Advertising and the Ambiguity of Product Experience." Journal of Consumer Research, Vol. XIII (September).

Hogarth, R. M. and Reder, M. W. 1986. "Perspectives from Economics and Psychology: Editors' Comments." Journal of Business, Vol. LIX (October).

Holt, C. A. 1986. "Preference Reversals and the Independence Axiom." American Economic Review, Vol. LXXVI (June).

Hotelling, H. 1932. "Edgeworth's Taxation Paradox and the Nature of Demand and Supply Functions." Journal of Political Economy, Vol. XL (October).

Houthakker, H. S. 1952. "Compensated Changes in Quantities and Qualities Consumed." Review of Economic Studies, Vol. XIX, No. 3.

Houthakker, H. S. 1961. "The Present State of Consumption Theory." Econometrica, Vol. XXIX (October).

Houthakker, H. S. 1950. "Revealed Preference and the Utility Function." Economica, Vol. XVII (May).

Howell, J. F. and Peristiani, S. 1987. "The Estimation of a Hedonic Asking and Offer Rent Equation Model: An EM Algorithm Approach." Empirical Economics, Vol. XII, No. 4.

Hui, J., McLean-Meyinsse, P. E. and Jones, D. 1995. "An Empirical Investigation of Importance Ratings of Meat Attributes by Louisiana and Texas Consumers." Journal of Agricultural Applied Economics, Vol. XXVII (December).

James, J. 1983. "The New Household Economics, General X-Efficiency Theory, and Developing Countries." Journal of Development Studies, Vol. XIX (July).

James, J. and Gutkind, E. 1985. "Attitude Change Revisited: Cognitive Dissonance Theory and Development Policy." World Development, Vol. XIII (October/November).

Johansen, L. 1979. "The Bargaining Society and the Inefficiency of Bargaining." Kyklos, Vol. XXXII, No. 3.

Johnson, H. 1971. "The Keynesian Revolution and the Monetarist Counter-Revolution." American Economic Association Papers and Proceedings, Vol. LXI (May).

Jones, L. E. 1988. "The Characteristics Model, Hedonic Prices and the Clientele Effect." Journal of Political Economy, Vol. XCVI (June).

Judd, J. P. and Scadding, J. L. 1982. "The Search for a Stable Money Demand Function." Journal of Economic Literature, Vol. XX (September).

Kaen, F. R. and Rosenman, R. E. 1986. "Predictable Behavior in Financial Markets: Some Evidence in Support of Heiner's Hypothesis." American Economic Review, Vol. LXXVI (March).

Kapteyn, A., Wansbeck, T. and Buyze, J. 1979. "Maximizing or Satisficing?" Review of Economics and Statistics, Vol. LXI (November).

Karni, E. and Safra, Z. 1987. "'Preference Reversal' and the Observability of Preferences by Experimental Methods." Econometrica, Vol. LV (May).

Karni, E. and Schmeidler, D. 1990. "Fixed Preferences and Changing Tastes." American Economic Association Papers and Proceedings, Vol. LXXX (May).

Keita, L. D. 1992. Science, Rationality, and Neoclassical Economics. Newark: University of Delaware Press.

Kim, T. and Richter, M. K. 1986. "Nontransitive-Nontotal Consumer Theory." Journal of Economic Theory, Vol. XXXVIII (April).

King, A. T. 1976. "The Demand for Housing: A Lancastrian Approach." Southern Economic Journal, Vol. XLIII (October).

Klamer, A. 1989. "A Conversation with Amartya Sen." Journal of Economic Perspectives, Vol. III (Winter).

Knez, P., Smith, V. L. and Williams, A. W. 1985. "Individual Rationality, Market Rationality, and Value Estimation." American Economic Association Papers and Proceedings, Vol. LXXV (May).

Knight, F. H. 1944. "Realism and Relevance in the Theory of Demand." Journal of Political Economy, Vol. LII (December).

Koopmans, T. 1957. Three Essays on the State of Economic Science. New York: McGraw-Hill.

Kotlikoff, L. J., Samuelson, W. and Johnson, S. 1988. "Consumption, Computation Mistakes, and Fiscal Policy." American Economic Association Papers and Proceedings, Vol. LXXVIII (May).

Kraft, A. and Kraft, J. 1975. "Specification of Commodity Subsets for Separable Utility Functions." Applied Economics, Vol. VII (December).

Kroll, Y., Levy, H. and Rapoport, A. 1988. "Experimental Tests of the Separation Theorem and the Capital Asset Pricing Model." American Economic Review, Vol. LXXVIII (June).

Kunreuther, H. and Slovic, P. 1978. "Economics, Psychology, and Protective Behavior." American Economic Association Papers and Proceedings, Vol. LXVIII (May).

Kuran, T. 1996. "The Discontents of Islamic Economic Morality." American Economic Association Papers and Proceedings, Vol. LXXXVI (May).

Ladd, G. W. and Suvannunt, V. 1976. "A Model of Consumer Goods Characteristics." American Journal of Agricultural Economics, Volume LVIII (August).

Ladd, G. W. and Zober, M. 1977. "Model of Consumer Reaction to Product Characteristics." Journal of Consumer Research, Vol. IV (September).

Laidler, D. 1980. "The Demand for Money in the United States Yet Again." In Karl Brunner and Allan H. Meltzer, eds., On The State of Macro-Economics, Vol. 12, Carnegie-Rochester Conferences on Public Policy. Journal of Monetary Economics, Supplement.

Lancaster, K. 1966a. "A New Approach to Consumer Theory." Journal of Political Economy, Vol. LXXIV (April).

Lancaster, K. 1966b. "Change and Innovation in the Technology of Consumption." American Economic Association Papers and Proceedings, Vol. LVI (May).

Lancaster, K. 1968. Mathematical Economics. New York: Macmillan.

Lancaster, P. 1969. Theory of Matrices. New York: Academic Press.

Leamer, E. E. 1983. "Let's Take the Con Out of Econometrics." American Economic Review, Vol. LXXIII (March).

Leamer, E. E. 1985. "Sensitivity Analyses Would Help." American Economic Review, Vol. LXXV (June).

Leamer, E. E. 1978. Specification Searches: AD HOC Inference with Non-Experimental Data. New York: Wiley.

Leibenstein, H. 1986. "On Relaxing the Maximization Postulate." Journal of Behavioral Economics, Vol. XV (Winter).

Leland, H. E. 1977. "Quality Choice and Competition." American Economic Review, Vol. LXVII (March).

Lenz, J. E., Mittelhammer, R. C. and Shi, H. 1994. "Retail-Level Hedonics and the Valuation of Milk Components." American Journal of Agricultural Economics, Vol. LXXVI (August).

Leontief, W. 1947. "Introduction to a Theory of the Internal Structure of Functional Relationships." Econometrica, Vol. XV (October).

Leontief, W. 1971. "Theoretical Assumptions and Nonobserved Facts." American Economic Review, Vol. LXI (March).

Lewin, Shira 1996. "Economics and Psychology: Lessons for Our Own Day from the Early Twentieth Century." Journal of Economic Literature, Vol. XXXIV (September).

Little, I. M. D. 1949. "A Reformulation of the Theory of Consumer's Behavior." Oxford Economic Papers, Vol. I (January).

Lucas, R. E. B. 1975. "Hedonic Price Functions." Economic Inquiry, Vol. XIII (June).

Luce, R. D. 1957. "A Probabilistic Theory of Utility." In R.D. Luce and H. Raiffa, Games and Decisions. New York: Wiley.

Lui, F. T. 1996. "Three Aspects of Corruption." Contemporary Economic Policy, Vol. XIV (July).

Machina, M. J. 1989. "Dynamic Consistency and Non-Expected Utility Models of Choice Under Uncertainty." Journal of Economic Literature, Vol. XXVII (December).

Mack, R. P. and Leigland, T. J. 1982. "'Optimizing' in Households, Toward a Behavioral Theory." American Economic Association Papers and Proceedings, Vol. LXXII (May).

Mäki, U. 1995. "Diagnosing McCloskey." Journal of Economic Literature, Vol. XXXIII (September).

Mäki, U. 1988. "How to Combine Rhetoric and Realism in the Methodology of Economics." Economics and Philosophy, Vol. IV (April).

March, J. A. 1982. "Theories of Choice and the Making of Decisions." Presented at the Annual Meeting of the American Association for the Advancement of Science, Washington, DC, January 5, 1982.

March, J. G. 1978. "Bounded Rationality, Ambiguity, and the Engineering of Choice." The Bell Journal of Economics, Vol. IX (Autumn).

Marschak, T. A. 1978. "On the Study of Taste Changing Policies." American Economic Association Papers and Proceedings Vol. LXVIII (May).

Mayer, T. 1993. Truth versus Precision in Economics. Aldershot, England: Edward Elgar Publishing Limited.

McAleer, M., Pagan, A. R., and Volker, P. A. 1985. "What Will Take the Con Out of Econometrics?" American Economic Review, Vol. LXXV (June).

McCloskey, D. N. 1995. "Modern Epistemology Against Analytic Philosophy: A Reply to Mäki." Journal of Economic Literature, Vol. XXXIII (September).

McCloskey, D. N. 1983. "The Rhetoric of Economics." Journal of Economic Literature, Vol. XXI (June).

McCloskey, D. N. 1988. "Two Replies and a Dialogue on the Rhetoric of Economics: Mäki, Rappaport and Rosenberg." Economics and Philosophy, Vol. IV (April).

McGuire, R. A. and Ohsfeldt, R. 1986. "Public versus Private Water Delivery: A Critical Analysis of a Hedonic Cost Approach." Public Finance Quarterly, Vol. XIV (July).

McMillan, M. L., Reid, B. G. and Gillen, D. W. 1980. "An Extension of the Hedonic Approach for Estimating the Value of Quiet." Land Economics, Vol. LVI (August).

Melitz, J. 1965. "Friedman and Machlup on the Significance of Testing Economic Assumptions." Journal of Political Economy, Vol. LXXIII (February).

Mendelsohn, R. 1984. "Estimating the Structural Equations of Implicit Markets and Household Production Functions." Review of Economics and Statistics, Vol. LXVI (November).

Meyer, R. J. and Sathi, A. 1985. "A Multiattribute Model of Consumer Choice during Product Learning." Marketing Science, Vol. IV (Winter).

Michael R. T. and Becker, G. S. 1973. "On the New Theory of Consumer Behavior." Swedish Journal of Economics, Vol. LXXV (December).

Miller, M. H. 1986. "Behavioral Rationality in Finance: The Case of Dividends." Journal of Business, Vol. LIX (October).

Miller, M. S. 1983. "Methodology and the Theory of Consumer Behavior." Review of Social Economy, Vol. XLI (April).

Miller, R. M. and Plott, C. R. 1985. "Product Quality Signaling in Experimental Markets." Econometrica, Vol. LIII (July).

Mishan, E. J. 1961. "Theories of Consumers' Behavior: A Cynical View." Economica, Vol. XXVIII (February).

Morgan, J. N. 1978. "Multiple Motives, Group Decisions, Uncertainty, Ignorance, and Confusion: A Realistic Economics of the Consumer Requires Some Psychology." American Economic Association Papers and Proceedings, Vol. LXVIII (May).

Mullen, J. D. and Wohlgenant, M. K. 1991. "The Willingness of Consumers to Pay for Attributes of Lamb" Australian Journal of Agricultural Economics, Vol. XXXV (December).

Muller, J. Z. 1993. Adam Smith in His Time and Ours: Designing the Decent Society. Princeton: Princeton University Press.

Murdoch, J. C. and Thayer, M. A. 1988. "Hedonic Price Estimation of Variable Urban Air Quality." Journal of Environmental Economics and Management, Vol. XV (June).

Muth, R. F. 1966. "Household Production and Consumer Demand Functions." Econometrica, Vol. XXXIV (July).

Nabers, L. 1966. "The Positive and Genetic Approaches." In The Structure of Economic Science: Essays on Methodology. Edited by Sherman Roy Krupp. Englewood Cliffs, New Jersey: Prentice-Hall.

Nagel, E. 1963. "Assumptions in Economic Theory." American Economic Association Papers and Proceedings, Vol. LIII (May).

Naylor, T. H. and Vernon, J. M. 1969. Microeconomics and Decision Models of the Firm. New York: Harcourt, Brace and World, Inc.

Nelson, J. A. 1995. "Feminism and Economics." Journal of Economic Perspectives, Vol. IX (Spring).

Nerlove, M. 1995. "Hedonic Price Functions and the Measurement of Preferences: The Case of Swedish Wine Consumers." European Economic Review, Vol. XXXIX (December).

Newell, A., Shaw, J. C., and Simon, H. A. 1960. "A General Problem Solving Problem for a Computer." Computers and Automation, Vol. VIII (July).

Newell, A., Shaw, J. C., and Simon, H. A. 1958. "Elements of a Theory of Human Problem Solving." Psychological Review, Vol. LXV.

Newell, A., and Simon, H. A. 1961. "The Simulation of Human Thought." In Current Trends in Psychological Theory. Pittsburgh: University of Pittsburgh Press.

North, D. C. 1994. "Economic Performance Through Time." American Economic Review, Vol. LXXXIV (June).

North, D. C. 1986. "The New Institutional Economics." Journal of Institutional and Theoretical Economics, Vol. CXLII (March).

Nozick, R. 1994. "Invisible-Hand Explanations." American Economic Association Papers and Proceedings, Vol. LXXXIV (May).

Odland, J. 1981. "A Household Production Approach to Destination Choice." Economic Geography, Vol. LVII (July).

Ohta, M. 1987. "Gasoline Cost and Hedonic Price Indexes of U.S. Used Cars for 1970-1983." Journal of Business and Economic Statistics, Vol. V (October).

Ozanne, L. and Malpezzi, S. 1985. "The Efficacy of Hedonic Estimation with the Annual Housing Survey: Evidence from the Demand Experiment." Journal of Economic and Social Measurement, Vol. II (July).

Palmquist, R. B. 1984. "Estimating the Demand for the Characteristics of Housing." Review of Economics and Statistics, Vol. LXVI (August).

Papandreou, A. G. 1963. "Theory Construction and Empirical Meaning in Economics." American Economic Association Papers and Proceedings, Vol. LIII (May).

Papandreou, A. G., et al. 1957. "A Test of a Stochastic Theory of Choice." University of California Publications in Economics, 16, No. 1.

Paque, K. H. 1985. "How Far is Vienna from Chicago? An Essay on the Methodology of Two Schools of Dogmatic Liberalism." Konjunkturpolitik, Vol. XXXI, No. 3.

Parsons, G. R. 1986. "An Almost Ideal Demand System for Housing Attributes." Southern Economic Journal, Vol. LIII (October).

Penrose, R. 1955. "A Generalized Inverse for Matrices." Proceedings Cambridge Philosophical Society, Vol. VI.

Persky, J. 1990. "Ceteris Paribus." Journal of Economic Perspectives, Vol. IV (Spring).

Persky, J. 1995. "Retrospectives: The Ethology of Homo Economicus." Journal of Economic Perspectives, Vol. IX (Spring).

Pessemier, E. M. 1978. "Stochastic Properties of Changing Preferences." American Economic Association Papers and Proceedings, Vol. LXVIII (May).

Phipps, A. G. 1987. "Households' Utilities and Hedonic Prices for Inner-City Homes." Environment and Planning A, Vol. XIX (January).

Pingle, M. 1992. "Costly Optimization: An Experiment." Journal of Economic Behavior and Organization, Vol. XVII.

Plott, C. R. 1986. "Rational Choice in Experimental Markets." Journal of Business, Vol. LIX (October).

Polasek, W. 1984. "Extreme Bound Analysis for Residential Load Curve Models: Empirical Evidence for a 16-Household Example." Empirical Economics, Vol. IX (3).

Pollak, R. A. 1978. "Endogenous Tastes in Demand and Welfare Analysis." American Economic Association Papers and Proceedings, Vol. LXVIII (May).

Pollak, R. A. and Wachter, M. L. 1975. "The Relevance of the Household's Production Function and Its Implications for the Allocation of Time." Journal of Political Economy, Vol. LXXXIII (April).

Pollak, R. A. 1985. "A Transaction Cost Approach to Families and Households." Journal of Economic Literature, Vol. XXII (June).

Popper, K. 1957. "The Aim of Science." Ratio, Vol. I (December).

Popper, K. 1968. The Logic of Scientific Discovery. London: Hutchinson.

Popper, K. 1969. "Three Views Concerning Human Knowledge." Conjectures and Refutations. London: Routledge.

Quah, E. 1986. "Persistent Problems in Measuring Household Production: Definition, Quantifying Joint Activities and Valuation Issues Are Solvable." American Journal of Economics and Sociology, Vol. XLV (April).

Quah, E. 1987. "Valuing Family Household Production: A Contingent Evaluation Approach." Applied Economics, Vol. XIX (July).

Ramezani, C. A. 1995. "Determinants of Nutrient Demand: A Nonparametric Analysis." Journal of Agricultural Resource Economics, Vol. XX (July).

Ratchford, B. T. 1975. "The New Economic Theory of Consumer Behavior: An Interpretive Essay." Journal of Consumer Research, Vol. II (September).

Rawls, J. 1971. A Theory of Justice. Cambridge: Harvard University Press.

Richter, M. K. 1966. "Revealed Preference Theory." Econometrica, Vol. XXXIV (July).

Riley, J. G. 1977. "Well-Behaved Preferences: An Expository Note." Economic Inquiry, Vol. XV (July).

Roberts, B. and Schulze, D. L. 1973. <u>Modern Mathematics and Economic Analysis</u>. New York: W. W. Norton and Company, Inc.

Robinson, J. 1962. <u>Economic Philosophy</u>. London: Watts and Co., Ltd.

Roley, V. V. 1985. "Money Demand Predictability." <u>Journal of Money, Credit, and Banking</u>, Vol. XVII (November).

Rose, A. M. 1957. "A Study of Irrational Judgments." <u>Journal of Political Economy</u>, Vol. LXV (October).

Rosenzweig, M. R. and Schultz, T. P. 1983. "Estimating a Household Production Function: Heterogeneity, the Demand for Health Inputs, and Their Effects on Birth Weight." <u>Journal of Political Economy</u>, Vol. XCI (October).

Roth, A. E. 1986. "Laboratory Experimentation in Economics." <u>Economics and Philosophy</u>, Vol. II (October).

Roth, T. P. 1973. "Classical vs. Process Analysis and the Form of the Production Function." <u>The Engineering Economist</u>, Vol. XIX (October-November).

Roth, T. P. 1977. "Imperfect Knowledge and the Problem of Choice Among Alternative Production Techniques." <u>The Engineering Economist</u>, Vol. XXII (Summer).

Roth, T. P. 1994. <u>Information, Ideology and Freedom</u>. Lanham, MD., New York and London: University Press of America.

Roth, T. P. 1975. "The Multi-Equation Utility Function, Information, and the Optimal Commodity Bundle." <u>Metroeconomica</u>, Vol. XXVII (May-December).

Roth, T. P. 1979. "On the Predictive Power of the New Approach to Consumer Theory." <u>Atlantic Economic Journal</u>, Vol. VII (July).

Roth, T. P. 1972. "The Subjective Production Function: An Approach to Its Determination." The Engineering Economist, Vol. XVII (July-August).

Rothschild, K. W. 1993. Ethics and Economic Theory. Hampshire, England: Edward Elgar Publishing, Limited.

Roy, R. 1947. "La Distribution du Revenu entre les Divers Biens." Econometrica, Vol. XV (January).

Russell, T. and Thaler, R. 1985. "The Relevance of Quasi-Rationality in Competitive Markets." American Economic Review, Vol. LXXV (December).

Samuelson, P. A. 1948. "Consumption Theory in Terms of Revealed Preference." Economica, Vol. XV (November).

Samuelson, P. A. 1947. Foundations of Economic Analysis. Cambridge: Harvard University Press. 9th edition, 1971.

Samuelson, P. A. 1938. "A Note on the Pure Theory of Consumer's Behavior." Economica, Vol. V (February and August).

Samuelson, P. A. 1963. "Problems of Methodology-Discussion." American Economic Association Papers and Proceedings, Vol. LIII (May).

Samuelson, P. A. 1965a. "Professor Samuelson on Theory and Realism: Reply." American Economic Review, Vol. LV (December).

Samuelson, P. A. 1956. "Social Indifference Curves." Quarterly Journal of Economics, Vol. LXX (February).

Samuelson, P. A. 1965b. "Using Full Duality to Show that Simultaneously Additive Direct and Indirect Utilities Implies Unitary Price Elasticity of Demand." Econometrica, Vol. XXXIII (October).

Sandmo, A. 1990. "Buchanan on Political Economy: A Review Article." Journal of Economic Literature, Vol. XXVIII (March).

Sargan, J. D. 1972. "Review of Lancaster (1971)." Economic Journal, Vol. LXXXII (March).

Sasaki, K. 1983. "A Household Production Approach to the Evaluation of Transportation System Change." Regional Science and Urban Economics, Vol. XIII (August).

Scotchmer, S. 1985. "Hedonic Prices and Cost/Benefit Analysis." Journal of Economic Theory, Vol. XXXVII (August).

Segal, U. 1988. "Does the Preference Reversal Phenomenon Necessarily Contradict the Independence Axiom?" American Economic Review, Vol. LXXVIII (March).

Sen, A. 1970. Collective Choice and Social Welfare. San Francisco: Holden Day.

Sen, A. 1995. "Rationality and Social Choice." American Economic Review, Vol. LXXXV (March).

Shaw, R. W. 1982. "Product Proliferation in Characteristics Space: The U.K. Fertilizer Industry." Journal of Industrial Economics, Vol. XXXI (September/December).

Shonkwiler, J. S. and Reynolds, J. E. 1986. "A Note on the Use of Hedonic Price Models in the Analysis of Land Prices at the Urban Fringe." Land Economics, Vol. CXII (February).

Shubik, M. 1970. "A Curmudgeon's Guide to Microeconomics." Journal of Economic Literature, Vol. VIII (June).

Siegel, J. J. and Thaler, R. H. 1997. "Anomalies: The Equity Premium Puzzle." Journal of Economic Perspectives, Vol. XI (Winter).

Simon, H. A. 1955. "A Behavioral Model of Rational Choice." Quarterly Journal of Economics, Vol. LXIX.

Simon, H. A. 1957. Models of Man. New York: Wiley.

Simon, H. A. 1978a. "On How to Decide What to Do." The Bell Journal of Economics, Vol. IX (Autumn).

Simon, H. A. 1956. "Rational Choice and the Structure of the Environment." Psychological Review, Vol. LXIII.

Simon, H. A. 1978b. "Rationality as Process and as Product of Thought." American Economic Association Papers and Proceedings, Vol. LXVIII (May).

Simon, H. A. 1986. "Rationality in Psychology and Economics." Journal of Business, Vol. LIX (October).

Simon, H. A. 1966. "Theories of Decision-Making in Economics and Behavioral Science." In Surveys of Economic Theory, Vol. III. New York: St. Martin's Press.

Sims, C. 1979. Review of Specification Searches: Ad hoc Inference with Nonexperimental Data by Edward E. Leamer. Journal of Economic Literature, Vol. XVII (June).

Singer, P. (ed.) 1993. A Companion to Ethics. Oxford, England: Blackwell Publishers, Ltd.

Slovic, P. and Lichtenstein, S. 1983. "Preference Reversals: A Broader Perspective." American Economic Review, Vol. LXXIII (September).

Smith, V. L. 1994. "Economics in the Laboratory." Journal of Economic Perspectives, Vol. VIII (Winter).

Smith, V. L. 1985. "Experimental Economics: Reply." American Economic Review, Vol. LXXV (March).

Smith, V. L. 1982. "Microeconomic Systems as an Experimental Science." American Economic Review, Vol. LXXII (December).

Smith, V. L. 1989. "Theory, Experiment and Economics." Journal of Economic Perspectives, Vol. III (Winter).

Sono, M. 1961. "The Effect of Price Changes on the Demand and Supply of Separable Goods." International Economic Review, Vol. II (September).

Stahl, D. O. II. 1984. "Cardinal vs. Characteristic Indices of Preference for Applied Welfare Economics." Public Finance Quarterly, Vol. XII (October).

Stanley, L. R. and Tschirhart, J. 1991. "Hedonic Prices for a Nondurable Good: The Case of Breakfast Cereals." Review of Economics and Statistics, Vol. LXXIII (August).

Stigler, G. and Becker, G. 1977. "De Gustibus Non Est Disputandum." American Economic Review, Vol. LXVII (March).

Stiglitz, J. 1993. "Post Walrasian and Post Marxian Economics." Journal of Economic Perspectives, Vol. VII (Winter).

Strotz, R. H. 1957. "The Empirical Implications of a Utility Tree." Econometrica, Vol. XXV (April).

Suppes, P. 1961. "Behavioristic Foundations of Utility." Econometrica, Vol. XXIX (April).

Tarr, D. G. 1976. "Experiments in Token Economies: A Review of the Evidence Relating to Assumptions and Implications of Economic Theory." Southern Economic Journal, Vol. XLIII (October).

Theil, H. 1975. Theory and Measurement of Consumer Demand, Volume I. Amsterdam: North Holland Publishing Company.

Thistle, P. D. 1985. "An Experimental Study of Consumer Demand Using Rats." Journal of Behavioral Economics, Vol. XIV (Summer).

Thompson, R. S. 1987. "New Entry and Hedonic Price Discounts: The Case of the Irish Car Market." Oxford Bulletin of Economics and Statistics, Vol. XLIX (November).

Throsby, D. 1994. "The Production and Consumption of the Arts: A View of Cultural Economics." Journal of Economic Literature, Vol. XXXII (March).

Triplett, J. E. 1986. "The Economic Interpretation of Hedonic Methods." Survey of Current Business, Vol. LXVI (January).

Tullock, G. 1996. "Corruption Theory and Practice." Contemporary Economic Policy, Vol. XIV (July).

Tversky, A. and Thaler, R. H. 1990. "Preference Reversals." Journal of Economic Perspectives, Vol. IV (Spring).

Tversky, A. and Kahneman, D. 1986. "Rational Choice and the Framing of Decisions." Journal of Business, Vol. LIX (October).

Unnevehr, L. J. 1986. "Consumer Demand for Rice Grain Quality and Returns to Research for Quality Improvement in Southeast Asia." American Journal of Agricultural Economics, Vol. LXVIII (August).

Uzawa, H. 1960. "Preference and Rational Choice in the Theory of Consumption." In Proceedings of a Symposium on Mathematical Methods in the Social Sciences. Stanford: Stanford University Press.

Veeman, M. M 1987. "Hedonic Price Functions for Wheat in the World Market: Implications for Canadian Wheat Export Strategy." Canadian Journal of Agricultural Economics, Vol. XXXV (November).

von Neumann, J. and Morgenstern, O. 1947. Theory of Games and Economic Behavior. Princeton: Princeton University Press.

Wagner, H. M. 1956. "An Eclectic Approach to the Pure Theory of Consumer Behavior." Econometrica, Vol. XXIV (October).

West, E. G. and McKee, M. 1983. "De Gustibus Est Disputandum: The Phenomenon of 'Merit Wants' Revisited." American Economic Review, Vol. LXXIII (December).

Whalley, D. 1985. "Hedonic Price Functions and Progressive Neighborhood Improvement: A Theoretical Exploration." Mathematical Social Sciences, Vol. X (December).

Wilde, K. D., LeBaron, A. D., and Israelson, L. D. 1985. "Knowledge, Uncertainty, and Behavior." American Economic Review, Vol. LXXV (May).

Williams, R. and Donath, S. 1994. "Simultaneous Uses of Time in Household Production." Review of Income and Wealth, Vol. XL (December).

Williamson, O. E. 1994. "Concluding Comment." Journal of Institutional and Theoretical Economics, Vol. CL (March).

Williamson, O. E. 1993. "Contested Exchange Versus the Governance of Contractual Relations." Journal of Economic Perspectives, Vol. VII (Winter).

Williamson, O. E. 1985. The Economic Institutions of Capitalism. New York: The Free Press.

Williamson, O. E. 1981. "The Modern Corporation: Origins, Evolution, Attributes." Journal of Economic Literature, Vol. XIX (December).

Williamson, O. E. 1987. "Transaction Cost Economics: The Comparative Contracting Perspective." Journal of Economic Behavior and Organization, Vol. VIII (December).

Wilson, J. Q. 1989. "Adam Smith on Business Ethics." California Management Review. Vol. XXXII (Fall).

Wold, H. and Jureen L. 1953. Demand Analysis. New York: Wiley.

Wolff, R. 1985. "On a Family of Utility Functions as a Basis of Separable Demand." Zeitschrift für Nationalökonomie, Vol. XLV, No. 2.

Wong, S. 1973. "The 'F-Twist' and the Methodology of Paul Samuelson." American Economic Review, Vol. LXIII (June).

Wu, S. and Pontney, J. 1967. <u>An Introduction to Modern Demand Theory</u>. New York: Random House.

Yezer, A. M., Goldfarb, R. S. and Poppen, P. J. 1996. "Does Studying Economics Discourage Cooperation? Watch What We Do, Not What We Say or How We Play." <u>Journal of Economic Perspectives</u>, Vol. X (Winter).

Index

Exogenous constraint, 139n5
Exogenous variable. *See* unidentified
Exogenously determined preference structure, 143
Expected utility theory, 47n13, 128n14
Experience, 5-6, 76, 83, 99, 118, 121, 143-44, 161n4, 163n24, 180n19
Experimental Economics, 27n25, 47n11
Explanation, 5, 7-8, 18-20, 26n21, 84, 90, 95, 99, 105, 112, 114, 119, 123, 129n18, 162n18
Explanatory power of models, 20, 25n9, 119
Explanatory power of theory, 11-12, 19, 34
Explanatory variable, 169
Explanatory view, 4-6, 18-20
Ex post rationalization, 26n21, 84
Extreme bounds analysis, 23, 169, 178n6

False assumption, 14, 17-18, 27n24
Falsification, 173
Freedom, 14, 92, 153-55
Free variable, 169
Full income, 94, 106, 112-13

General possibility theorem, 153
Generative assumption, 14, 16, 19-20, 28n31, 33, 36, 39, 98, 104, 116, 119-20, 122, 129n18, 131, 137, 143, 158
Global sensitivity analysis, 169
Goods indeterminacy, 55-56, 59, 61, 64, 68n3, 105. *See also* multiple dimensions of goods

Habit formation, 143, 152-53
Habits, 158

Higher-order preference, 144
Homo economicus, 47n10, 141-42, 146
Household behavior, 95-96
Household production function, 21-22, 89-91, 93-95, 97, 100n6, 105-6, 165
Human capital, 96, 100n6, 101n12, 102n15,
Human problem solver, 116, 118
Hybrid model, 136
Hypotheses. *See* scientific tests of

Impartial spectator, 159
Implications. *See* designed and undesigned class of
Indirect utility function, 2, 41-42, 101n11
Indivisible commodity, 43
Information asymmetry, 22, 124, 138-39, 142, 144-45, 148, 150, 156, 158
Information diffusion, 163n25
Institution, 132, 135, 139n3, 156, 159, 163n29
Instrumentalism, 4, 12, 19, 20, 28n40, 179n16
Instrumentalist, 6-8, 10-14, 16-18, 25n15, 110, 143
Interdependency, 156
Internal conflict, 21, 87n8, 144, 148, 152
Interpersonal relationship, 21, 145, 148
Interpersonal utility comparison, 153
Interpretive rule, 8-12, 14, 20, 23, 26n21, 35-36, 45, 48n16, 69n17, 83, 86n6, 87n6, 98, 106, 122, 165, 168, 170, 172-75, 177
Intertemporal phenomena, 153
Introspection, 13, 176, 178n8
Irrationality, 22, 102n13, 129n19,

27n25, 35

About the Author

Timothy P. Roth is currently A. B. Templeton Professor and Chairman, Department of Economics and Finance, the University of Texas at El Paso. He served for two years as Senior Economist, U.S. Congress Joint Economic Committee. More recently, he was Executive Director of President Reagan's Steel Advisory Committee, Senior Economic Advisor in the Office of the Secretary of Commerce, and Consultant to President Reagan's Cabinet Council on Economic Policy.